STUDYING PAUL'S LETTERS

STUDYING PAUL'S LETTERS

CONTEMPORARY PERSPECTIVES AND METHODS

Joseph A. Marchal, Editor

Fortress Press

Minneapolis

Library of Congress Cataloging-in-Publication Data
Studying Paul's letters : contemporary perspectives and methods / Joseph A. Marchal, editor.
p. cm.
Includes bibliographical references.
ISBN 978-0-8006-9818-8 (alk. paper)
1. Bible. N.T. Epistles of Paul—Criticism, interpretation, etc. I. Marchal, Joseph A.
BS2650.52.S783 2012
227'.0601—dc23
2011047081

16   15   14   13   12   1   2   3   4   5   6   7   8   9   10

CONTENTS

Acknowledgments

The process of bringing this collection together began and now ends as a primarily pedagogical and frequently collective effort. Thus, the main test for this book is still to come, as I hope that reading and working with (and through) its content proves useful to those who encounter it. But, in the meantime, it must be acknowledged how many people worked to bring this to completion and how many encountered this work in its many preliminary, intermediate, and penultimate forms.

The idea for this collection started with a teaching problem and project. I puzzled over the problem of what I thought students or new readers of Paul's letters need to know, or perhaps, more appropriately, do. I immediately thought of a range of issues and a number of my colleagues in biblical studies, but the trick was to make the latest and most relevant critical perspectives accessible to the novice. So to begin, I really must acknowledge all of my students over the years who experienced firsthand, and in turn contributed to, my own sense of the positively puzzling and trenchantly troubling aspects of studying biblical materials (not just Paul's letters). The test and opportunity of teaching students in seminaries, small liberal arts colleges, and state universities across the U.S. has proven invaluable, in courses quite Pauline or otherwise. If my own writing has improved at all in reaching people new to these questions and concerns, it is almost certainly due to my own learning with and from students.

This collection took more specific shape, though, in the particular context of Ball State University, where my students have been enthusiastic, honest, hilarious, maddening, and gladdening participants in a number of activities that directly impacted this book. My experiences in these activities have been exhilarating, harrowing, and even humbling and thus immensely useful for the scholarly teacher I aim to be. In particular, students in a course titled "Paul and the Politics of Gender, Ethnicity, and Empire" (Spring of 2011) read and tried to use early versions of many of these chapters. This often led to surprising results, but their input was always valuable to me and to many of the authors. One of the goals for this book is to make something useful for classes and, with these students' help, the book is much closer to this now, even as many of them seemed to prefer (or even thrilled over) drafts and chapters in development. The planning for this particular course and the resulting collection were ineluctably shaped and supported by resources at Ball State. Participating in a seminar on teaching upper-level, discipline-specific reading skills—led by my colleague Dave Concepción—and in the university's diversity associates program provided insights and support in key phases without which this book would not have been completed. It is wonderful to be in a department and university where there are so many formal and informal occasions for reflecting upon pedagogies, which also made my ongoing teaching and learning conversations with local colleagues at Butler University and a wider circle of colleagues from Wabash Center workshops all the more valuable.

The collection also benefited from the occasions where I have presented or led learning opportunities in a number of different contexts, with a number of community organizations (religious and otherwise). The chance to speak, teach, and learn with these kinds of "novice readers" reinforces why it is important to grapple with the ongoing religious, political, and cultural authority ascribed to Paul (and his letters). In particular, the contemporary biblical scholars forum at North United Methodist Church in Indianapolis keeps inviting and engaging me, even as the sessions I lead tend to be neither particularly Methodist nor methodical! Nevertheless, they know well how invested I am in talking about methods and their effect on our understanding, the kinds of effects about which they and many communities so deeply care. This book is meant for communities like this, those who want to see and use texts and traditions we have inherited differently.

Most of the chapters in this collection began as presentations in two consecutive sessions on "Paul and the Politics of Introduction" at the Society of Biblical Literature annual meeting in Atlanta, Georgia, in November 2010. Thanks, then, must also go out to my colleagues on the steering committee of the Paul and Politics Section who graciously appreciated the potential of these sessions and set this time aside for scholars with cramped schedules to meet, present, and interact with each other and many more beside. Many of the chapters were improved by these initial presentations and conversations, and my own work benefitted from additional opportunities to present at the University of Oslo and Marian University. I must admit, with regret, that efforts were made to feature chapters on still more approaches and perspectives that, for one reason or the other, were not feasible to include at this point. Given time and space, one could certainly notice that even more questions could be asked, and still other critical perspectives could be adopted, which this book most certainly encourages. In the end, I am confident that collectively we offer the most relevant set of approaches and perspectives for this edition of the book. This confidence feels increasingly appropriate given the work done on this book by the fine staff at Fortress Press, who have managed yet again to prepare a fine resource for engaging Paul's letters. Thanks must again be given to my editor, Neil Elliott, who immediately understood this project's potential impact and import and has supported it in ways only he knows. Hope seems less ridiculous in the light of his attentive eye and patient correspondence. I would be remiss if I did not also acknowledge the rest of the team at Fortress Press who worked on the manuscript, including Marissa Wold, Sally Messner, Susan Johnson, and Jessica Hillstrom. Their support is unmatched, even as my partner, friends, and family (many of whom are teachers themselves) have found unparalleled ways to give their own kinds of support. I admit I am too silently grateful to these who surround me physically, virtually, even phantasmically in their own forms of constancy. They are the greatest critical thinkers, teachers, and activists in my life—the greatest, the closest, and the most constant of these being my partner tascha.

But in the end, I must most fully acknowledge and thunderously thank the scholarly teachers and learners, in and out of the classroom, who were most directly involved in creating this book. This of course begins with the colleagues who so carefully wrote the various chapters of this book. It can be a real challenge to switch codes and write for different kinds of audiences, making important academic ideas accessible. I am forever grateful, then, that each of these colleagues agreed to work with me on this collection and graciously accepted me as their editor and fellow collaborator (sometimes in multiple senses). It is my genuine hope that their patience, trust, and fortitude in this project and with their own students, each other, and this editor are rewarded by the results in this book. When I imagine bringing people into the most important critical conversations, about Paul's letters and many other things, I imagine them interacting with this fine collection of scholars, teachers, and people. Lastly, one of those aforementioned Ball State students, Kelsi Morrison-Atkins, helped all of us push these entries through middling, muddling, and penultimate stages as my student editorial assistant for this book. Ms. Morrison-Atkins spent many a sun-filled summer day inside, reading over drafts and comments, and then working over the pages with me. She has proven generous yet critical in all the right ways, with a good ear for audience and an eagle eye for detail. She exemplifies how the line or, rather, the movement from novice to scholar is finer, quicker, and stranger than many of us often realize as teachers and learners. She is both of these, as are so many others new and "new" to these ways of approaching authoritative materials. This work is dedicated then to those, like Kelsi and the contributors, who are dedicated to such movements toward teaching, learning, and critical engagement.

Contributors

Cynthia Briggs Kittredge is Ernest J. Villavaso Jr. Professor of New Testament and Academic Dean at the Seminary of the Southwest and is the author of *Conversations with Scripture: The Gospel of John* (2007) and *Community and Authority: The Rhetoric of Obedience in the Pauline Tradition* (1998). She coedited *The Bible in the Public Square: Reading the Signs of the Times* (Fortress Press, 2008) and *Walk in the Ways of Wisdom: Essays in Honor of Elisabeth Schüssler Fiorenza* (2003).

Pamela Eisenbaum is Associate Professor of Biblical Studies and Christian Origins at Iliff School of Theology and is the author of *The Jewish Heroes of Christian History: Hebrews 11 in Literary Context* (1997), *Invitation to Romans* (2006), and *Paul Was Not a Christian: The Original Message of a Misunderstood Apostle* (2009).

Melanie Johnson-DeBaufre is Associate Professor of New Testament and Early Christianity at Drew University and is the author of *Jesus among Her Children: Q, Eschatology, and the Construction of Christian Origins* (2006) and the coauthor of *Mary Magdalene Understood* (2006). She coedited *Walk in the Ways of Wisdom: Essays in Honor of Elisabeth Schüssler Fiorenza* (2003) and serves as the coeditor of the *Journal of Feminist Studies in Religion*.

Davina C. Lopez is Assistant Professor of Religious Studies at Eckerd College and the author of *Apostle to the Conquered: Reimagining Paul's Mission* (Fortress Press, 2008). She coedited a double issue of the *Union Seminary Quarterly Review* 59:3–4 (2005) on "New Testament and Roman Empire: Shifting Paradigms for Interpretation" and coauthored *De-Introducing the New Testament*.

Joseph A. Marchal is Associate Professor of Religious Studies at Ball State University and the author of *The Politics of Heaven: Women, Gender, and Empire in the Study of Paul* (Fortress Press, 2008) and *Hierarchy, Unity, and Imitation: A Feminist Rhetorical Analysis of Power Dynamics in Paul's Letter to the Philippians* (2006).

Laura S. Nasrallah is Professor of New Testament and Early Christianity at Harvard Divinity School and the author of *An Ecstasy of Folly: Prophecy and Authority in Early Christianity* (2004) and *Christian Responses to Roman Art and Architecture:*

The Second-Century Church amid the Spaces of Empire (2010). She coedited *Prejudice and Christian Beginnings: Investigating Race, Gender, and Ethnicity in Early Christian Studies* (Fortress Press, 2009) and *From Roman to Early Christian Thessalonikē: Studies in Religion and Archaeology* (2010).

PETER S. OAKES is Greenwood Senior Lecturer in New Testament at the University of Manchester and the author of *Reading Romans in Pompeii* (Fortress Press, 2009) and *Philippians: From People to Letter* (2001). He also edited *Rome in the Bible and the Early Church* (2002) and coedited *Torah in the New Testament* (2009).

TODD PENNER is Gould H. and Marie Cloud Associate Professor of Religious Studies at Austin College, author of *In Praise of Christian Origins: Stephen and the Hellenists in Lukan Apologetic Historiography* (2004) and *The Epistle of James and Eschatology: Rereading an Ancient Christian Letter* (1996), and coauthor of *Contextualizing Gender in Early Christian Discourse: Thinking beyond Thecla* (2009) and *De-Introducing the New Testament* (forthcoming). He coedited *Contextualizing Acts: Lukan Narrative and Greco-Roman Discourse* (2003), *Moving beyond New Testament Theology? Essays in Conversation with Heikki Räisänen* (2005), *Her Master's Tools: Feminist and Postcolonial Engagements of Historical-Critical Discourse* (2005), and *Mapping Gender in Ancient Religious Discourses* (2007).

JEREMY PUNT is Professor of New Testament at the University of Stellenbosch in South Africa and the author of numerous articles on hermeneutics, cultural studies, and the use of the Bible in Africa. He coedited *The New Testament Interpreted: Essays in Honor of Bernard C. Lategan* (2006).

SZE-KAR WAN is Professor of New Testament at the Perkins School of Theology, Southern Methodist University, and the author of *Power in Weakness: Conflict and Rhetorics in Paul's Second Letter to the Corinthians* (2000). He edited *The Bible in Modern China: The Literary and Intellectual Impact* (1999).

DEMETRIUS K. WILLIAMS is Associate Professor in the Department of French, Italian, and Comparative Literature and director of the Religious Studies Program at the University of Wisconsin-Milwaukee. He is the author of *"An End to This Strife": The Politics of Gender in African American Churches* (Fortress Press, 2004) and *Enemies of the Cross of Christ: The Terminology of the Cross and Conflict in Philippians* (2002) and coeditor of *Onesimus Our Brother: Reading Religion, Race, and Culture in Philemon* (Fortress Press, 2012).

Figures

Chapter 3

Fig. 1: *The World according to the USA* (detail). Illustration by Yanko Tsvetkov, "Mapping Stereotypes: The Geography of Prejudice." Reprinted by permission of the artist.

Fig. 2: *View of the World from 9th Avenue*. Illustration by Saul Steinberg, *The New Yorker*, March 29, 1976. Reprinted by permission of the Saul Steinberg Foundation.

Fig. 3: Plan of Philippi in the second century. Modified from Michel Sève, "Le côté nord du forum de Philippes," *Bulletin de correspondance hellénique* 110, no. 1 (1986). Published with thanks to Chaido Koukouli-Chrysanthaki and the Presidential Information Technology Fellow program at Harvard University.

Fig. 4: Augustan coin from Philippi. Printed courtesy of the Bibliothèque nationale de France, Paris.

Fig. 5: Augustan coin from Philippi, 27 BCE – 14 CE. Printed courtesy of the Bibliothèque nationale de France, Paris.

Chapter 5

Fig. 1: Statue of Augustus of Prima Porta. Braccio Nuovo, Vatican Museums, Rome. Photo by Davina C. Lopez.

Fig. 2: President George W. Bush boards the *USS Abraham Lincoln*, May 1, 2003. United States Navy Photo by Photographer's Mate Third Class Tyler J. Clements. Public Domain.

Fig. 3: Statue of Augustus of Prima Porta. Braccio Nuovo, Vatican Museums, Rome. Photo by Davina C. Lopez.

Fig. 4: Relief of an allegorical personification thought to be the nation of Hispania (Spain), Hadrianeum. Capitoline Museum, Rome. Photo by Davina C. Lopez.

Fig. 5: Keystone depicting a crouching woman, perhaps the personification of Dacia, from the Trajanic period. Capitoline Museum, Rome. Photo by Davina C. Lopez.

Fig. 6: Relief depicting the defeat of Germania (Germany) under the emperor Domitian, found at Ostia. National Museum of Rome at the Baths of Diocletian. Photo by Davina C. Lopez.

Fig. 7: Relief featuring a winged figure, perhaps the goddess Victory, flying in to announce the end of war with a Roman standard in her arms. National Museum of Rome at the Baths of Diocletian. Photo by Davina C. Lopez.

ASKING THE RIGHT QUESTIONS?

Perspective and Approach

JOSEPH A. MARCHAL

WHAT AND WHY?

What does one need to know when beginning to study Paul's letters? Typically, I find it annoying when someone asks a question for which they really want or expect only one answer. It is something I try to avoid doing (and not always with great success). Happily, I believe, asking this opening question means I have managed not to repeat this odd pattern of speech. This kind of question is the preoccupation of this book, its various chapters, and its various authors (often because it is also central to our occupations). In short, answering this kind of question is not always as straight-forward as you might think. Even just perusing the table of contents that precede this introduction or skimming the pages that follow it, you, dear reader, are likely to realize that there are some very different perspectives and approaches presented in this volume. Certainly, they will be different from each other but quite possibly also different from what you might first expect when learning about Paul's letters.

Perhaps at this point, the more pressing question for you then is: Why? Why study Paul's letters at all? In doing so, why think about these approaches and perspectives? For these questions I admit that I most certainly have a first response, but the book itself reflects others besides this and, in engaging these responses, your encounter with this book might spark still more responses to such *why* questions. My answer is based upon what people have said about and done with Paul's letters.[1] People have variously argued that Paul's letters tell us what to think about women, slaves, gays and lesbians, Jews, foreigners, "pagans," the poor, children, and even the government (among other things). Perhaps these uses of the letters have conditioned your own impressions of Paul, either positively or negatively. You might be aware of the heightened role Paul's letters played in some historical debate; you might have felt the sting of condemnation or stereotype much more recently while others might be unaware of such impacts; or you still could insist that these are peripheral to what you feel is the main point of those letters. I won't be so foolish to ask you to "bracket" these experiences and impressions. However, this book will also ask you to think some more and, at one or several points, in different ways about how to approach these letters. Anything worth thinking, believing, or doing is worth further thought and reflection, particularly when it is related to something with so great an impact personally and publically.

Indeed, it is important to grapple with Paul's letters because they do continue to be used; they are not just epistles from the past, creating arguments with and for others long ago. This also suggests that Paul's letters are not just for Christians or even for people living in Christian-majority cultures. Because biblical ideas have become central to the most populous religion, and because people from Christian-majority cultures have gone virtually everywhere else on the planet (with otherwise good or bad intentions), it would be inadvisable to ignore the impact of biblical, and especially Pauline, image and argument. Whether you or I see it as legitimate or not (or ourselves practice it or not), people continue to use Pauline arguments and images to found or reinforce a variety of practices and standards, including those that have destructive and dehumanizing effects. With the help of the critical approaches and perspectives to follow, studying Paul's letters can make us savvier about such dynamics, certainly when biblical claims or worlds are being deployed but also more generally when appeals are made to any kind of authority or "foundation" in culture.

This sounds like a good reason "why" to study these letters, particularly with the help of the approaches and perspectives introduced in this book. As I noted above, it may not be your initial number one "why," but I do think there are good reasons this "why" can otherwise interact with, complement, or comment on other whys, likely including yours. Reflect and test these reasons as you continue reading; think critically and carefully about what perspectives and approaches are useful and relevant in addressing the whys of the world today.

WHERE TO BEGIN?

So, I return again to the question first posed in this introduction: What does some-one studying Paul's letters need to know before beginning? The trick is, though, that we have already begun, in the book, sure, but also in the world. For instance, one thing you might have already noticed, either about this introduction or even the title of the book itself, is that we don't study Paul—we study Paul's letters. Fur-ther than this, when someone starts to study these letters, she or he is also starting to study the way people have made meaning in their encounter with these letters. In stressing this, though, you might also notice that I have managed to introduce something about Paul after all: he wrote letters. Furthermore, the above discussion refers to the way many cultures have treated these letters and their author. Describ-ing this author simply as Paul might even strike you as odd, as if it were only the second half of the name for someone more commonly called Saint Paul. This Paul becomes a sanctified figure for many reasons, but highest among them are the let-ters that we attribute to him, letters that are preserved in some variation within the canonical scriptures of most Christian groups and cultures (in the Christian versions of the Bible). Deciding what counts as a central or necessary idea for our beginning is no neutral or objective activity, because these activities and attribu-tions of authority precede us. Already, the "basics" have been colored in particular shades and hues. Simply the fact that these were saved and treated in specific ways suggests to us certain reasons for their worth and relevance. The starting point or initial perspective on Paul's letters condition what seems important to tell you or anyone, in the beginning or in any time.

Therefore, it is important to recognize how one's starting point or perspective (yours, mine, a particular tradition's, or various authors', included or not in the chapters of this book) affects how one sees Paul's letters. But, for the moment, I can at least begin from what I have already noted: Paul's letters. Of course, almost immediately I will need to tell you that most scholars think only some of the four-teen letters later attributed to Paul are authentic or "undisputed" in authorship. Very few would consider the pastoral letters of 1 Timothy, 2 Timothy, and Titus as authentically from Paul, but a few more still think that Ephesians, Colossians, and 2 Thessalonians could be, while Hebrews seems completely different from all of the other letters. This leaves us with seven letters: Romans, 1 and 2 Corinthians, Gala-tians, Philippians, 1 Thessalonians, and Philemon. Even this process of discerning which letters are Pauline can reflect particular goals or histories. One could note that the assumption driving this process, a process of extracting the work of the "real Paul" from his imitators (or even students), is that it is important to find out which are from this "real Paul," all the better to follow and be instructed by him (as Saint Paul). Even as this might not be your or my operating assumption for why we are studying these letters, the division has proven to be a convenient one, for historical, rhetorical, cultural, and theological purposes, so it is one that this book mostly maintains and reflects.

Starting from another angle, I could emphasize that letters of course have audiences, so one then asks about these recipients in places like Galatia, Corinth, Philippi, or Rome. However, what one pursues or notices about these audiences also affects how they look. For example, Paul's letters often describe their intended recipients as the Gentiles to whom Paul was sent (see Rom. 1:1-6; or Gal. 1:15-17; 2:7-9). But even the choice of how to translate the Greek term for this group, *ta ethnē*, changes one's perspective on the letters. Should we imagine them as "the Gentiles," all the ancient peoples who weren't Jewish? Or should we talk about Paul as the apostle to "the nations," including the Jews and all of the other nations subject to the Romans?[2] From this point of view, it might become clear that Paul himself was Jewish, even a Pharisee (see, for instance, Phil. 3:4-6). However, this apparently obvious scholarly commonplace could be surprising, considering how many Christian traditions depict him as the Christian convert par excellence. Is it important then to introduce first an idea like this that conflicts with received traditions or dominant assumptions?

Circling back around to the subject of the letters, though, perhaps it seems more relevant that they were written in an ancient form of Greek. The letters, then, reflect the process called Hellenization, the way Greek rulers encouraged all they conquered in the eastern part of the Mediterranean to adapt to and participate in Greek culture. Of course, the letters reflect not only this linguistic system but also the wider cultural practices of presentation and argumentation, called rhetoric. Perhaps a more responsible introduction to Paul's letters should begin with an introduction to the exercises and figures of a rhetorical education so we can understand how they argue before we begin pulling out particular ideas or claims. Yet, the relevance of these figures and exercises is also rightly disputed, as scholars wonder whether Paul or his audiences would have received such an education, or whether certain ways of speaking or arguing were "in the air" when one went to markets and squares in the cities of the time.

It should now be apparent that depending upon where you begin, different elements of Paul's letters will end up being stressed or downplayed. Accordingly, the letters present a range of opportunities as well as a set of challenges. Indeed, since they are directed to particular communities at particular times, they present exciting possibilities for what they can tell us about these places and times that were key in the years before something like the earliest Christianities emerged. This is yet another reason why Paul's letters are important to study. However, the letters give and the letters take away. Not only are the letters written from some distance (Paul was not in Corinth, for instance, when he wrote to the Corinthians), but they also do not function like historical records or theological treatises. The letters were written occasionally in at least two senses of the word *occasional*: not systematically but every now and then, and for a specific reason or purpose. Often, it is not easy to discern what the occasion was for sending a letter, all the more so because Paul might not have been the most consistent or systematic letter writer. Nevertheless, given their density and their impact, studying Paul's letters provides us with our own occasion to reflect on a range of issues.

Such reflection could make us look at a number of factors in a new light. For instance, it might seem totally justified to introduce certain ideas like Hellenization, rhetoric, Paul's Jewishness, or his audience as Gentiles/nations in the discussion thus far. But how strange would it be for me to insist on introducing this letter writer as male? Certainly, some might say that this is an exercise in stating the obvious. Yet, its significance may not always be clear, not the least because often what we mean by maleness and femaleness, or masculinity and femininity, is actually pretty complex in its particularities. Not only were many of the concepts of gender in the ancient world different from our time, they were also themselves complex.[3] This gives us some new perspective on Paul's arguments, even when they seem to be universal, apparently directed to all, regardless of their gender (among other factors). The "packaging" for this universal message is typically directed in androcentric language (focused on, or from the perspective of, males). If I assume that females were present in the audience, what should I think about or even do with the language Paul uses from this androcentric perspective? Women in the audiences are named in several of Paul's letters (see Rom. 16:1-15; 1 Cor. 1:11; 16:19; Phil. 4:2-3; and Philem. 2), and issues about women's participation are discussed in general in several more places. Does this mean I should translate the Greek term *adelphoi* inclusively as "brothers and sisters" or preserve the androcentric sense of this language and translate it only as "brothers"? Does the second option exclude females now or simply raise our awareness of how problematic many language systems are (including ancient Greek)? Without paying attention to the specific issues of women's roles or gendered language, such ideas and questions would likely go unnoticed (as they did for many of Paul's interpreters and users throughout the centuries).

So, what is important enough to introduce when one is first starting to study Paul's letters? Beginning with the seemingly "new" or the apparently "obvious" gives us different results, but results that seem interesting, even compelling. As the above example demonstrates, rethinking factors that are taken for granted can be illuminating. In fact, one of the more interesting recent trends in Pauline scholarship is to rethink the specifically imperial aspect of living and working in the Roman Empire. One could argue that you cannot get more obvious than asking who the rulers were, yet it took more recent work to highlight the imperial resonance of many key Pauline terms like *righteousness* or, in the imperial light, the more pointedly political *justice*. Yet, it is important to consider how our ideas about these letters change if one introduces another topic, like Paul's "job." "Apostle" isn't exactly a job title, and according to some it doesn't pay very well, so highlighting that Paul and other members of these communities worked with their hands, likely as tentmakers, throws the letters into new light again. If Paul is primarily talking to people from such lower status groups, not middle- or upper-class people, then what we imagine we think of an assembly community in Rome will be different from more contemporary images of "church."

In this introduction I am not going to tell you which of these ideas should be the starting point. However, by starting with this selection of issues, the introduction (and this collection of chapters as a whole) is unlike many previous treatments of Paul's letters. As a result, I am also not going to tell you that something like faithfulness, or grace, or the law, are *the central* concepts for understanding Paul's letters, because frankly I am not convinced that they are. These are traditional and tricky concepts, with their own weighty religious history and theological significance, and you will see that they will be treated at various points in this book. However, if you have encountered them before, the authors in this book are likely to present them to you in fresh ways. Likewise, some have become accustomed to hearing or using Paul's letters as demonstrating that Paul is for or against women, slaves, LGBTIQ folks, imperial subjects, or the poor. Occasionally, the chapters to follow will argue similarly, but mostly they will complicate any simple pro- vs. anti- claims about Paul's arguments, while making it clear that the responsibility for dealing with these topics is now ours. Learning about and with the critical approaches and perspectives of this book will help take us to a more accountable place than simply attributing certain features to a letter or person from the past.

WHY AGAIN?

These are some of the reasons this book presents such a variety of critical perspectives and approaches. What one knows and does with Paul's letters depends upon the perspective from which one proceeds. This is why approach and perspective are one of the most pressing points of divergence as well as importance when it comes to understanding and using biblical texts. In short, complexity, questioning, and cross-conversations are all part of what biblical studies (or the most interesting part of it) looks like right now. Thus, this book will not be an "everything you ever needed to know about" Paul or Paul's letters, or even how to study them. The chapters in the book do not pretend to be comprehensive, claiming to "cover it all," quite possibly because such a claim would be pretending, given its impossibility. These chapters do aim, though, to help you and me comprehend what we are doing. The chapters make important ideas comprehensible, all so that one can become critically reflective about what it is that people (including ourselves) do when they use Paul's letters.

The images and arguments in these letters, and the worlds that they reflect and construct, are both like and unlike more contemporary images, arguments, and worlds. On the one hand, studying Paul's letters is like reading someone else's mail. On the other hand, as I have explained above, these letters are part of a crucial heritage religiously and culturally, a heritage that is both ours and not ours at the same time. Thus, we would be wise to engage them carefully and conscientiously. Still, one cannot help to note the resonances between Paul's world and the world many currently occupy. Both ancient and contemporary audiences are living in a context with both multicultural and monocultural impulses. Just like many of those who first read (or more likely heard) these letters, many of us today regularly interact with people, ideas, and practices from many different cultures. Yet, just as the Roman Empire promoted one dominant vision for how to live around the Mediterranean (what they called *mare nostrum*, or "our sea"), a larger corporate entertainment and communications network now aims to achieve its own singular kinds of market saturation and import its point of view around the world. Negotiating such contexts provided then and offer now opportunities for connection and disillusion, realizations and misunderstandings, often while exacerbating traditional divides and ongoing inequalities.

Given such conditions, the goals for this book are not simply to pass along information but to encourage a more critical and creative formation and even a transformation in how people negotiate their contexts. Certainly, I think it will be useful to develop an understanding of the academic approaches and perspectives presented in this book. This understanding will allow you to interpret these letters in new ways and see how the ideas in the various chapters are useful and relevant for a range of topics. More so, I think that engaging these perspectives and approaches can foster one's own critical abilities for using and evaluating images and arguments, in both approaches and applications.

The model for learning presented here in *Studying Paul's Letters* is not simply a master-disciple or an information acquisition model. As you read some of these chapters, you might become convinced to interpret Paul's letters more like the authors. Or you might encounter new ideas or concepts, ideas we are happy for people to learn. However, I wouldn't say that either of these is a primary goal of a collection like this. Rather, I hope that this book helps with the development of one's own critical abilities, considering how to use and also weigh and evaluate what one learns, questioning its utility for a variety of situations. Yes, each chapter presumes you can learn about a particular critical perspective or approach, giving you an idea of how to "do" that kind of reading or interpretation. Just as importantly (or even more so), the book encourages us to question and to construct a more meaningful present and future. Such questioning means evaluating and repositioning, likely so that we start doing things differently.

The book, then, offers the reader an opportunity for reflection, particularly on what conditions the way you or I think and act. What approach or perspective do you or I or another that we encounter take? Discerning and then evaluating these perspectives highlights why method matters, because it can indicate the mindset from which someone proceeds. Indeed, this helps to explain why so many of the debates about "what the Bible really says" often involve people speaking right past each other: their positions and claims reflect their difference in perspective or approach. This is one of the reasons why it is important to consider one's starting points, why this book foregrounds approach and perspective. Once people become more explicit and conscious about what their perspectives are, they become accountable not only for their perspective or approach but also for the results. One can imagine how differently some of these debates and discussions might look if they focused on this level of reflection. This is why we aim to learn more than just how to recount facts or ideas but to be more careful, conscious, critical, and creative users of authoritative traditions or foundational texts, whether they are biblical or otherwise.

Certainly, this could help in any efforts to go some place other than where people have gone in the history of uses of Paul's letters. Indeed this is an urgent and ethically compelling task for a number of reasons. For instance, developing such skills can help one address those uses that were part of my initial answer to "why" one should study Paul's letters in this way. It is important to grapple with how people have used biblical and specifically Pauline argumentation in dominating, destructive, and dehumanizing ways. Given the effects of these uses, feminist biblical scholar Elisabeth Schüssler Fiorenza has famously argued that the contents of biblical texts should be marked with the label: "Caution, could be dangerous to your health and survival."[4] Schüssler Fiorenza is not alone in making such a determination. As another scholar (and prominent religious leader), Krister Stendahl, wrote years ago: "I would guess that the last racists in this country, if there ever be an end to such, will be the ones with Bible in hand. There never has been an evil cause in the world that has not become more evil if it has been possible to argue it on biblical grounds."[5] Such an assertion haunts many of our attempts more responsibly to understand and use Paul's letters or, indeed, any text that is treated as uniquely meaningful or instructive. Yet, as you will also see (or might already know), biblical texts have also been used to argue against such destruction and domination. Indeed, these uses are why I often describe the Bible as part of a "mixed heritage" culturally and religiously.

Because of these historical and contemporary uses of biblical argumentation, many have called for changes in how people engage biblical images and arguments. As early as her 1987 public address as the president of the Society of Biblical Literature (the main academic association for biblical scholars), Schüssler Fiorenza has argued for "an ethics of accountability that stands responsible not only for the choice of theoretical interpretive models but also for the ethical consequences of the biblical text and its subsequent interpretations."[6] This, then, becomes a matter not just of how "the church" lives with the text but also of a responsibility to a wider public. Because all kinds of social, cultural, and political arguments often make public claims using the Bible and, thus, shape social and political life, responsible and responsive students of biblical scholarship must address a wider audience than just religious and academic institutions.

HOW TO USE THIS BOOK

This book aims to address wider audiences and an extensive set of issues and ideas. Indeed, the chapters to follow represent many of the latest and most important trends in biblical studies. Each chapter in this book aims to exemplify what a difference in perspective or approach can make for understanding the use and interpretation of Paul's letters. In doing so the chapters will not be mechanical in form; they are not simply a "how to" instruction manual. Rather, they will be focused upon clearly communicating what each critical approach or perspective is, why it matters, and how it works when engaging an instance of a chapter (or so) of Paul's letters. Each of these can also work on other Pauline texts and typically other biblical texts as well, which is why this book also functions as a good "crash course" on theories and methodologies for biblical studies in general. The overall structure of the book reflects not only the most relevant or recently emergent work in Pauline studies, but it is also organized so that one can engage a new reading every week or so, especially (but not only) if you are using this in a course or with a study group.

Structurally, this *could* mean that one reads the chapters of this book in a sequence going from front to back. In fact, the first full chapter that follows my introduction, on historical approaches, is instructive for the way it foregrounds what are often a series of unspoken assumptions about how to understand and use biblical and specifically Pauline texts. It critically reflects upon the position of historical criticism and qualifies how else one can ask questions about history. Many of the chapters after that exemplify particular ways to pursue different historical questions, or simply begin from the starting point that historical information is crucial in the study of Paul's letters. However, some of these chapters will not strictly, or even particularly, be interested in making historical claims or pursuing historical reconstructions.[7] Therefore, it could also be instructive to explore other chapters first and come back around to ones like the "Historical Approaches" chapter. As a result, there is no particular reason why one must read one chapter before any other, including even this introduction. One can start in the middle and work outward, go from back to front, or simply browse the chapter titles and contents and start where you are most excited, confused, enraged, or simply curious.

The nature of this book allows for multiple uses precisely because, as you will notice, there are quite a few overlaps, resonances, and conversations between these chapters and their authors. The "Historical Approaches" chapter, for instance, contextualizes historical pursuits in terms of recent questions and challenges posed from feminist, Jewish, political, and other communal perspectives, questions and challenges described in chapters like "Feminist Approaches," "Jewish Perspectives," and "Postcolonial Approaches," but reflected in virtually all of the other chapters. Many of the chapters address how Pauline letters and interpretations function as arguments, while some even indicate how seemingly neutral or passive parts of culture, like visual images or urban architecture, themselves reflect and construct particular arguments (see the "Visual Perspectives" and "Spatial Perspectives" chapters). Yet, such a topic is most closely treated in a chapter on rhetorical approaches. One might assume, given the history of how Paul's letters were used to explain or condemn the Atlantic slave trade, that slavery would be an important issue in a chapter on African American approaches, but slave images and contexts are addressed in the "Feminist Approaches" and "Queer Approaches" chapters as well. One might think that the roles of women or gendered language are of interest only to those last two chapters mentioned, nevertheless they play key roles in considering a range of conditions in the "Economic Approaches," "Rhetorical Approaches," and "Visual Perspectives" chapters. Paul's Jewishness is an important element not only for the "Jewish Perspectives" chapter but also for the "Asian American Perspectives" chapter (among others).

A discussion of such overlaps, conversations, and interconnections based upon topics, commitments, concerns, or procedures could go on for much longer. Indeed, this might not be a bad topic of conversation for you and others to consider as you encounter the perspectives and approaches of this book. The resonances between these chapters indicate that these authors (and coauthors) are not just expert scholars and teachers in the particular approaches or perspectives they introduce in this book. In fact, each of them could have just as easily written one of the chapters besides the ones they have done here. This underscores how a lot of the more interesting and important work in biblical studies does not proceed from just one starting point.

While in some ways it is a bit easier at first to learn each of these "on its own," these interconnections should also encourage you to explore and experiment with how these ideas and procedures can interact with and contribute to each other. Try reading two or more of these approaches or perspectives together, in order to look for things like the economic impact of spatial arrangement (or the spatial impact on one's economic place). How might this be further complicated if you recall imperial or colonial contexts, then or now? Do these have different impacts for those who have been constructed and treated as racial or ethnic minorities? Do such groups have different perspectives on elements of history, art, or architecture?

Such experimentation and exploration can apply to how one looks at Paul's letters, and which parts of them. Each of the chapters spends some time showing how one might use or apply the practices and concepts from certain perspectives or approaches to one particular passage from the letters. However, these are not meant to indicate that one cannot just as easily and constructively apply or use them with many other parts of Paul's letters (or the wider biblical corpus). Several of the chapters offer examples along the way of the relevance of their approaches or perspectives for other passages. Yet, even when they do not, it is both relevant and rewarding to explore and experiment with using these in different ways, at different times, on different passages or topics (and, then, in continued conversation with other chapters). In fact, most of the letters treated in this book are engaged in more than one chapter: Romans (Economic and Feminist), Galatians (Visual, Jewish, Asian American, and Queer), Philippians (Rhetorical and Spatial), 1 Thessalonians (Historical and Postcolonial), and Philemon (African American). (While the Corinthian correspondence is not the primary focus for any of these, key issues for these letters are raised in several of the chapters, including the Economic, Feminist, Postcolonial, and Queer chapters.) Thus, even just comparing how different chapters talk about the same letter can prove illuminating, since each changes the focus and method for engaging the letter.

Each of these chapters aims to be detailed enough to be accurate and illuminating but still focused enough to be accessible and clear. As a result, I cannot pretend to tell you that what is presented in each of the chapters are the only important things to know and do for those approaches or perspectives. The longer you spend and the closer you attend to these chapters, the more you will certainly notice that even more questions can be asked, and still other critical perspectives or approaches could be adopted. Efforts were made to include entries on as many relevant approaches and perspectives as possible, while still keeping the book manageable to read and use. It is certainly my hope that the interested reader, student, or even teacher might "talk back," then, with their own issues and questions for the traditions of interpretation, the letters themselves, and even the chapters of this book. This might also be sparked by the clear ways in which the various authors of these chapters work out of different contexts, including their teaching and learning contexts. Such differences are useful, as you or I can use them as an occasion to reflect upon the particularities of our own contexts, to think about commitments, and to consider how those would differ in still other settings or times (for you, me, or others).

Thus, I would describe each of these chapters as a "good faith" effort (if you'll pardon the expression) to help us focus upon what they see as the most relevant issues, concepts, and practices for these approaches and perspectives. The reader should flip back to the endnotes, particularly when you find the chapter you are reading especially interesting.[8] Because there is always more to know and to read, each chapter also suggests some selections for further reading that would reward your additional exploration, consideration, and evaluation. I hope that such aims and aids help to make this book a resource deserving careful study and reuse.

The perspectives and approaches presented in this collection present not only the state of the issues in Pauline studies, they also reckon with and beckon beyond the boundaries of such scholarship. This book is reflective *and* suggestive, characterizing the present *and* propelling us users of the book into an anticipatory future that is more consistent in its theoretical nuance and critical reflexivity. I hope that you will find these good, preliminary reasons for how, where, and why to study Paul's letters in the ways offered here.

NOTES

1. For an engaging overview of the interpretations of Paul's letters over the centuries, see Robert Paul Seesengood, *Paul: A Brief History* (Malden: Wiley-Blackwell, 2010).

2. On Paul as the apostle to the nations, see Davina C. Lopez, *Apostle to the Conquered: Reimagining Paul's Mission* (Minneapolis: Fortress Press, 2008). There has also been some debate about whether and when to translate the Greek term *Ioudaios* as "Jew/Jewish" or "Judean." See, for instance, Denise Kimber Buell and Caroline Johnson Hodge, "The Politics of Interpretation: The Rhetoric of Race and Ethnicity in Paul," *Journal of Biblical Literature* 123, no. 2 (2004): 235–51; Amy-Jill Levine, *The Misunderstood Jew: The Church and the Scandal of the Jewish Jesus* (San Francisco: Harper, 2006); and Caroline Johnson Hodge, *If Sons, Then Heirs: A Study of Kinship and Ethnicity in the Letters of Paul* (Oxford: Oxford University Press, 2007), especially 11–15.

3. See, for example, the discussion in Caroline Vander Stichele and Todd Penner, *Contextualizing Gender in Early Christian Discourse: Thinking beyond Thecla* (London: T&T Clark, 2009).

4. See Elisabeth Schüssler Fiorenza, *Rhetoric and Ethic: The Politics of Biblical Studies* (Minneapolis: Fortress Press, 1999), 14.

5. See Krister Stendahl, "Ancient Scripture in the Modern World," in *Scripture in the Jewish and Christian Traditions: Authority, Interpretation, Relevance*, ed. Frederick E. Greenspahn (Nashville: Abingdon, 1982), 201–14, 205. Stendahl was a well-known figure in both Europe and the U.S., as a prominent professor at Harvard Divinity School and as the Bishop of Stockholm, indicating that asking such questions or pursuing these sorts of issues are not strictly only academic or religious.

6. See Schüssler Fiorenza, *Rhetoric and Ethic*, 17–30, 28. Reprinted from *Journal of Biblical Literature* 107, no. 1 (1988): 3–17.

7. For example, see also the assertion made by John D. Caputo: "What the later tradition makes of foundationalist texts is both necessary and necessarily anachronistic—it departs from the original text and context. That is to say, later generations are nourished by the foundational texts in ways that meet the needs of their times and reflect their own standpoints as much as, and perhaps more than, the foundational texts themselves. That is as it should be. The tradition is marked by geniuses who give strong misreadings of foundational texts which shape their own times and that of subsequent generations." See Caputo, "Introduction: Postcards from Paul: Subtraction versus Grafting," in *St. Paul among the Philosophers*, ed. Caputo and Linda Martín Alcoff (Bloomington: Indiana University Press, 2009), 1–23, 18.

8. Over the years, a number of my students have assured me that students never read footnotes or endnotes. Let the recommendation of this introduction suffice to underscore, though, the potential utility of checking them, if, for nothing else, the possibility that teachers are taking students' input seriously!

1

HISTORICAL APPROACHES

Which Past? Whose Past?

MELANIE JOHNSON-DEBAUFRE

The present changes our past. How is that possible? How can new developments today change the past? The answer is simple and you may have already guessed it. What happened in the past is only available to us through history, through the stories, charts, images, and objects that describe and represent the past.

Imagine telling about your day today in one story. Which moments will you tell about and which will you skip over? How do you decide what is worth telling about your day? Which objects that you used or touched should be associated with you and with this day? In the future, your story of this day might be changed because of things that happen. If you become a leading historian, someone might find this book filled with your marginal notes and argue that your love of history began when you read a book about Paul. What if society in the future is concerned about different realities than you are concerned about now? Your version of the day's story probably does not mention that people picked up your garbage on the curb today. But if in the future your city is overrun by waste or a sanitation workers' strike, your town might implicate you in its history of wasteful self-destruction or in its habit of paying low wages to essential but unskilled labor. With these kinds of changes, your future self might no longer recognize your own story, or you may now remember your past differently.

This chapter explores changes in the discipline of biblical studies that have altered the history we tell about the letters of Paul. Because the story of the past is constantly being rewritten in new times and from different perspectives, you too can enter the critical discussion about the history of Pauline communities and why it might matter to tell it differently.

THE BROAD CONTEXT

For much of the twentieth century, virtually the sole approach to the academic study of the Bible in Europe and the U.S. was *historical criticism*, which privileges interpreting biblical texts "in their historical contexts, in light of the literary and cultural conventions of their time."[1] This approach emerged in the European Enlightenment largely among Protestant theologian-scholars seeking religious and intellectual freedom from church authorities. It was thus part of a shifting approach to knowledge: "where medieval culture had celebrated belief as a virtue and regarded doubt as a sin, the modern critical mentality regards doubt as a necessary step in the testing of knowledge."[2] This introduced a separation between the history *in* the text and the history *of* and *around* the text. For example, historical-critical scholars began to distinguish among a scholarly history of the figure of Jesus, the story of Jesus in the Gospels, and the history of the writing of the Gospels. Phenomena like Jesus' miracles began to be doubted as historical because they violate the laws of nature and reason. Although biblical critics in this period still largely viewed the book of Acts as presenting the history of Paul's travels, there was significant effort to *prove* that it is historical, a project that presupposes that Acts might not be historical. Influential studies of Paul that explained his life and thought in terms of the religion and culture of the first century also emerged with this approach.

Although some people still find it unsettling, asking historical questions has become the standard scholarly approach to the Bible. Most of the reference works in the field, from dictionaries and commentaries to introductory textbooks and websites, have been produced with the historical-critical toolbox, which contains such tools as textual, source, form, and redaction criticisms, archaeology, epigraphy, and historically-focused versions of literary and sociological analysis.

However, in the past forty years, the landscape of biblical interpretation has begun to change. With the rise of diverse social movements claiming rights and recognition for groups of people traditionally excluded from the power structures of society, white women and various minority men and women in Europe and the U.S. began to enter the academy. On a global scale, nationalist and liberationist movements redrew the global map. From the 1970s on, the presence of and attention to diverse perspectives have multiplied, and new methods that take seriously the way knowledge and meaning is always produced in cultural contexts have proliferated in the field of biblical studies. Many of these approaches are represented in this volume.

Both the history of western colonialism and the social movements of the twentieth century have had an impact on Western thinking regarding the modernist approach to knowledge and authority. The broadest term one might use to describe the shift is *postmodernism*.[3] Generally speaking, a postmodern way of thinking questions a modern privileging of traditional order, scientific rationality, and scholarly objectivity. A postmodern worldview highlights the way that knowledge—and even reality itself—is much more varied and contested than in a modernist view. The diversification of voices and shifting ideas about the nature of language and the politics of scholarship has produced an exciting intellectual context in biblical studies characterized by multiplicity and possibility. The next section introduces three basic principles that reflect these changes and that reorient how we might approach history in relation to the letters of Paul.

THREE BASIC PRINCIPLES FOR A CRITICAL PRACTICE OF HISTORY

Language Shapes Reality

One of the most far-reaching ways to generate new historical questions is to remind ourselves constantly that language does not describe or reflect reality, it creates and shapes reality. From a traditional historian's point of view, Paul's letters are evidence of what happened in Corinth or Philippi or Galatia. But words do not refer to external realities in any simple way; rather, they participate in constituting that reality. Taking this distinction seriously is commonly called *history after the linguistic turn*, because it recognizes that our understanding of the past is always mediated by and as texts, both ancient and modern. Even material remains from the past must be interpreted as and by texts.

Consider a simple example of this principle: when Paul exclaims "O foolish Galatians!" (Gal. 3:1a), it is hardly a straightforward *fact* that the Galatians are fools. We should ask: How and why did Paul try to shape how the Galatians saw themselves? Do we know that any of them understood themselves as fools? How does Paul's language shape how *we* understand them? You would be surprised how many interpreters of Galatians subtly assume that Paul is right and the letter's audience is religiously or intellectually deficient. They do not see that they are taking Paul's evaluations at face value. Many descriptions of the situation Paul addressed in the Galatian community replicate his negative evaluation of his audience. Paul is speaking rhetorically, that is, he is seeking to *persuade* his audience (see the "Rhetorical Approaches" chapter). Classifying his language within the types of ancient rhetoric helps our understanding, but it does not give us access to how the Galatians understood themselves, nor does it expose that Paul is making a power play that may or may not have succeeded.[4]

The one-sided nature of Paul's letters presents a challenge to historians because texts can only succeed in producing reality if the readers grant authority to the text.

Readers consent to or resist the text and thus participate in its production of meaning. Indeed, texts need readers to internalize and reproduce their ideas in order to have meaning and an impact on the world. This insight has been invaluable to feminist biblical scholars who take a posture of *suspicion* toward the biblical texts and their interpretations because their construction of reality is male-centered and promotes hierarchical structures of power and privilege based on categories like gender, race, and class. For example, when Paul says, "I want you to understand that the head of every man is Christ, the head of a woman is her husband, and the head of Christ is God" (1 Cor. 11:3), in what sense do these words describe an ancient reality? Can we be sure that this is how everyone saw humans and the divine? If so, why does Paul say "I want you to understand"? Some historians might use 1 Corinthians 11:3 to demonstrate that the ancient Pauline communities were hierarchical with regard to gender. Others might use the same text to propose that the ancient Corinthian community was so fervently engaging issues that touched on women's status that Paul (re)asserted a gendered hierarchy in response.

What You See Depends on Where You Stand

Disrupting an easy relationship between language and reality leads quickly to issues of perspective and authority. Just as the text is not automatically a description of the way things are, so the historian is not an objective describer of the past. He or she is always located. Even the concept of scientific objectivity emerged in a particular context. As discussed above, getting critical distance from the text and appealing to a scientific approach to knowledge freed biblical scholarship to pursue its questions independent of church approval. However, the impulses toward rooting authority in reason and the pursuit of objective Truth emerged at the same time as modern Western racism and colonialism, which often vilified or romanticized the "Other"—that is, the non-white, non-Christian, non-Western—as irrational, inferior, and uncivilized (and thus in need of civilizing). This claim to objectivity thus also served to authorize Western imperialism and racism, presenting Western ways of knowing and being as if they were and should be universal (see, for instance, the "African American Approaches" and "Postcolonial Approaches" chapters).

Reminding ourselves that *what we see depends on where we stand* interrupts any illusions of objectivity and raises the question of alternative and multiple ways of thinking. There are many handbooks, dictionaries, and textbooks that describe the history of the Pauline communities in impartial tones and as a set of relatively stable facts. It is quite easy to forget that these resources present the composite results of a series of scholarly arguments, interpretive decisions, and even unseen prejudices and assumptions. How often do we examine *how* these resources tell history and from what perspective?

For example, it is very common for New Testament scholarship to miss its Christian bias. The pro-Christian perspective of histories of the first century is often (but not always) quite apparent to non-Christians. Some members of minority groups and people from postcolonial contexts likewise have seen the way the Mediterranean past has been claimed as the history of white and western peoples.[5] Recognizing that all history writing is selective and perspectival raises political and ethical questions that can be asked by anyone: Whose history has been told? Who has benefitted from this telling of the past? How has this telling been blind and/or harmful? How does your own context shape your view of Christian beginnings? These are questions you can ask in your study of both the letters and the history of interpretation of Paul.

History Is an Interpretation of the Past, Not the Past Itself

If you were to write a history of the Pauline communities, you would need to make some basic decisions. What materials will you use? Will you use all thirteen letters attributed to Paul? Or, will you accept the arguments of previous scholars and use only the seven letters understood to be "authentic" Pauline letters? How will you use the book of Acts? For other literature of the period, will you look at mostly Jewish sources—since Paul was Jewish—or at Greek and Roman literature since Paul wrote in Greek and presents himself as an apostle to the many peoples (Gentiles) of the Roman Empire? What about archaeological remains and other material artifacts? Which scholarly histories will you consult? According to what criteria will you select them?

Thinking about these basic questions reminds us that the past is lost to us except through some texts and material remains and the decisions we make about them. Whatever we say we know about the past is always a narration or a text of the past and not the past itself. If all our histories are particular interpretations of the past, then alternative narrations are always possible; not only ones that might arguably aim to be more accurate than the alternatives but also ones that might be *as* accurate but might narrate history from a different point of view or with a different goal. Taking a critical approach to history means examining the interests and assumptions of the histories that we have received from previous generations. It draws our attention not only to a history's content but also its infrastructures, such as its large-scale models, terminology and categories, periodization, selection of relevant events and texts, choice of analogies, and theories of cause and effect.

One model of history that has been very influential in modernist historical criticism is the privileging of origins as the place to find the true essence of Christianity. The modern roots of this model are in the Reformation. Martin Luther championed (his interpretation of) the Pauline churches as the place where true Christianity emerged as a religion of freedom and faith defined over and against laws and works. From this view, the Judaism that came before Paul is often characterized as anemic and legalistic, and the Roman Catholic Christianity that came after is seen as both legalistic and also as polluted with pagan ideas, such as that the divine needs demonstrations of piety. Many historical narratives of the Pauline churches still replicate the notion that an ideal Pauline Christianity fixed and replaced Judaism and/ or eventually declined into Roman Catholicism.

Both interpretations of the past—a model of progress and/or decline—are grand fictions. They organize events in a particular way, minimize any contradicting evidence or perspectives, and valorize particular versions of Christianity. In the postmodern context discussed above, suspicion of such grand narratives has come from many fronts. Such totalizing stories miss the ways that we use history to organize a past that is much messier, mundane, and multidirectional. We often organize the past in order to say something to and about our own present contexts. What is at stake in how you explain Christian beginnings? What debates and ideas today might revise and revitalize how we narrate the past? The next section introduces three trends in historical approaches to Paul that represent larger scale shifts away from the traditional narrations of early Christian history.

THREE TRENDS IN PAULINE HISTORIOGRAPHY

De-Christianizing Paul

In an introduction to the Bible course that I used to teach at an undergraduate institution, I would regularly give an introductory lecture on Paul entitled, "Paul was not a Christian." I made the case that Paul lived and died a Jew simply by reviewing Paul's self-description, the absence of the term "Christian" from the Pauline letters, and the preponderance of Jewish traditions and questions discussed in the letters. This lecture always caused a commotion among the students. Many of us instinctively assume that mid-first-century people who understood Jesus as the Christ are basically the same as those who later called themselves Christians, and that Christianity is the result of specifically Christian ways of thinking put forth by certain notable people, such as the apostle Paul. We assume that without such thinkers there would be no Christianity. Because Paul has long been a figure in Christian history, he has been effectively converted into a Christian despite the ways these are plain anachronisms.

A significant corrective trend in the historical study of the letters of Paul can be broadly characterized as an effort to de-Christianize Paul by re-Judaizing him. Revising this picture of Paul has required deeper and more detailed knowledge of first-century Judaism, rethinking Paul's major concepts as fully within the range of Jewish thought in his time, and even retranslating words and phrases that have been heavily Christianized by centuries of Christian interpretation. Although scholars do not agree on all the details, the results of this trend—often called the "New Perspective on Paul"—represent a significant new historical picture of Paul as a fully Jewish thinker engaging Gentile audiences.[6] The traditional Paul introduces religious innovations to Judaism and is seen as radically breaking with Judaism. This view of Paul is built on and perpetuates a prejudicial Christian caricature of Jews and Judaism as legalistic and ethnocentric. By contrast, the New Paul is not a Christian critiquing Judaism. Rather, he addresses issues of social, ethnic, and cultural difference and group identity and solidarity from his Jewish perspective, which is also an ethnic-cultural identity in antiquity.

In this frame, Paul's thinking about faith, the Law, Gentile salvation, and Christology has its home in Jewish thought (see the "Jewish Perspectives" chapter). The conflicts and authority struggles so apparent in Paul's letters prove that there was a lively debate within the Christ communities about the relationship of the peoples of the nations (Gentiles/*ethnē*) to the God of the Judeans, the Judean people and their traditions, and the rest of the people of the nations and their gods and traditions. Although many scholars still view Paul as a religious or cultural hero—recall the foolish Galatians example—taking this new approach helps us see that there was not one Jewish or "Christian" or Gentile position in the Christ communities on these issues. The valorization and magnification of Paul's view as *the* Christian view is the result of the interpretive process of history, not a fact of history. As you study Paul's letters and read scholarship interpreting them, pay close attention to how much your (or their) view of Paul resembles later Christian theology and Christian attitudes toward Jews and Judaism.

Why is this important? One reason is because we might be able to produce new historical narratives that are arguably more accurate, that is, they can make better sense of the texts of the past than the narratives of previous generations. Another is because the telling of history is not only about the past, it is also about the present. After one of my "Paul Was Not a Christian" lectures, my coteacher overheard a student ask another student: "Is she Jewish?" Why would an academic lecture about the historical Paul being Jewish result in someone speculating about my own religious affiliation? Apparently, the student needed to make sense of why I would tell history in this way. Indeed, the student's instinct that something in the present must be motivating me was correct in general if not in the specifics. Teaching at a church-related college, I felt that it was my responsibility as an educator to encourage critical thinking about the Christian tradition and its complicity in such social violence as anti-Semitism. Telling history differently exposes the way that Christians have made Paul a spokesperson for Christian prejudice against Jews. In this way, the needs of the present inform the way we rethink the past. Indeed, the New

Perspective on Paul emerged in response to the Holocaust among Western Christian biblical scholars investigating the roots of Christian anti-Semitism and among historians seeking to understand Paul's Jewish context on its own terms rather than in the service of progressive narratives of Christian supersession of Judaism. These two goals—better history and more responsible history—are echoed in the words of John Gager, a historical-critical scholar who has proposed one of the more radical reinventions of the Jewish Paul: "My argument is that the dominant view of Paul across nearly two thousand years is both bad, in that it has proved harmful, and wrong, in that it can no longer be defended historically."[7]

Politicizing Paul

If you take a college course on Paul, who is more likely to teach it: a religion professor or someone in a department like political science, classics, literature, or history? Although your professor might have a literary or historical focus, most academic classes on Paul are religion courses (of course, this is also true by default in seminary classes). Being part of the Christian canon, the letters of Paul are usually viewed as religious texts that need to be studied theologically and/or within the history of religions. This creates at least two problems. First, it predetermines that when we read Paul's letters, we expect to find religion and to ask questions about religion. Second, it splits off religion as a category of human experience somehow separate from the other aspects of culture. Is it your experience that people's religion today can be easily separated from their politics, economics, social habits, or even their taste in art and literature? Although the historical-critical method requires attention to the social-political context of the New Testament, this historical work often serves as background in which to find the religious meanings of the text and in which to set a narrative of the emergence of the Christian religion.

A second significant trend in a historical approach to the Pauline letters has been to repoliticize Paul, that is, to consider the ways that Paul's letters can be read as instruments of political and economic organizing and ideology rather than as theological treatises.[8] One increasingly common way of taking this approach to Paul entails significant attention to the context of the power relations and propaganda of the Roman Empire, as well as an understanding that ancient religion was thoroughly a part of ancient social, political, and economic life. This does not mean ancient religion is somehow false religion, that is, simply politics masking as religion. We can only make this value judgment if we have a presupposition that true religion is somehow *not politics*. In the ancient world these separate categories: "politics" and "religion"—or "state" and "church," or "secular" and "religious"—simply did not exist.

A now classic example of religious language resonating with social-political meaning and values is 1 Thessalonians 4:13–5:11. This passage has traditionally been read (1) as Paul's pastoral care for grieving Thessalonians, assuring them of life after death, and (2) as Paul's Jewish apocalyptic (thus religious) announcement of the second coming of Christ, promising the rescue (or rapture) of faithful Christians before God's judgment of a sinful world. Both themes emphasize the personal and spiritual over the social and political. However, much of Paul's imagery and vocabulary here echoes royal pageantry and military readiness. Death and grief are addressed at the same time that proclamations of "peace and security" (5:3), common themes in Augustan imperial self-promotion, are exposed as empty promises (see the "Postcolonial Approaches" chapter). In this context, Paul's apocalyptic future takes on very present political implications. Is the coming Lord an alternative to the reigning Caesar? In what ways did the letters of Paul reorient their audience to prevailing systems of justice, patronage, and political loyalty? What if Paul's letters attest not to a new religious movement but to the formation of alternative communities of resistance and solidarity against the false advertising of the Roman peace?

If we told the history of early Christianity primarily as political history rather than religious history, then the growth of Western Christianity defined as individual beliefs concerning spiritual—not political—matters would also have to be seen as having a political impact. Postcolonial biblical scholars have made this point in relation to the efforts to re-politicize Paul. Although we might convincingly reconstruct the Pauline assemblies as communities of colonized people responding to the Roman Empire, we also have to tell the history of Paul's letters being used to authorize Western projects to missionize, and, therefore, aid in the colonization of Africa, Asia, and the imperial ambitions of the West. In this sense, even the religious readings of Paul have always been political.

Changing the Subject: People's History and De-Centering Paul

You have probably heard the expression, "History is written by the winners." History is also written *about* the winners, about great men and their public deeds, such as their political or military accomplishments. Since the 1970s, historians and other academics have pointed out the way that this kind of history focuses on the elites of a past society and usually serves the elites of the present society. In this sense, history is also written *for* the winners. A familiar case in the United States is the way that school history books have treated the presence and lives of people of African descent in North America. Telling history in a way that treats slavery as a problem overcome by leaders of the past with little attention to its ongoing social, political, or economic effects can subtly relieve contemporary people, particularly those who benefit from white privilege, from examining the structural aspects of racism in the present day. National programs such as Black History Month (or Women's History

Month) attempt to fill in the common omissions in U.S. history, even while their existence proves that certain people have populated our narratives of the past much more than others. Some projects attend more to class than to gender or ethnicity and race, tracing a "People's History" that focuses on the lives of everyday people— rather than the "great men"—as well as the struggles of the working class in the face of the rise of industrialization and capitalism. The ideological critique of history and the efforts to restore a range of people to history together represent a wide- ranging effort to *change the subjects* of history, that is, to reconsider who benefits from the telling of history and to revise whose past we tell.

These larger trends appear in the study of Paul's letters in a few ways. Feminist scholars made early and influential contributions both to the history of women in the Pauline communities and to methodologies that expose and counter the male-centeredness (or androcentrism) of both the biblical texts and the traditions of interpretation (see the "Feminist Approaches" chapter). Using social scientific methods and the study of visual and popular culture, some scholars have turned from an interest in the history of Christianity to the history of Christians, in which everyday Christians become the subjects of history and are considered social, political, and economic actors in their societies.[9] Given that the vast majority of the textual remains and the most visible material remains of the ancient world are products of elite culture, this effort to tell a history of everyday people is difficult. Some scholars of the New Testament have suggested that Paul's letters represent a rare opportunity to glimpse everyday ancient people because they were produced in and for communities of non-elite people.

Changing the subjects of history means taking marginalized perspectives seri- ously as well as resisting the powerful tendency to focus on great men. This can be difficult because Paul's letters present only his point of view. Our eyes are drawn to Paul because of the canonization of his letters, the hero stories in Acts, and the Christian tradition's own tendency to tell its history in terms of great men and their victories. Changing the subject means making some effort, for example, to think about the impact of Paul's teaching on slave members of the communities or about how slaves might have re- or even mis-interpreted his words.

Another way to think about changing the subject of history is to consider de- centering Paul from the stories we tell.[10] How can we approach the letters of Paul as attesting to connections and debates among different people and communities rather than as repositories of one person's vision? The history of social movements is often told as the history of great visionaries. These histories do not tell the stories of the myriad of people that come together to make common cause, deal with their disagreements, and often unwittingly and over time produce new ways of thinking and living. If we interpret Paul as part of the communities of Christ rather than as their creator and sole spokesperson, he does not have to always be right or the hero of the story. Because the writing of history is never only about the past, this de-centering of Paul makes room for contemporary people to engage the questions of the communities of Christ as they resonate in new but equally diverse social contexts rather than to focus on what Paul alone thought or did.

EXPLORING LARGE SHIFTS WITH A SMALL TEXT: 1 THESSALONIANS 2:14-16

Thinking with Basic Principles

Let's turn to a Pauline text to see how thinking with these basic principles and larger trends might spur our historical imagination and critical thinking. Paul's first letter to the Thessalonians has a small section comparing the suffering of the community to that of the Christ communities in Judea. Spend some time comparing a few translations of 1 Thessalonians 2:14-16. What differences do you see? What questions do you have? Even if you do not know Greek, examining small differences among translations can immediately remind us that texts do not reflect reality in a straightforward way.

First Thessalonians is often seen as evidence for and interpreted with two historical generalizations: that the early Christians faced opposition from Jews and that they were persecuted for their faith. Applying the basic principle that *language shapes reality*, however, paints a much less clear picture. For example, the assertion in 2:15 that "Jews" "oppose everyone" (NRSV) is not a neutral description but a negative generalization. Why does Paul describe Jews in this way? Did his view resonate with his audience?

Many commentaries and textbooks on 1 Thessalonians say that the community was experiencing persecution. But the letter does not give any details of this suffering. If we take Paul's words in 2:14 literally, we still have to fill in the gaps: what kind of suffering? How much? From whom or what? Often we depend upon those very commentaries and textbooks to fill in these gaps. But, they do not have more direct evidence of this particular community than you and I have, that is, 1 Thessalonians itself. Paul is choosing (consciously or unconsciously, it really does not matter) to describe the community in this way. Thus, our verses are not automatically evidence that the Thessalonians *have suffered*, rather they are evidence of the community *being interpreted as sufferers* and being invited to see themselves in that way. This language may shape how the audience and later readers view their experiences. It may also influence how they and we view Paul. In this sense the text does not even have a direct relationship to the real Paul of the past; what we think we know about Paul is also shaped by Paul's language and the texts—the biblical ones and our own.

At minimum, we can say that 1 Thessalonians 2:14-16 proves that some Christ followers (or at least one) in the mid–first century expressed very negative generalizations about (some) Jews and interpreted their own experiences through the deaths of Jesus and some unnamed prophets. Traditional historians will make some attempt to say—judiciously—what actually happened. Historians after the linguistic turn are more likely to remain agnostic about just how much we can know about the Thessalonian community or the mind of Paul and rather explore the predecessors, relatives, and after-effects of this kind of rhetoric (see further below). One can also explore the ways that polemical language against Jews and viewing the representation of the Christian as a sufferer became common ways for ancient Christians to interpret their world.

In the last forty years, many interpreters of this passage have been preoccupied with a particular historical question: Was Paul anti-Semitic? The appearance of this question in scholarship, where it did not appear before, demonstrates the principle that *what you see depends on where you stand*. While previous generations had not been particularly troubled by what was taken as a declaration of God's judgment on Jews, the violence of the Holocaust jolted many Western theologians and historians into examining the Christian past for the roots of modern anti-Semitism. Because 1 Thessalonians has been viewed by scholars as the earliest surviving "Christian" text, these few verses raise the question whether anti-Semitism has infused Christian thought from the very beginnings. It was not scholars' evolving objectivity that produced and compelled new questions. It was precisely their self-reflective subjectivity—their experience of shame and responsibility in the face of the horrors of the Holocaust—that changed the way they thought about the past.

The principle that all perspectives are located opens up new ways to think about familiar texts, but it also resists the idea that the corrected perspective is now somehow fully objective or simply factual. For example, examining the text with the question of anti-Semitism in mind, this passage begins to stick out as odd.[11] This is the only place in the authentic letters where Paul says that "the Jews" killed Jesus and where Paul seems to pronounce God's wrathful judgment on the Jews as a people. The text also seems to contradict Paul's climactic statement in Romans 11:26 that "all Israel will be saved" (see Rom. 9:3-5; 11:17-31). Some scholars have thus argued that part or all of 1 Thessalonians 2:13-16 is an interpolation, that is, an addition by a later scribe. However, given the Western tendency to locate ideal Christianity at its origins, it seems convenient that this theory locates 1 Thessalonians 2:14-16 within the history of Christian anti-Semitism but not with Paul or in the 50s CE. This seeming bias does not make the thesis automatically wrong, but it does remind us to continually turn the analytical eye on the desires, choices, and assumptions of particular versions of history. A critical approach to history reframes scholarship as a deliberation on the plausibility and effectiveness of our interpretations of the past rather than as a scientific and objective quest for the past itself.

History is always an argument about the past, a selection and interpretation of events. This applies to history within the text as well. These few verses interpret the past from a theological perspective. The suffering of the Christ communities are located within a chain of violence beginning with the death of Jesus and the prophets, continuing to Paul's being opposed and driven out of Judea, and culminating in God's wrath coming upon the perpetrators. The Judean past is thus presented as a general story of violence. Are there other stories that could have been told? In what sense is it a plausible historical statement to say that "the Jews," as a whole people, killed Jesus? There had been thousands of crucifixions of other Jews in the years before and after the death of Jesus. Why does Paul describe the Jewish story as one of killing and opposition rather than as one of suffering? Why does he interpret the present of "the Jews who killed Jesus and the prophets" as receiving God's well-deserved wrath? Is there something about Paul's rhetorical interests that relies on this interpretation of the Jews' past as one of violence and retribution? A common answer to this question is that Paul is locked in a battle with Jews who disagree with his mission to the nations. Criticizing what he perceives as sinful obstruction of God's mission to the Gentiles, Paul characterizes the story of the Jews as a sweeping and polemical story of violence and opposition. As the study note on verses 14-16 in the *New Oxford Annotated Bible* (RSV, 1973) suggests: "the severe language reflects the strenuous struggle between Paul and the Jews (Acts 14:2, 5, 19; 17:5, 13; 21:21; 25:2, 7)."[12]

By now, however, these cross-references to Acts should also raise questions. Acts has been very influential in framing the grand narrative of Christian history; thus, we must scrutinize its role in our interpretations. Indeed, the historicizing narrative in Acts often simply becomes the historian's description of what actually happened in the city before the writing of the letter.[13] But, there is nothing in 1 Thessalonians to corroborate the idea that Paul began his preaching in the synagogue or that some jealous Jews in the city were causing problems for him. And Acts repeatedly describes Paul's missionary strategy and the opposition he faces in the same way: beginning with the synagogues and drawing violent Jewish opposition. Why would this be? One explanation is that Paul and mobs of Jews were very consistent from city to city. Another more likely explanation takes seriously that the entire narrative of Luke-Acts structures its story of the Way as beginning among the Jews and, because of negative responses of jealous and violent Jews, moving out to the nations where it is received positively. Acts does not record history; it invents history in order to shape its readers' view of the past. When we use Acts as history, we often unconsciously replicate its interpretation of the past, that is, we repeat its early version of the grand narrative of the progress of Christian truth beyond the confines of Judaism and its triumph among the nations despite the violent opposition of the Jews.[14]

This analysis suggests that we know much less about the events preceding the writing of 1 Thessalonians than we think we know. Accepting this lack of knowledge of the past is one way to resist the ideological force of the grand narratives that shape modernity and that undergird Christian anti-Semitism and triumphalism. However, by putting 1 Thessalonians 2:14-16 and Acts 17:1-10 alongside each other, we can also produce alternative knowledge. Both texts demonstrate that interpreting the Jewish past was an important piece of the emergence of Christian identity and self-understanding by the end of the first century. 1 Thessalonians shows how a particular construal of the death of Jesus, that is, that the Jews killed Jesus, served as a lens with which to cast negative light on one's opponents' past, present, and future. Acts 17:1-10 shows how a story-like narration of the experiences of Paul created a Christian version of the Jewish past that made the triumph of the Way of Christ appear self-evident and inevitable.

Thinking with Trends in Pauline Historiography

So far in our discussion of 1 Thessalonians 2:14-16, we have spoken largely in terms of "Christians" and "Jews," with some mention of "Gentiles." However, the word "Christian" does not appear here or in any of Paul's letters. This raises the challenge of thinking historically about Paul as Jewish and not Christian. While this passage has been seen as distinctly un-Pauline, in certain ways it fits within Paul's regular rhetorical practices and theological assumptions: the use of Hebrew scripture to interpret events, a view of the divine as the final arbiter and enactor of justice, and an expectation that the God of Israel will bring salvation to the nations. All of these are rooted deeply in Jewish tradition. If Paul shares a great deal with other Jews, why is he so polemical? The answer may be linked to his passion for the mission to the Gentiles. A key principle of the New Perspective understands Paul as speaking to Gentiles about Gentile issues. In the case of 1 Thessalonians, the negative portrayal of Paul's opponents primarily bolsters his own relationship with the community by urging his audience to view those who oppose him in the same way he does. In other words, this depiction of a history of violence creates insiders—the audience and Paul and his coworkers—by condemning outsiders.

Outsiders to what? Insiders to what? Is Paul somehow now Christian because he has criticized other Jews as violent and wrong? No. Indeed, the antecedents and relatives of this kind of polemic locate the text fully *within* the Jewish tradition. Announcing God's judgment on Israel for killing its own prophets appears in the Hebrew scriptures (for example, Neh. 9:26; Jer. 2:30; 2 Chr. 36:16) as well as in Jewish writings from before the time of Paul (*Jub* 1.12; *T.Levi* 16.2). This idea of Jewish suffering being a result of Jewish rejection of God's prophets also appears in the traditions of Jesus' sayings (Luke 11:49-51; Matt. 23:34-36) as well as in the book of Acts (7:51-53) and may have been used both to interpret the death of Jesus and, later, the destruction of Jerusalem.[15] While the Gospels and Acts would eventually use the tradition in a way that begins to *make a difference* among "the Jews" and Christ followers ("the Way" in Acts), Paul's use of this Jewish interpretation of suffering and violence does not map onto a division between "Jews" and "Gentiles," let alone a division between "Jews" and "Christians."

A close look at the text supports this point. Verse 14 compares communities in different geographic regions. What makes the Thessalonians like the communities of God in Christ Jesus in Judea is that they *both suffer at the hands of their own people.* The logic of the comparison depends on the Christ communities *sharing* a social identity with those who are being accused of violence. Thus the opponents of the Thessalonians are other Gentiles and the opponents of the Christ-identified Judeans are other Judeans. Indeed, in Greek, the word Judea and the word translated "Jews" are two versions of the same noun: *Ioudaia/Ioudaioi.* The first refers to the geographic region of Judea and the second to the people associated with that geographic region and their traditions. Would your understanding of the text change if it was translated this way?

> For you, brothers and sisters, became imitators of the churches of God
> in Christ Jesus that are in Judea, for you suffered the same things from
> your own people [in Thessalonikē] as they did from the Judeans who
> killed both the Lord Jesus and the prophets, and drove us out.

This translation emphasizes the shared ethnic-geographic identity of the groups in Thessalonikē and Judea. In addition, removing the comma after the word "Judeans" means that verse 15 describes—if you know your grammar—*those particular Judeans* (the ones who killed and have driven out), not all Judeans. There are now "Judeans," or Jews, as we translate the word *Ioudaioi* today, on both sides, exactly as in the Jewish tradition about the death of the prophets.

This suggests that interpreting (and punctuating) verse 15 as a condemnation of "the Jews" represents a misreading or, better, an *overwriting* of the text (and not a neutral or innocent one). Revising it in the way above brings into view a much messier picture than Christians versus Jews. Indeed, our text now attests to the lack of a coherent "Christian" identity within and among the Pauline communities. This disrupts any easy claim to the inevitability of the emergence of Christianity over and against Judaism as it comes to be defined later. The first ancient readers' response to this text (which is lost to us), the later canonization of it by Christians, and even the punctuation and the translation of *Ioudaioi* as Jews (instead of Judeans) are all part of the process of inventing a Christianity separate from Judaism. But thinking about the past is always bound up with the present. Thus our revision of historical narratives of first-century Jewish-Christian identities as a fluid and complex interplay of ethnic, geographical, and religious identities both draws on and can further expose the ways that religious identities today are never pure or unrelated to racial-ethnic or geographic differences.

And what if the differences being set up by our text are not primarily religious differences? In many ways, the focus on anti-Semitism and the relationships among Christians and Jews, or Gentiles and Jews, perpetuates an interpretation of the letter in distinctly religious terms. Although the events that Paul interprets as suffering are unknown to us, do we still assume that they are related to religion? Why? If the religious aspects of ancient life cannot be separated from the social, political, and economic, then the struggles of the Thessalonians may have been experienced in social, political, or economic terms. Some scholars have shifted the terms of analysis in just this way, interpreting the ancient audience of 1 Thessalonians as poor artisans who gathered together to remedy poverty with economic mutuality, to counter social invisibility with in-group respect and status, and to survive imperial violence and disinformation by dreaming of the arrival of a just, true, and peaceful ruler. Changing our interpretation of the past in this way can shift how we think about religious change over time; perhaps religious differences, in this case practices and ideas identifiable as distinctly Christian, are the *result* of social, economic, and political forces and differences rather than the cause of them.

From this perspective, Paul's construction of common struggle across geography and ethnicity in 1 Thessalonians 2:14-16 takes on a distinctly political flavor. The Pauline letters may represent efforts to build networks of social-political solidarity across ethnic-religious lines, such as among Judeans and the various peoples and cities of the Roman Empire. This interpretation leads to a different explanation of Paul's condemnation of Judean violence as a "political critique of local accommodationist practices."[16] Placing the text on a trans-local map of resistance that includes Judean resistance to Rome, 1 Thessalonians 2:14-16 becomes "neither an interpolation nor an anti-Jewish statement but Paul's critique of pro-Roman forces in Thessalonika through an analogous critique of pro-Roman forces in Judea."[17] Thus Paul condemns some Judeans who killed Jesus and the prophets and some Gentiles who oppress the Thessalonians because they perpetrated injustice. However, Paul's blaming of some Judeans for the death of Jesus also points to the power of empire to proliferate divisiveness among subject peoples (particularly considering how only Roman authorities could order the crucifixion of people in their empire).

Rethinking the Pauline communities as responding to and shaping people's social, economic, and political lives as much as cultivating a religious identity draws our attention to a wider range of people than are usually the subjects of history. For example, imagining the suffering of the Thessalonian community as the everyday struggles of the non-elite for survival and recognition resonates with the letter's discussion of manual labor and a concern for the opinions of outsiders. In this light, 1 Thessalonians 2:14-16 uses the Judean prophetic tradition to make sense of senseless social violence. However, if we think about telling the history of Christians rather than Christianity, we still have to contend with the way that this non-elite theological thinking, when canonized and naturalized, became a site for ongoing violence against Jews.

Attempting to change the subjects of history as we approach 1 Thessalonians also brings to our attention the considerable difficulty of doing so with Paul's letters. We have no idea whether there were women or slaves in the community who might have had significantly different experiences of daily struggle and suffering than Paul knows about or has in mind. In what ways does the text's free-male-centered language and kyriarchal imagery participate in the erasure of some people from history even as it can be effectively used to change the subjects of history away from religious or elite histories? Do we reinscribe a "great man" approach to history when we focus solely on the perspective of Paul? How can we approach the letters of Paul as products of community issues and relationships?

CONCLUSION

With the three basic principles described above and some sense of the major trends in Pauline historiography, you can analyze the historical narratives and assumptions that you encounter in the standard scholarly resources as well as in popular knowledge. You can also ask historical questions of your own about the letters of Paul. Taking a critical approach to history requires a considerable amount of imagination, persistence, and comfort with not knowing. Indeed, some newer approaches in biblical studies have set aside historical questions altogether, as some of the following chapters might do. A historical approach does tend to restrict the text's meaning to the past and to one geographic region when it actually has been and continues to be signified in various communities. However, even these new approaches can unwittingly perpetuate dominant assumptions about the past and problematic habits of narrating Christian history. Thus, it is important to continue to ask critical questions about history, although they may not be the same as the questions of the past.

FURTHER READING

Within the Discipline of History

Iggers, George G. *Historiography in the Twentieth Century: From Scientific Objectivity to the Postmodern Challenge*. Middletown: Wesleyan University Press, 2005. Overview of the changes in the philosophy of history in the twentieth century.

White, Hayden. *The Fiction of Narrative: Essays on History, Literature, and Theory, 1957–2007*. Edited by Robert Doran. Baltimore: Johns Hopkins University Press, 2010. Signal essays from the most influential historian of the linguistic turn.

Rethinking the Discipline of History in Biblical Studies and Early Christianity

Castelli, Elizabeth and Hal Taussig. "Drawing Large and Startling Figures: Reimagining Christian Origins by Painting Like Picasso," in *Reimagining Christian Origins*, edited by Elizabeth Castelli and Hal Taussig, 3–20. Minneapolis: Fortress Press, 1990. Outlines several important propositions for reimagining Christian beginnings.

Clark, Elizabeth. *History, Theory, Text: Historians and the Linguistic Turn*. Cambridge: Harvard University Press, 2004. Explains shifts in the philosophy of history in relation to the study of Late Antiquity.

King, Karen. "Which Christianity?" In *The Oxford Handbook of Early Christian Studies*, edited by Susan Ashbrook Harvey and David G. Hunter, 66–86. Oxford: Oxford University Press, 2008. Overview of the emergence of a multilocational model of diversity in early Christian studies over linear models of orthodoxy and unity.

Schüssler Fiorenza, Elisabeth. *Rhetoric and Ethic: The Politics of Biblical Studies*. Minneapolis: Fortress Press, 1999. Signal essays on the shifts in the field, the paradigms and ethics of interpretation, historiography, and power-attuned rhetorical criticism.

Segovia, Fernando. "'And They Began to Speak in Other Tongues': Competing Modes of Discourse in Contemporary Biblical Criticism," in *Reading from This Place* Vol. 1, edited by Fernando Segovia and Mary Ann Tolbert, 1–32. Minneapolis: Fortress Press, 1995. An influential mapping of the methodological and political changes in the discipline.

Vander Stichele, Caroline and Todd Penner, "Mastering the Tools or Retooling the Masters? The Legacy of Historical-Critical Discourse," in *Her Master's Tools? Feminist and Postcolonial Engagements of Historical-Critical Discourse*, edited by Caroline Vander Stichele and Todd Penner, 1–29. Atlanta: Society of Biblical Literature, 2005. Introduction to the interruption of the objective and universalist claims of the elite male Western view of history by a range of scholars claiming alternative experiences.

On 1 Thessalonians

Johnson-DeBaufre, Melanie. "A Monument to Suffering: 1 Thessalonians 2:14-16, Dangerous Memory, and Christian Identity," *Journal of Christian History* (2011). In-depth discussion of 1 Thessalonians 2:14-16 as a site of collective Christian memory.

———. "Gazing Upon the Invisible: Archaeology, Historiography, and the Elusive Women of 1 Thessalonians," in *From Roman to Early Christian Thessalonikē*, edited by Laura Nasrallah, et al, 73–108. Cambridge: Harvard University Press, 2010. Examines the problem of the (in)visibility of women in the Thessalonian community, the letter, Pauline scholarship, and archaeology.

Smith, Abraham. "The First and Second Letters to the Thessalonians," in *A Postcolonial Commentary on the New Testament Writings*, edited by Fernando Segovia and R. S. Sugirtharajah, 304–22. London and New York: T&T Clark, 2007. Interprets 1 Thessalonians and its history of interpretation using postcolonial criticism.

NOTES

1. John J. Collins, *The Bible after Babel: Historical Criticism in a Postmodern Age* (Grand Rapids: Eerdmans, 2005), 4.

2. Ibid., 5.

3. For an extended treatment of the interaction of biblical studies with these philosophical and theoretical trends, see Bible and Culture Collective, *The Postmodern Bible* (New Haven: Yale University Press, 1995).

4. For a discussion of politically attuned rhetorical analysis, see Elisabeth Schüssler Fiorenza, *Rhetoric and Ethic: The Politics of Biblical Studies* (Minneapolis: Fortress Press, 1999), 129–48.

5. See Brian K. Blount, et al., "Introduction" in *True to Our Native Land: An African American New Testament Commentary* (Minneapolis: Fortress Press, 2007), 1–10; R. S. Sugitharajah, *The Bible and the Third World: Precolonial, Colonial, and Postcolonial Encounters* (Cambridge: Cambridge University Press, 2001); and Shawn Kelley, *Racializing Jesus: Race, Ideology, and the Formation of Modern Biblical Scholarship* (New York: Routledge, 2002).

6. For an overview of this scholarly trajectory, see John G. Gager, *Reinventing Paul* (Oxford: Oxford University Press, 2000).

7. Gager, *Reinventing Paul*, viii.

8. See the three volumes edited by Richard Horsley and published by Trinity Press International: *Paul and Empire: Religion and Power in Roman Imperial Society* (Harrisburg: Trinity Press International, 1997); *Paul and Politics: Ekklesia, Israel, Imperium, Interpretation; Essays in Honor of Krister Stendahl* (Harrisburg: Trinity Press International, 2000); *Paul and the Roman Imperial Order* (Harrisburg: Trinity Press International, 2004); and all of the books in the Paul in Critical Context series from Fortress Press.

9. See the People's History of Christianity series from Fortress Press, especially Richard Horsley, ed., *Christian Origins*, Vol. 1 (Minneapolis: Fortress Press, 2005), and Virginia Burrus, ed., *Late Ancient Christianity*, Vol. 2 (Minneapolis: Fortress Press, 2010).

10. See Melanie Johnson-DeBaufre and Laura S. Nasrallah, "Beyond the Heroic Paul: Toward a Feminist and Decolonizing Approach to the Letters of Paul," in *The Colonized Apostle: Paul through Postcolonial Eyes*, ed. Christopher Stanley (Minneapolis: Fortress Press, 2011), 161–74.

11. Even in 1 Thessalonians, chapter 2 reads quite nicely without verses 13-16, as verse 17 returns to the themes of 2:9-12. Strangely, the preceding verse seems to introduce a second thanksgiving (v. 13; see 1:2) after the body of the letter had already begun in 2:1. Also, the criticism of the Jews for the death of Jesus and the idea that God's judgment is upon them sounds more like the Gospels and other texts written after the destruction of the Temple and Jerusalem in 70 CE than it does like anything in the Pauline letters.

12. *New Oxford Annotated Bible with the Apocrypha, Revised Standard Version*, ed. Herbert G. May and Bruce M. Metzger (New York: Oxford, 1977), p. 1434.

13. For an example, see the discussion of Paul's abrupt departure from the city (2:17) in *The HarperCollins Study Bible* (NRSV), ed. Harold W. Attridge and Wayne A. Meeks (New York: Harper Collins, 1993), p. 2218.

14. See Shelly Matthews, *Perfect Martyr: The Stoning of Stephen and the Construction of Christian Identity* (Oxford: Oxford University Press, 2010). For a discussion of the gospel tradition, see Melanie Johnson-DeBaufre, "The Blood Required of this Generation: Interpreting Communal Blame in a Colonial Context," in *Violence in the New Testament*, ed. Shelly Matthews and Leigh Gibson (New York: T&T Clark, 2005), 22–34.

15. Ibid., 71–72.

16. Abraham Smith, "The First and Second Letters to the Thessalonians," in *A Postcolonial Commentary on the New Testament Writings*, ed. Fernando F. Segovia and R. S. Sugirtharajah (London and New York: T&T Clark, 2007), 304–22, 310.

17. Ibid., 314.

2

RHETORICAL APPROACHES

*Introducing the Art of Persuasion
in Paul and Pauline Studies*

TODD PENNER AND DAVINA C. LOPEZ[1]

RHETORICALLY INTRODUCING RHETORIC

Shortly after United States Marines killed Osama bin Laden on May 1, 2011, the al-Qaida organization elected his successor. Ayman al-Zawahiri, al-Qaida's "second-in-command" at that time, emerged as the new leader of the movement. Robert Louis Gates, the United States Defense Secretary, offered a public statement on June 16, the day the al-Qaida announcement became public. Following initial commentary on the continuing gravity of the "terror threat" al-Qaida presented, Gates quipped: ". . . [it is] probably tough to count votes when you're in a cave."[2] While this off-handed statement can be read as a wry comment on the situation of those living in hiding and secrecy brought about by American military intervention in Afghanistan and Northern Pakistan, we highlight here the caricature his statement reinforces. This "humor" is based on the idea that there cannot be a real election if a group secrets itself in vastly dispersed caves. The joke's power rests on elements describing an "enemy" as cowardly, weak, powerless, and, by implication, effeminate. They are not "real men"—"real men" live publicly and vote freely in a democracy. Knowing that "al-Qaida" signifies "terrorism" as well as a long-term opposition to the United States government (and people) provides Gates's statement with some persuasive force. Additionally, Gates's rhetorical statement situates hearers in specific positions. There is an "us" and a "them"—and, as people living in the "West," in "America," we are positioned as those "not in caves" who "live openly." We are "real men." We vote "freely" and "in public."

Even cursory analysis of Gates's statement yields layers of complexity that Gates may not have intended. The most simple of pronouncements can be rhetorically weighty. Precisely this issue is of most interest to us here: how rhetoric forms the very fabric of our communicative practices. Rhetoric is not just about the words we use and the contexts in which we use them, but concerns the fundamental shape of our social interactions, self-perceptions, and belief systems. While we may use the term "rhetoric" to denote banal claims by colleagues or friends ("give me a break, that's all rhetoric"), the act of designating claims as "rhetorical" is itself a rhetorical maneuver. The strategic negative use of the word *rhetorical* is already based in pejorative characterizations of persons and manners of speaking. In this way, al-Zawahiri's response to Gates could be "here we go again: more American rhetoric!" And he would be right.[3]

We discuss Gates's comment in this context because it helps illuminate Paul's use of rhetoric. Before we shift to Paul, however, it is necessary to understand "rhetoric" further. Rhetoric permeates all of life—human lived reality is, at its base, rhetorically constructed and mediated. Ancient rhetoricians—who practiced "rhetoric" professionally—defined it as "the art of persuasion." These teachers and practitioners located the "art of persuasion" in various spheres of social and political engagement: law courts, political assemblies, and public memorializing events, such as funerals. Greeks like Aristotle and Romans like Quintilian wrote treatises on rhetoric, delineating the minute instructions on everything from how one should look and perform to how one should build arguments, compose persuasive sentences, organize a deliverable and compelling product, and appeal to an audience's logic and emotions. It took years of training to master rhetoric. Again, rhetorical situations determined which rhetorical techniques and forms were appropriate. Law courts required "judicial" rhetoric, which was deemed inappropriate for the public assemblies of free men. In the latter, persuasion took a different form designated as "deliberative." The "accusation" of the law court was out of place in a context where decisions had to be weighed based on evidence and the rational processes involved in the evaluation of arguments. When memorializing an important person such as a hero, king, or sage at a funeral, though, neither judicial nor deliberative rhetoric would suffice; a speaker was required to extol the deceased's virtues and achievements using "epideictic," or "praise and blame," rhetoric. If the speaker disliked the dead individual, he would use invective to denigrate the character of the departed.

While ancient discussions of rhetoric often limit application and analysis of rhetorical form and practice to specific settings, such observations are easily extended. Contemporary scholars such as Vernon K. Robbins have sought to demonstrate how all social spheres of existence elicit forms of persuasion.[4] The "art of persuasion" developed attendant themes and tropes not only in law courts, public assemblies, and funerals, but also in homes, bathhouses, religious assemblies, schools, and so forth. Expanding the more formal analysis of ancient Greek and Roman teachers of rhetoric, Robbins asserts that all of life is infused with rhetoric, taking on different forms and modalities based on where we are, what aims we have there, what expectations there are of us, and the relationships we have with those places and with those whom we "persuade." This volume you are holding (as a printed or electronic book) seeks to persuade you that (1) Paul (and, by extension, early Christianity) is worth studying and that (2) it helps to have a range of clearly delineated and separate methodologies to inform your interpretation when studying Pauline literature. We seek to persuade you in this chapter that rhetoric is essential not only for studying Paul but also for you, the reader, in terms of how you think about the world and your place in it (and the choices you make, individually and collectively, both consciously and unconsciously). That, in a nutshell, is what rhetoric is about. Everything you have read so far in this chapter is part of a rhetorical argument that seeks to move you toward an intended end. It remains to be judged, of course, whether the rhetorical construction is persuasive or just minimally effective.

The "art of persuasion" is ideological in nature; it cannot be viewed as unbiased or apolitical. If communicative practices and actions proceed from a set of presuppositions about how the world operates and our placement therein, then the "art of persuasion" will always embed values, assumptions, and principles of social action that shape the content, form, and execution of our rhetoric. The contours of this ideology differ dramatically from person to person, context to context, genre to genre, and so on. A newspaper contains subtle forms of "bias" in terms of "reporting" what "really happened." A political speech against an opponent offers a series of statements that, while often taken at face value, upon closer analysis reveal rhetorical flourishes not necessarily found in newspapers. Both enact the "art of persuasion." The difference lies in the premises, values, and purposes that shape the rhetoric.

If all persuasive statements and actions are contextual, then the logical conclusion is that someone in a distinctly different context will possess an alternate set of values and premises that will lead to distinctive rhetorical expressions and forms. Gates and al-Zawahiri do not share the same worldview. Their rhetoric appears radically different, so the dilemma is: who is right? As Stanley Fish observes: ". . . it would seem . . . that something is always happening to the way we think, and that it is always the same something, a tug-of-war between two views of human life and its possibilities, no one of which can ever gain complete and lasting ascendancy."[5] In our view this is both true and not true. Tropes and persuasive ends might differ, but the structures, logics, forms, inherent politics, and themes elaborated for argumentation are, in effect, rather similar. Bruce Lincoln aptly demonstrates this point in a persuasively argued piece in which he rethinks religion and politics after the events of 9/11.[6] Considering the speeches of Osama bin Laden and President George W. Bush, Lincoln shows that, while on the surface the rhetorical nature of each speaker's form and content of persuasion related to the world (what is good, what is evil, and concomitant social configurations) appears to be substantively divergent, a closer look at the structure of the embedded *logos* (the rhetorical term for "rational argumentation" or "argumentative logic") suggests an overarching similarity. Bush and bin Laden seem "worlds apart" and yet say something analogous about the world and their place in it. Importantly, despite apparent difference, there is similarity at the structural level.

Such observations, however, do not permit a lapse into rhetorical relativism. Feminist theologian and biblical interpreter Elisabeth Schüssler Fiorenza has argued that scholars of the Bible and religion are obligated to reflect ethically on their discourses and performances of the "art of persuasion." After all, aside from a *logos*, rhetorical constructions embody an *ethos*. That is, alongside the logic of the argumentative process, which is itself open to scrutiny and to ethical evaluation, there lie embodied political, social, and personal ethics in rhetoric. These are praxis-oriented ways-of-being-in-the-world with and for others that rhetorical speech acts and performances inculcate, nourish, and sustain, most often unbeknownst to us. Thus, even if forced to attest to the relativity of rhetorical contexts that shape who we are as "persuaders" and "those persuaded," we can reflect ethically on the alignment of our purported value-systems with those promoted by our own rhetoric. Lest one thinks there is a space that exists outside of the rhetorical world we inhabit, we submit that the powerful political and social forces that shape our lives dwell everywhere, even in spaces where we believe they do not and cannot exist. The innocuous front pages of the *New York Times* or *The Washington Post*, and the ways in which we respond to and are shaped by that rhetoric, might say more about who we are in this world than the rhetoric of religious communities. That we might not notice "persuasion" operative in newspapers evokes a larger point: we tend not to recognize rhetoric operative and deployed in sources and contexts that we assume are objective, neutral, universal, normative, natural, and absolute. The call to be ethically engaged in assessing and analyzing our own rhetorical strategies, contexts, and influences, then, is critical for being a socially aware member of a democratic society. Thus, engaging the study of rhetoric as it occurs in Paul's writings can be illustrative for individuals in living a "bible-affirming" culture such as ours. Seeing it work "there" might help us better assess how it operates "here."

ENGAGING PAUL IN RHETORICALLY CRITICAL WAYS

Given the above discussion, it stands to reason that Paul, like us, lived in a world imbued with and animated by rhetoric. At one level, it matters little whether Paul had formal rhetorical training. His writings that we have, those designated as either "authentic" or "deutero-Pauline," evidence what we might expect: Paul performs the "art of persuasion," regardless of whether his "art" would be judged as "adequate" or "superior" by, say, Quintilian or Stanley Fish. Paul's letters promote arguments to various communities and individuals—sometimes forcefully and angrily (as in Galatians), other times sublimely if not seductively (as in Philemon). Paul seeks to persuade those to whom he writes both to believe certain principles and to act in specific ways. He instructs, admonishes, and exhorts. He includes lists of vices and virtues; things to do, things not to do. He expresses shock, disgust, and heart-brokenness. He just as readily communicates joy, elation, and sentiments of solidarity. As quickly as he extols mutuality, he commends hierarchies—with him on top, right below the divine. Although Paul draws on the Hebrew Bible, he more frequently uses Christ as an exemplary figure, along with himself. There is no place outside of rhetoric in Paul's letters. Every word links with other words, forming series of statements that play a role in making arguments that Paul, presumably, finds important to share with his recipients. When we ask "what did Paul mean?" by this line or phrase, or "what did Paul intend?" by that paragraph or concept, we are essentially asking questions about his rhetoric. What argumentative aim—what persuasive end—did Paul have in mind? How did he achieve that end? Was the argument persuasive? If so, under what terms and conditions?

It is critical to understand, moreover, that just because an argument is persuasive, and just because we might find a compilation of arguments compelling *from an argumentative standpoint*, it does not thereby follow that said argument is "true." Paul may make a convincing and moving case that Christ's suffering and death brought about redemptive benefits for the human race. It is another matter to assess the veracity of that claim. For ancient orators, the indicator of a rhetorician's success was whether the audience was convinced to accept the account. An orator could argue against what he or she knew to be true—it only mattered that the audience was swayed. We are not suggesting that Paul used cunning rhetoric to trick ancient people into accepting a gospel he did not think was true. Rather, we are stating that a rhetorical-critical approach to Paul is not invested in the truth claims of Paul's gospel per se. To be sure, many people who study Paul's rhetoric do believe that Paul wrote "truth" about God, Christ, and humanity. We understand such commitments to be separate from analyzing Paul's "art of persuasion."

Let us give an example: in Romans 1:18-32, Paul argues forcefully that Gentiles were given over to their "depravity" because they knew but failed to worship the one true God (of Israel). Now, an interpreter might concur that Paul builds a persuasive argument based on the premises he utilizes, but that does not mean they must accept those claims as "true." Whether any case that Paul makes is found to be convincing or wanting largely depends upon a reader's willingness to grant validity to its argumentative substructure. If one does not believe that dead people can rise up post-mortem, it is unlikely Paul's appeal to such a claim as part of a larger argument (1 Cor. 15) will be persuasive. If one does not think that "all people have sinned and fallen short of God's glory" (Rom. 3:23), then Paul's use of a string of Hebrew Bible scriptural passages (Rom. 3:10-18) to support his claim of a universal human condition will not be persuasive. If a Stoic, for instance, believes that one imitates God by imitating nature, then nature cannot be corrupt as Paul states—and people are not helpless apart from Christ. If someone worships Isis, it is unlikely that a demand to worship only the "true" God of Israel would be persuasive. Such people may already believe they are leading a moral life regardless of what Paul says.

Whether readers find arguments persuasive depends upon their relationship with various rhetorical contexts and their pre-commitments to particular world-views. It should not be surprising—but it does provide cause for reflection—that many people in our world who encounter Paul's letters generally accept Paul's discourse and argumentation as persuasive and compelling. Paul's rhetorical formulations and argumentative aims are part of a biblical tradition that historically informs our culture in deep and profound ways. Our interactions with Pauline rhetoric would be entirely different had we not been exposed to his discourse in one way or another beforehand. Think of a new religious movement in our world—one that espouses belief in aliens, perhaps that humans have descended from an alien race of long ago and that the goal of human existence is to rejoin that alien race. Many in our society would find such a community's persuasive strategies rather unconvincing, perhaps even alarming. This raises, then, several interesting questions for us regarding our interactions with Paul's rhetoric. Our biases with respect to the Bible—our own faith commitments, by choice or absorption—shape how we analyze the persuasive quality of Paul's letters. We should understand that, as much as Paul's discursive world may seem familiar, it might have struck ancient people as strange—much like what we might experience with an alien-oriented new religious movement. It is thus helpful to create some critical distance between accepting or disavowing particular "truth claims" and analyzing argumentative strategies used to achieve specific rhetorical ends. Understanding at a distance is an essential principle of the Humanities as a disciplinary analytic orientation. We can try to follow Paul's argument, even if we cannot follow Paul by committing to whatever his argument demands of us. It is not a matter of accepting the verity of the argumentation itself. It is a matter of seeking to understand the argumentation, which does not mean, however, that ethical reflection and interrogation cannot take place as a secondary step.

If our goal is to understand the rhetorical structure and content, and ultimately to evaluate the argumentative "success," of Paul's letters, it stands to reason that there might be better and worse ways to do so. The task of "exegesis," which attempts to draw out a text's inherent meaning, is the first step toward situating the rhetorical contours of a text. Before scholars became interested in formal aspects of Paul's rhetoric, interpreters were already engaged in examining Paul's argumentative structures. One of the first enterprises in which biblical scholars were engaged was philology, the task of which is dedicated to analyzing words and their historical development as language. It matters that Paul wrote in Greek, and knowing Greek makes a difference for understanding what Paul wrote. Understanding something about the culture in which Paul lived and wrote also matters, for only then can one more fully locate the rhetorical nature and ends of his letters. Earlier scholars thus paid significant attention to the language Paul used and the socio-historical world in which he wrote. Further, many scholars, at least those initially interested in the rhetorical structure of Paul's letters, have been curious about just how advanced his rhetorical training might have been. Can we compare Paul's letters with formal oratorical compositions (those influenced by Greek and Roman teachers of rhetoric) in order to help us understand his arguments?

It is also significant where Paul grew up, where he travelled, and whom he met. It is by piecing together not only a thought-world but also something of "real" social interactions and historical circumstances that we can begin to illustrate the context in which Paul's rhetoric occurs, revealing the external influences on that rhetoric. Those "influences" include concepts taken from the broader philosophical, social, and cultural environments, redeployed and reused in service of promoting Paul's burgeoning "gospel movement." It is also important to know if and to what extent Paul borrowed language and ideas from the Greeks or Romans, and if he, as a Jew, used Jewish scriptures, idioms, and theological concepts and ethics. While such "borrowing" might make his arguments all the more persuasive, we cannot in fact know how (un)successful Paul's ancient rhetoric was. We assume he convinced many—that he and his letters gained widespread influence well after his death. In fact, his greatest influence came with Luther in the Reformation period and later—so Paul's rhetoric "won the day" at some point in Western human history. However, we cannot know how many early communities read Paul's letters, and we cannot even be certain that any of the letters were actually ever sent. Still, we have these letters, and we read them now. For all intents and purposes, then, we are Paul's audience.

Further along these lines, even though we cannot know much about them, scholars maintain that the historical context of the communities to which Paul wrote matters. The "rhetorical situation" informing a letter makes a difference for what Paul argues and how he does so. Knowing something about the social and cultic life of cities like Corinth, and inferring something about the Corinthian community from Paul's two surviving letters, may help us understand Paul's argument better. For instance, certain portions of 1 Corinthians (11, 14) contain seemingly vehemently argued cases for restrictions on female participants in the assembly of believers. Antoinette Clark Wire has proposed that a group of female prophets was asserting power and authority in the Corinthian community, and that Paul sought to suppress these specific women (see also the "Feminist Approaches" chapter).[7] Constructing a rhetorical situation such as this might, some would argue, help us to understand the persuasive strategies that Paul employs. Or, alternately, perhaps knowing that there were particularly prominent Roman women in Corinth who did not maintain traditional standards of proper decorum might help us to assess how Paul's rhetorical strategies unfold in these chapters and whether they might be judged "successful."[8]

Constructing a "rhetorical situation" is mostly guesswork and often circular: we use Paul's rhetoric to reconstruct the rhetorical situation to which he then responds. In Galatians, at least, Paul notes something of a rhetorical situation through minimal traces of purported actual "events" lurking in the background: Peter's withdrawal from eating with Gentiles in Antioch upon the arrival of Jews from Jerusalem. We also find hints of "motivation." In Romans, for instance, he attempts to explain his "gospel," while in many of his other letters, like 1 Corinthians, Paul seeks to sustain community cohesion. Even as we cannot know to whom Paul wrote or the exact specifics regarding the occasion of the letter, we can surmise that he attempts to persuade readers of the veracity of his agenda. Does context matter? Most assuredly it does. Ancient rhetorical teachers suggest that the best rhetorical practices, including the rhetorical construction and strategies used for argumentation, will befit the contexts and occasions to which one is attending. Just as one does not give a funerary speech in a courtroom, so Paul responds to potential insurgency in a community differently depending on that community's relationship to him. The question remains, however, to what degree we can legitimately and accurately reconstruct contexts for Paul's letters and whether Paul's own rhetoric makes such reconstruction difficult, if not impossible.

In the ancient world, "truth" and "facts" were contingent upon the argumentative aims to be achieved, which may be difficult to accept in a culture like ours that is ostensibly committed to "truth" and "facts" as essential elements in determining what kind of rhetoric is "good." "Truth" was a malleable concept for the ancients. One might articulate this conceptual world as one in which "the end justifies the means." That said, the character of "facts" and "truth" is always inherently rhetorical, and, while they are useful within various socio-historical contexts to differing persuasive ends, "facts" and "truth" are ultimately tropes that have to be contextualized within wider systems of meaning-making in order to be more fully understood.[9] Readers must therefore become critically aware of how statements and tropes of argumentation are utilized toward particular ends, since the "truth" of a rhetorical figuration is intimately tied to its effectiveness in creating "factual" impressions.

For example, one ancient rhetorical strategy was known as *ekphrasis*, or "vivid description," wherein an orator described an event in such a manner that hearers would feel like they were seeing it themselves. *Ekphrasis* was successful if it made an event so alive that it was impressed in a dramatic way upon the audience's minds. It was not enough for the audience to hear about the event—it had to have an emotional impact. This strategy demonstrates that what mattered was convincing the audience of a particular point by whatever means necessary, including a dramatic appeal to the emotions. At the same time, plausible argumentation was highly valued. Descriptions had to be "true enough" to an audience's experience—the more plausible the description, the more "true" it would appear. In discussing the virtues of a warrior, it would have been unseemly to speak of how he slew mythic dragons. A noble warrior killed real, live, and fierce human beings, worthy opponents who confirmed the mastery of the one being praised. All of this means, though, that we cannot draw a one-to-one correspondence between what is stated and what is "real."

Understanding rhetoric is important for understanding Paul because it means that the most we can access in Paul's letters is what Paul constructs rhetorically. In ancient courtrooms two or more parties argued different sides of a case. In Paul's letters, however, we have only his "voice." Given the importance of performance in rhetoric, the orator was to perform as a "true man"—but we cannot say that the "Paul" of the letters, the voice projected in and through his words, is what "Paul" was really like. We have access to a persona, one constructed in, through, and for the persuasive ends of the arguments being made. Paul's literary persona need not align with his "authentic" identity, even as "authenticity" may be a valuable modern rhetorical construction. Paul thus projects the image of himself that is deemed appropriate to the argumentative ends he seeks to achieve. The "art of persuasion" is not just about words and their uses. Authorial performance is a key component in achieving rhetorical ends. The audience's perception of the person using those words represents a major factor in whether they will be convincing. As we already noted, the same principle applies to the construction of a "rhetorical situation." Paul's letters grant access to a rhetorical construction of a "rhetorical situation," but we do not have unmediated access to a pristine, unbiased, objective world behind the texts of Paul. Just as we do not have access to a "real Paul"—only a projected rhetorical persona—so also we only have the ability to speak and think about a text's rhetorical constructions of meaning and purpose.[10]

The field of New Testament studies has largely been committed to a wholly different enterprise than the one we are describing here. Most scholars of Pauline literature, for example, are invested in constructing "real" history and belief systems in and behind the texts we possess. In the contemporary world we prize "the true story," that which "actually happened." There is nothing wrong with that orientation. The issue, however, is whether our sources can support the "truth" we desire (see the "Historical Approaches" chapter). Furthermore, we cannot divorce our own rhetorical self-constructions—whom we desire to project to ourselves and others as interpreters of a text—from the act of engaging Paul's "art of persuasion." This is not a matter of what we believe, or our own ideological presuppositions, but of how we rhetorically project who we are as interpreters and readers of Paul. Do we project a sober historical investigator persona? Do we project a flippant "I do not believe any of this crap" persona? Do we project a sophisticated persona of someone who is rhetorically attuned to the complexity of Paul's rhetoric, to its ins and outs, its reversals and gaps? Whatever else we can say about Paul's "art of persuasion," our determinations of the latter are not in small part dependent upon our rhetorical constructions of our self (and that self's relation to others).

Sustained attention to rhetorical constructions of self and other, in texts and by readers thereof, can and should result in an increased awareness of the ethical dimensions of rhetoric, as well as the rhetoric of ethical interestedness. To illustrate how highlighting ethics deepens an understanding of rhetorical analysis and constitutes a type of rhetorical persona in its own right, we consider the rhetorical approaches of the two New Testament scholars mentioned at the outset of this chapter, Robbins and Schüssler Fiorenza. Albeit in differing ways, both interpreters place significant accent on the embodied ethics in the rhetoric deployed in texts. Robbins is interested in the worlds sustained by the "art of persuasion," and the typologies of persons and communities created in and through rhetorical ends of arguments. In other words, Paul's rhetoric is not an innocuous ancient composition. When we engage Paul's texts, we are moved to become a particular kind of person and to enact a specific kind of communal ethic. We may, of course, resist, critique, and/or embrace those engagements. Most frequently, however, the effects of the rhetorical worlds we enter are unknown to us. Robbins is most interested in the kinds of social responses to the world that rhetoric inspires and promotes, and he would likely nuance this perspective by narrowing the range of effects to a specific socio-historical context: that out of which and to which "Paul" wrote. This principle still holds regardless of whether we can reconstruct that ancient socio-historical context or not.

Similarly, Schüssler Fiorenza encourages—perhaps even demands—that readers of, in this case Paul's, rhetoric engage the ethics engendered by such texts. As noted earlier, rhetorical means and ends, and their interconnections with power and authority, inculcate within audiences particular ethical stances. The critical issue for interpreters of rhetoric, then, is assessing what type of worlds—and personal and communal embodiments thereof—are created, nurtured, and sustained by Paul's rhetoric. Robbins aims to discern the stance in and of itself, partially because he projects a persona of "belief" in the well-intentioned nature of Paul's texts and, as a result, power issues in the texts themselves are less pressing for him.[11] Schüssler Fiorenza, on the other hand, projects a "hermeneutics of suspicion" persona that subjects texts to critical scrutiny concerning their interconnections with systems of domination and oppression. She presumes that texts mask power structures articulated and mediated by rhetorical strategies and ends.[12] It is insufficient, in her view, to ask what kind of world is created through rhetoric or what kind of people we are called to be. Rather, one must also query: Is it a world we want to live in? Are these people we want to be?

THE PHILIPPIANS HYMN:
BEING LIKE CHRIST, RHETORICALLY SPEAKING

Scholars of early Christianity often consider the so-called "Christ Hymn" in Philippians 2:6-11 to be a pre-Pauline liturgical composition that has been appropriated and placed in the center of a discussion on community behavior. Regardless of its origin (for our argument here, it matters little whether Paul wrote it himself or not), these six poetic verses comprise one of the most (over-)interpreted passages in New Testament literature. The hymn or poem is significant primarily because it uses the term *kenosis*, a Greek word that is critically important for the history of Christian theology.[13] *Kenosis* means something like "self-emptying," and is vital in discussions of Christ's incarnation in the person of Jesus. Theologians and scholars of early Christian beliefs have deemed this hymn essential for reconstructing core aspects of ancient Christian understandings of Christ. Was Christ God? Did he give up divinity to become human? What was the purpose of "self-emptying"? Theological questions abound. Paul's rhetorical constructions, then, become battlegrounds of modern scholarly inquiry; much is at stake theologically for our understandings of who early believers thought Jesus/Christ was (with obvious implications for contemporary believers).

We submit that couching ideological investments in theological terminology obfuscates the more interesting aspects of Paul's rhetoric. Thus, our interest here is in examining the rhetoric of the hymn as it functions within the larger rhetorical context of Philippians 2. For brevity, we leave to one side how this chapter might function within the letter as a whole. Whatever else the hymn is, it is part of an argument that Paul develops in Philippians 2:1-18. It is framed by a discussion with or an exhortation to (notice that both forms of interaction involve different rhetorical orientations to the material) the letter's audience, whom Paul encourages to "have the same mind" (2:1) and treat each other well, prioritizing the interests of others (2:4). Philippians 2:5 introduces the hymn. Using his own resultant "joy" (2:2) as an example, Paul urges unity. At the end of the hymn, Paul returns to the discussion of community behavior, requesting that people not "murmur" or "argue" (2:14) but, again, demonstrate cohesion. Importantly, Paul uses himself as an example, stating that the community's unity will ensure that he has not "run in vain." As Paul is "being poured out as a libation over the sacrifice" of the community's faith (2:17), so the audience should give him hope by "obeying" (2:12) his exhortation. We have used a range of signifiers to delineate the kind of rhetorical aim employed here, and it is important to keep in mind that whatever terms are used to describe the rhetorical aim will shape the rhetorical analysis of the text.

Our summary of rhetorical context does not do justice to the complexly nuanced rhetorical strategy present in this text. It is fair to say that this section of Philippians is "dripping" with Pauline rhetorical "sweat": Paul is working hard to enforce his appeal in a variety of ways. We may in fact consider this text rather cloying and over the top. Nonetheless, it offers a rather clear context in which to situate the "Christ hymn." Closer examination would determine an even more precise rhetorical agenda. Is Paul angrily exhorting or condemning the audience? Then this would be a form of invective epideictic rhetoric (with spatial traces of the law court or the public forum). Is Paul persuading people toward praiseworthy and community-strengthening behaviors? Then this unit might be like a Sunday morning sermon, an epideictic composition encouraging adherence to already-affirmed community values. Is Paul asking people to consider his argument, to see whether they agree with the general premise based on his various supporting claims? Then this unit would be deliberative in orientation.

Rhetorical motivations or intentions make a difference. Contemporary readers are at a disadvantage, as it is difficult to ascertain "original" motivations and intentions precisely. That said, given the intriguing, if also annoying and perhaps (passive-)aggressive combination of "friendly" and "forceful" rhetorical tropes in Philippians 2 (that is, "obey me," "follow my example," and "become one-minded amongst yourselves"), it seems most likely to us that the first option is probably the way to go: Paul demands behaviors from his community, using Christ and himself as didactic examples to show how the community is currently behaving in a contrary way to what he desires. Regardless of whether we have discerned the precise nuance of the rhetorical unit correctly, the hymn's broader contextualization looks the same: it offers a model to follow (as 2:5 makes clear: "let the same mind be in you that was in Christ Jesus"). Within this context, and in terms of ancient and modern rhetorical categories, we would label the hymn an *exemplum*, the classical rhetorical term for "example." The core of Paul's argumentative strategy here seems to lie in his use of the term "mind of Christ" as a model, followed by representing himself as a further *exemplum*. Paul can command, exhort, and even "yell" at his audience. "Christ" tops all examples in this strategy—the community cannot refute it. According to the logic of the "art of persuasion," this reference at this juncture is apt because Paul's audience accepts (we presume) the basic premises and rationales embedded in the conceptual category of "Christ as model."

Regardless of a reader's orientation to the presumed theological heft of the words in the "Christ hymn," we submit that the precise meaning of these words, their broader ideological import, and the background (re)sources for fleshing out the concepts in the text are relatively irrelevant. One can ascertain the hymn's basic logic at a cursory glance: Christ had higher status than humans; that status was closely related to God's; Christ gave up that high position in order to become human; human status was significantly lower than that of Christ's former position (Paul uses a simile to denote just how low a status: like a "slave"); Christ continued on a humiliating path (as if becoming human was not enough!); through his obedience (presumably to God) he endured one of the lowest forms of death ("on a cross"); as a result of Christ's willingness to give up his high status and become humiliated, God "exalts" Christ, restoring him to his previous position, perhaps taking on an even higher rank as a result. Such is the hymn's basic argumentative texture. As a single unit one would read this as an epideictic composition praising Christ. That is, the hymn exalts the exalted one, explaining the greatness of the figure being worshipped. In its larger context the hymn signifies something different, as it provides an example for how a community should act. It does not take professional training in New Testament studies to deduce that Paul urges his audience to be humble—to act lowly, to be slaves to others, to put others first, to be the "least of these"—and, following that logic, they will likewise be exalted by God (and Christ and Paul). Paul may not mean to suggest that those following Christ's model will be exalted to the status of a deity (it is possible, of course, that he did). However, this rhetoric suggests that good things come to those who act according to the model of Christ. Moreover, because Christ was willing to humiliate himself (even becoming slave-like), it is not a loss in worldly status or social positioning to follow this model that, on the surface, would promote a way of being in the world that stands opposed to that of the conceptions of the larger culture (where giving up high social status would be unthinkable).

Similarly, since Paul's example, Christ, is the cultic object of worship, following this model is not shameful. His argument is based on axioms the community would already accept prior to his deployment of the *exemplum*. Paul's rhetorical force can thus be stronger because he does not have to argue the merit or worthiness of the logic that underpins the argument and makes it "true" and "correct." Effective rhetoric operates by utilizing an audience's shared values and socio-cultural assumptions toward the desired argumentative end. The modeling of Christ fits perfectly with various points Paul raises in the unit's opening and closing regarding how he wants the community to behave. Whether the community actually acted "like Christ" in the end is beyond our ken. We can say, however, that this rhetorical unit is well-constructed and well-argued. It is "convincing" and "true," and the audience of the letter may have found it to be so as well. In fact, some contemporary communities, when not focusing on the embedded christological claims at stake, continue to find it a persuasive argument regarding preferable conduct in religious and other settings.

Scholars interested in theological themes might notice that specific rhetorical features of the hymn enhance reconstructions of early beliefs about Jesus. For instance, 2:10-11 comprises a rather adept rhetorical move wherein a citation from Isaiah about Yahweh (45:23) is reconfigured so as to apply to Christ: he is now worshipped as Yahweh was in Isaiah (whether the audience recognized such Jewish Bible references is an open question). In the hymn's logic, God exalts Christ to the same stature as God. Is there a higher status than that of Yahweh? Such rhetorical excursions into a conceptual world certainly demand further exploration.

We, however, are more concerned with the final aspect of our rhetorical analytical approach, that of ethics. In our view, it is inadequate to leave rhetorical analysis at the textual level. We must also assess the ethical program of the rhetorical end (the politics embedded in the rhetoric), which we may choose to reject should we find it incongruous with our own ethical and social orientation. For instance, Americans who embrace Ayn Rand's ethics would find the Pauline ethic outlined here rather problematic. Thus, we emphasize the final element of rhetorical analysis: what kind of world is envisioned in this text? What kind of way-of-being is modeled? We stress that the text's purported ethic may actually contradict its achieved results. Matters get somewhat complicated when we engage in such meta-critical reflection, which means acknowledging that, while Paul's *exemplum* logically coheres with his argumentative aim, it could also contain problematic political and social embodiments. Whether Paul intends what his rhetoric implies is a matter for debate—his rhetoric may mean more than he means, or fashion a different world from his own intentions. To illustrate our point, we shall take two angles on the ethics of Paul's rhetoric, exploring two emergent possibilities, underscoring what we consider to be the most critical point in rhetorical analysis: the act of moving beyond surface appearances of textual rhetoric to the deep-rooted ideological texture of the rhetoric itself.

One way to enter into the world embodied in the Pauline unit under examination, along the lines of Robbins' model outlined earlier, is to contextualize Paul's rhetoric within the rhetorical environment of which he was a part. One rhetorical framework, particularly for those educated and trained in rhetorical practice, was that of *mimesis*, or imitation. Greeks and Romans considered education to be an enculturating process—one was pulled into social, political, and cultural life through pedagogy. Even as we cannot know Paul's educational level, if we are willing to grant that he wrote, or dictated, letters like Philippians, then he likely had access to some formal education. Although it is unlikely that he had "professional" oratorical training, at the minimum Paul would have been exposed to practices from ancient elementary educational training manuals, some of which survive. Called *progymnasmata*, these offered beginning lessons for younger students, comprising series of exercises demonstrating how to develop arguments and compose basic elements of speech. These manuals focused on providing basic knowledge in the service of argumentation, which ancient Greeks and Romans considered to be a primary means of enculturation. The *progymnasmata* prioritized imitation. Unlike our individualistic culture, where each person is characterized by an "authentic," unique self, in Paul's world the highest praise went to those who best imitated predecessors, those who could "pass" as the "greats."

One can see why it is difficult to tell "authentic" Pauline letters (for example, Galatians) from those who wrote like him and in his name (for example, 1 and 2 Timothy). The more one seemed to be like a predecessor, the greater their rhetorical prowess was determined to be. Ancient students transcribed the words of great figures like Socrates and then reworded them in alternate ways. They composed "speech-in-character," which meant that they created speeches that would pass for the kind that Socrates would utter. *Progymnasmatic* education makes sense in a world where imitating greatness makes one great, where imitating cultural values integrates one into that culture. Acting like and speaking like cultural heroes and representatives brought students into that great tradition of "real men." Rhetorical training, then, was more than just teaching people how to argue. It was an induction into the world of *mimesis*, of imitating classical virtues and great individuals who defined what was understood to be the "true essence" of their socio-cultural environment.[14]

How would such a context make a difference for understanding the "Christ hymn" in Philippians 2? One might recall Paul's use of Christ as a model. We would say "Christ is a model worth imitating"—but that goes "without saying" in Paul's text. Given this claim's self-evident nature we might catch a glimpse here of "Christian" (not just "Pauline") enculturation, which would be a process of inducting, or introducing, an audience (in)to inhabiting specific kinds of Christian identity and community/social formation. We further observe that *mimesis* in this instance urges a specific community identity: not one of hierarchy and social privilege but one of selflessness and service to others. "Like Christ," the Philippians are herein inculcated into a system of being-in-the-world where the "last becomes first." In a culture materially dependent upon the maintenance of hierarchies through master-slave relationships, such imitation represents a radical reorientation of existence. This rhetoric, thus, could be read as producing a world and ethic that offer a different mode of personal and communal relations. Indeed, and this cannot be overstated, the rhetorical move herein emphasizes a model for imitation (Christ's suffering, even unto death) that would signify, in the larger cultural context, a shameful and degrading form of existence. Unlike Socrates or Augustus, this model encourages one to be humiliated "like a slave," to be penetrated by the multiple mechanisms of the state. Interestingly, though, in this rhetorical unit, what "is shameful" from an outsider perspective is viewed quite the opposite from within the community. The text could posit, then, a potentially resistant ethic. We additionally suggest that here lies the formation of a significantly divergent type of ancient rhetoric and embodied social identity: in the process of laying out being "like Christ" as a model, such people as Paul were rhetorically reshaping ideologies and remapping (themselves in relationship to their place in) the world. As Penner and Vander Stichele note: "Christians grew adept at blending and reconfiguring public and private space, lower and upper social status, civic and barbaric identities, male and female roles, and even going as far as redeploying unsavory Greco-Roman topoi to new and potent ends. . . . There are thus complex social crossings that get mapped onto the rhetoric of the early Christians."[15] This rhetorical process blends broader cultural elements, resulting in the production of different, even subversive, ways of thinking and acting.

Reading the world embodied in the "Christ hymn" as subversive is not the only option, however. If we adopt a "hermeneutics of suspicion" approach, along the lines of Schüssler Fiorenza's model outlined earlier, our initial proposal regarding the ethics of the rhetoric would be turned upside-down. A critically interrogative reading of the hymn assumes that power relationships are always being reconstituted even as they appear to be eradicated. In this light, the world and ethic embodied in this rhetoric might thus be viewed as oppressive and insidious, given that it purports to be about mutual submission. After all, rhetorical strategies promoting "mutuality" and "community submission" could in fact reinstate hierarchies and power relationships whilst seemingly challenging and undermining them.[16] Hierarchies were overtly celebrated in the ancient world, unlike in our modern democratic system, which tends to mask such structures by ostensibly extolling equality and egalitarianism. The ancient emperor was on top, and everyone else stood in relationship to others in descending order. "Penetration" (physical, social, rhetorical) was considered virtuous—a *vir bonus*—we might say, a "real man"—was one who retained his hierarchical position. To be "penetrated" was, in effect, to move downward within the hierarchy (see also the "Queer Approaches" chapter).

In light of this framework, it is possible that, while Paul "orders" his community to follow the "mind of Christ," he remains "on top" in Philippians. Thus, throughout the larger unit for which the "Christ hymn" serves as a rhetorical *exemplum*, Paul asserts his authority and stature within the community, using theological premises that his audience would have accepted as ideal. We might say that submitting to Paul is functionally what is at stake in modeling Christ, or that being "like Christ" is in effect submitting to Paul. Christ becomes a means by which Paul enforces control over his communities. Paul is the "penetrator" in this text—rhetorically, the broader culture's hierarchies are not eliminated but reconfigured in a carefully masked way so as to reinscribe Paul as the ultimate authority, placing the audience under him. Whether Paul intends his rhetoric to function in this manner is somewhat beside the point. In an ideological examination of rhetoric, reinscribing dominant power relationships whilst seeming to decenter or eradicate them can be an unconscious act. The ethics of the rhetoric need not be intentional to be effective; power is inscribed most vigorously where it appears not to be, where even the one doing the reinscribing is unaware of the rhetoric's effects. Assuming someone always gains and someone always loses through human rhetorical interactions, the most potent and insidious forms of power are those to which we are most oblivious, for these are precisely the forms of power with which we are most compliant and complicit. In other words, Paul might be a victim of his own cultural codes as much as we might be of Paul's rhetorical ones.

CONCLUSION

There are many other ways of examining the ethics of this rhetorical unit of Philippians. Our aim is to be illustrative, not exhaustive. One need not be a specialist in New Testament studies to identify ways of reading the "Christ hymn," perhaps finding a "middle path" between the two (somewhat polar) possibilities we have mapped out here. More importantly, and in line with the main thrust of this chapter, one need not have expertise in ancient rhetoric and its cultural environment to read New Testament texts critically. Understanding rhetoric's pervasiveness in our daily lives—that everything is rhetorical, and everything is about persuasion and argumentation, often unbeknownst to us—enables us to assess the role(s) rhetoric plays in Paul's letters.

That rhetoric pervades every aspect of our lives ultimately affords ample opportunity not only to understand rhetorical aspects of ancient texts and traditions, but also to understand how we rhetorically configure the methods we use and study. To that end, one productive rhetorical effect engendered by encountering the disciplinary configuration concerned with rhetorically introducing Paul's rhetoric is to position the discipline itself as a means to reflect on its contemporary agenda and ethics. In turn, this becomes a site from which to better understand the place of Pauline studies, as a project of the Humanities, in our socio-political, religious, and higher-educational landscape today. That is to say, a truly critically engaged exploration of rhetoric and Paul (and Pauline rhetoric) will necessarily move beyond noticing specific tropes in his letters and making decisions about the ethical programs he did and did not intend. Rather, exploring rhetoric ought to help us reassess the rhetorical constructions of our own sense of "self" and everyday lives in relation to others, using Paul, and studies of Paul, to do so.[17]

By examining the past and probing Paul, even in the perfunctory way we have done here, we gain some distance from ourselves—even as we come face to face with our own assumptions about and interactions with the effects of Paul's rhetoric. And seeing how rhetoric "drips" off the pages of Paul's letters helps us reflect on how our world is similarly rhetorically saturated. We may well inhabit a socio-cultural environment that masks rhetoric, that makes it more subtle than what we find in Pauline literature. The challenge that studying Paul's rhetoric provides, then, is to similarly engage our world. Moreover, in higher-education contexts we have an opportunity to juxtapose Paul's rhetorical constructions with our own without having to submit to Paul as a means of showing deference to ecclesiastical authorities. Studying the rhetoric of Paul in an educational setting should be comparative in nature, for it is often through such comparisons that we are able to see more clearly the contours of our own systems of meaning-making. Ultimately, in the pedagogical context we are envisioning herein, studying Paul is not about locating a theology and/or ideology we might recover for, and redeploy in, our world. Although advocating assent to a

Pauline program might be legitimate in some contexts, it is not one in which we are engaged in this chapter. Rather, comparative analysis empowers us to map our own systems of rhetoric and ideology, to delineate the outlines of persuasive systems in which we are always—frequently unwittingly—involved and complicit.

Ultimately, studying Paul is about studying ourselves, it is about using rhetorical analysis to better understand our world, not his. It is essentially a process of encountering our own humanity whilst encountering aspects of Paul's. It is, finally, a reinscription of the humanizing project of education itself, of encountering ourselves at our best and our worst. And, not to miss the point of this chapter, everything you have just read is, of course, rhetorical! Just rhetoric? Or a form of just rhetoric? Readers will need to make that determination for themselves, through analyzing the ethics of the rhetoric we have deployed in these pages, and, finally, discerning their own desire for and orientation towards particular ways of being in this world.

FURTHER READING

Butler, Judith. *Giving an Account of Oneself.* New York: Fordham University Press, 2005. Focuses on the rhetorical situations where subjects are formed through responding to accusations. Reflects on what it can mean to be human in contexts that deny the complexity of humanity. Redefines "ethics" as critical engagement of the social norms that implore us to act, rather than a set of rules that create and maintain such norms.

Kennedy, George A. *New Testament Interpretation through Rhetorical Criticism.* Chapel Hill: University of North Carolina Press, 1984. A classic introduction to rhetorical criticism. Engages the idea that authors wrote to persuade audiences of the "truth" of their claims by deploying ancient rhetorical conventions. Applies these concepts to the interpretation of New Testament texts.

Lincoln, Bruce. *Holy Terrors: Thinking about Religion after September 11th,* 2nd ed. Chicago: University of Chicago Press, 2006. Argues that, when rhetorical analysis yields structural commonalities between seemingly divergent figures in a post-9/11 world, there is a need to clarify what the study of religion does in a postcolonial landscape characterized by illusory distinctions between religion and politics.

Mack, Burton. *Rhetoric and the New Testament.* Guides to Biblical Scholarship, New Testament Series. Minneapolis: Fortress Press, 1990. Builds the case that rhetoric is about persuasive argumentation, and engages rhetorical criticism as a matter of critical biblical hermeneutics. Relates categories from classical rhetoric to the interpretation of New Testament texts.

Martin, Ralph P. *A Hymn of Christ: Philippians 2:5-11 in Recent Interpretation and in the Setting of Early Christian Worship.* Downers Grove: InterVarsity, 1997. Provides a detailed history of scholarship on Philippians from a variety of angles. Situates the Christ hymn as a set of codes utilized by early Christians. Originally published in 1967 (Cambridge University Press), it has been updated by a series of prefaces in 1983 and 1997.

Pernot, Laurent. *Rhetoric in Antiquity.* Translated by W. E. Higgins. Washington: Catholic University of America Press, 2005. Introduces the theory and practice of rhetorical performance from Homer to Augustine. Argues for rhetoric as a pervasive component of human society.

Robbins, Vernon K. *The Invention of Christian Discourse.* Volume 1. Blandford Forum: Deo, 2009. Demonstrates how the New Testament was the product of religious thought, belief, and practice in the ancient world that, building on an Israelite-Jewish heritage, blended and reconfigured rhetorical forms into new types of discourse.

Schüssler Fiorenza, Elisabeth. *Democratizing Biblical Studies: Toward an Emancipatory Educational Space.* Louisville: Westminster John Knox, 2009. Proposes shifting scholarly focus to a meta-discourse about how proponents of such approaches are shaped in institutions of graduate education. A "radical democratic ethos" emphasizes opening alternative rhetorical spaces for creating a vision of a different world.

Vander Stichele, Caroline and Todd Penner. *Contextualizing Gender in Early Christian Discourse: Thinking beyond Thecla.* New York: Continuum/T&T Clark, 2009. Uses constructions of gender as a prism through which to examine how ancient and modern rhetorical formations and social actions create, and are created by, patterns of engaging ancient Christian texts in modern contexts.

Wire, Antoinette Clark. *The Corinthian Women Prophets: A Reconstruction through Paul's Rhetoric.* Minneapolis: Fortress Press, 1990. Uses feminist criticism to analyze Pauline passages pertaining to female prophets in Corinth in order to discern a historical and religious environment behind Paul's rhetoric where women's agency is valued and encouraged.

NOTES

1. We are grateful to Joseph Marchal for inviting us to contribute to this volume, as well as for his gracious editorial engagement. We also appreciate the work of Kelsi Morrison-Atkins, an undergraduate student at Ball State University, who read through our piece with a fresh pair of eyes. As teachers of biblical and religious studies at liberal arts colleges who are still committed to, and invested in, the Humanities as a means of learning about and critically interrogating differing ways of embodying human relationship in this world, we embrace the opportunity to think about Paul and method in a context such as this. Portions of this chapter were presented in a much earlier form at the "Paul and the Politics of Introduction" panel at the November 2010 Annual Meeting of the Society of Biblical Literature (Atlanta). During that session, we realized that our interpretive and pedagogical priorities did not fully align with some of the other panelists, who were teaching in different institutional settings than the two of us. We are thankful for such articulations of difference, as they have helped us to clarify some of the positions we attempt to inhabit in the present chapter. We are also indebted to the thoughtful conversation engendered by the undergraduate participants in Davina's "Apostle Paul: Religion and Politics" seminar at Eckerd College in Spring 2011. Lauren Bridge, Natasha Gregory, Will McCann, and Matthew Rodahaver were most willing to think with us on ways to explore Paul as an exercise in cultivating an expansive critical imagination in the service of civic and social engagement. Finally, this chapter is dedicated to the memory of Hamza Ali Al-Khateeb (1997–2011) from Al Jeezah in Syria, in the steadfast hope that a commitment to a radical ethic (in word and deed) can change how humans choose to act in this world and the next. May his final hours of terror

terrorize us all, shoring up our resolve to understand and assess rhetorical practice and performance as the first step toward creating more sustainable and just forms of human interaction and relationship.

2. "US says 'we will kill Zawahiri just like bin Laden,'" *The Telegraph*, June 17, 2011. Cited December 1, 2011: http://www.telegraph.co.uk/news/worldnews/al-qaeda/8581122/US-says-we-will-kill-Zawahiri-just-like-bin-Laden.html

3. For a larger context in which to situate this form of communicative practice, with an ethical engagement of the issues at stake, see Judith Butler, *Giving an Account of Oneself* (New York: Fordham University Press, 2005).

4. See his earlier work, Vernon K. Robbins, *The Tapestry of Early Christian Discourse: Rhetoric, Society and Ideology* (London: Routledge, 1996).

5. Stanley Fish, "Rhetoric," in *Critical Terms for Literary Study*, 2nd ed, ed. Frank Lentricchia and Thomas McLaughlin (Chicago: University of Chicago Press, 1995), 203–22, 221.

6. Bruce Lincoln, *Holy Terrors: Thinking about Religion after September 11th*, 2nd ed. (Chicago: University of Chicago Press, 2006).

7. Antoinette Clark Wire, *The Corinthian Women Prophets: A Reconstruction through Paul's Rhetoric* (Minneapolis: Fortress Press, 1990).

8. Bruce Winter, *Roman Wives, Roman Widows: The Appearance of New Women and the Pauline Communities* (Grand Rapids: Eerdmans, 2003).

9. For further discussions on these various threads of rhetoric in antiquity, see Todd Penner, *In Praise of Christian Origins: Stephen and the Hellenists in Lukan Apologetic Historiography*, Emory Studies in Early Christianity, Vol. 10 (New York: Continuum/T&T Clark, 2004), 104–222; and Mark Given, *Paul's True Rhetoric: Ambiguity, Cunning, and Deception in Greece and Rome*, Emory Studies in Early Christianity, Vol. 7 (New York: Continuum/T&T Clark, 2001).

10. For fuller discussion, see Todd Penner and Caroline Vander Stichele, "Unveiling Paul: Gendering Éthos in 1 Corinthians 11:2-16," in *Rhetoric, Ethic, and Moral Persuasion in Biblical Discourse: Essays from the Heidelberg Conference 2002*, ed. Thomas H. Olbricht and Anders Eriksson (New York: T&T Clark, 2005), 214–37.

11. For a general introduction, alongside *Tapestry of Early Christian Discourse*, see Vernon K. Robbins, *Exploring the Texture of Texts: A Guide to Socio-Rhetorical Interpretation* (Harrisburg: Trinity Press International, 1996).

12. For a good example of her approach, see Elisabeth Schüssler Fiorenza, *The Power of the Word: Scripture and the Rhetoric of Empire* (Minneapolis: Fortress Press, 2007).

13. For a history of the interpretive issues and differences of opinion in modern scholarship, see Ralph P. Martin, *A Hymn of Christ: Philippians 2:5-11 in Recent Interpretation and in the Setting of Early Christian Worship* (Downers Grove: InterVarsity, 1997).

14. See further, Todd Penner, "Reconfiguring the Rhetorical Study of Acts: Reflections on the Method in and Learning of a Progymnastic Poetics," *Perspectives in Religious Studies* 30 (2003): 425-39.

15. Todd Penner and Caroline Vander Stichele, "Rhetorical Practice and Performance in Early Christianity," in *The Cambridge Companion to Ancient Rhetoric*, ed. Erik Gunderson (New York: Cambridge University Press, 2009), 245–60, 255.

16. For more on this point in relation to Philippians, see Joseph A. Marchal, *The Politics of Heaven: Women, Gender, and Empire in the Study of Paul* in Paul in Critical Contexts (Minneapolis: Fortress Press, 2008).

17. For further consideration, see Davina C. Lopez, "Pedagogy with the Repressed: Reflections from a Post-9/11 Biblical Studies Classroom," in *Faith, Feminism, and Scholarship: The Next Generation*, ed. Melanie L. Harris and Kate Ott (New York: Palgrave MacMillan, 2011), 163–80.

SPATIAL PERSPECTIVES

Space and Archaeology in Roman Philippi

LAURA S. NASRALLAH

At the heart of questions of resistance lie questions of spatiality—
the politics of lived space.[1]

New Testament scholarship has long experienced a tyranny of the book or tyranny of the word. We have been more interested in its words than its places. Why?
Perhaps our logocentrism emerges from the commonly held idea that the New
Testament or the Bible is a unified book, its words uttered by God or imparted by
the Holy Spirit. Or perhaps it emerges from ancient and modern practices of writing commentaries or our disciplinary training in philology; we plumb the depths
of each and every word (see the "Visual Perspectives" chapter). Thus the w/Word
begets words, untethered in time and space. Or perhaps our logocentrism is the
result of a New Testament that *looks* like stable words. This is especially true in
translations, but even Greek editions of the New Testament organize the untidy
scatter of manuscripts, pushing debate and minority voices to the page's apparatus. The text is made legible, thankfully, but its words are also made to look
stable.

But these New Testament texts—and texts they are, many letters and books, not
to mention fragments of papyrus and vellum pieced together—came from a variety
of times and places. And where they came from matters. To whom they were sent
matters. Place matters. This chapter will explore the topic of place and Paul's letters,
using Roman Philippi and the letter to the Philippians as a case study.

PLACE, SPACE, POWER

New Testament scholars have long argued that we should not read Paul's letters as a unified corpus or as systematic theology but as *occasional letters*. That is, Paul and his coworkers addressed particular people in particular places with dynamic situations. Paul's arguments and emphases shift, depending upon his audience, their location, their struggles, what they had to think with, and his own place among those *ekklēsiai* or assemblies.

A logical extension of the principle that Paul's letters are occasional and specific is that *the places to which they were sent matters*. If we are interested in how the earliest communities in Christ developed, we need to ask what was going on politically, socially, economically, theologically in cities such as Corinth, Antioch, and Thessalonikē. These places matter for their own sake and as nodes in Paul's and others' travels. When Cephas came to Antioch, when Paul left Corinth, when some in Thessalonikē died, changes took place in these cities. Authorities rose and fell, people ate together and stopped eating together, men were circumcised and not circumcised, people argued over whose vision of being in Christ was correct, people mourned and worked, and they did so whether Cephas and Paul were around or not. They walked the streets of their cities, to work, to temple, to home, past the civic center, past the butcher, past the imperial cult temple, and, departing the city gate, past the necropolis, the "city of the dead." Depending on their status, their sex, their ethnicity, their civic roles, they would walk quickly or slowly. They might use tactics to avoid certain routes, or they might walk confidently, acquiescing to the strategies that had produced this civic organization.[2] With the (relative) ease of travel in the Roman Empire, their bodies might map not only paths in the city but also paths between cities.

To take seriously each letter of Paul's *in its place* is to turn away from the one toward the many, the less powerful, the cacophony of voices that inspired Paul's letter and received each letter in its place. It is to think about the possibilities of interpretation in that place. The first objective of my chapter is to demonstrate that place matters, and to argue that we should not glance into the texts of the New Testament, or even dig deep within them, and think that we have done enough if we have attended to word alone.

Place matters, but so too do our conceptions of place. Thus space matters. Discussing this idea is the second objective of my chapter. We might think of place as objective and factual: I stand at a certain longitude and latitude; my position on the earth can be plotted according to geometry; or, more subjectively, there are mountains nearby; from my window, I can see the water and hear the dockworkers at the bay. Certainly, geographical theory long engaged in such abstract definitions, even in the Roman imperial period, when Claudius Ptolemy used astronomy to map the terrestrial world in his second-century CE *Almagest*, or when we find *periploi* and geographies, itineraries from travelers on land and sea. Yet a second-century CE writer like Ptolemy knew that there were other ways to map the world: his *Tetrabiblos* characterizes each *ethnos* (nation or race) according to what he claims are its physiological, moral, and other characteristics, arguing about the planets and gods that govern each people.

In our own time, theorists like Henri Lefebvre have challenged abstract ideas of geography, as his title *The Production of Space* shows. Sensitive to capitalism's effects on conceptions of space and on concrete productions of space, Lefebvre leads the reader away from a simple binary of epistemological *or* social notions of space. That is, he moves away from the idea that space is either abstractly, mathematically, concretely defined *or* only defined by human relations within it. He develops a "perceived-conceived-lived triad."[3] Edward Soja expounds upon this triad, using the term trialectics or "Thirdspace," as he thinks about the city of Los Angeles. This concept encompasses conceived space (which he defines as space as it is) and perceived space (which he defines as space as it is imagined or theorized) into "a fully *lived space*, a simultaneously real-and-imagined, actual-and-virtual locus of structured individual and collective experience and agency."[4]

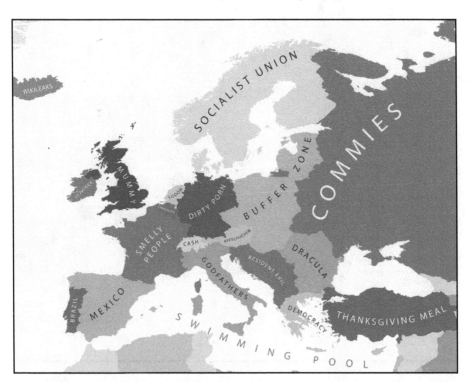

Figure 1. Detail of Yanko Tsvetkov's *The World according to the USA*, from the project "Mapping Stereotypes: The Geography of Prejudice," reprinted by permission of the artist.

To understand how abstract notions of space intersect with this idea of space's *production*—let's call it the spatial imaginary—we can look to the lighthearted and satiric "The World according to the U.S.A." in artist Yanko Tsvetkov's larger project "Mapping Stereotypes: The Geography of Prejudice" (fig. 1). We may have in our minds a map of the world, which geographers since Claudius Ptolemy and even earlier have tried to map out with mathematical precision, struggling to project the roundness of the globe onto our flatter experiences of ground and map. Yet superimposed upon that map are our ideas, our prejudices, our experiences, as Tsvetkov makes clear. Or an entirely new way of mapping might emerge—one that has

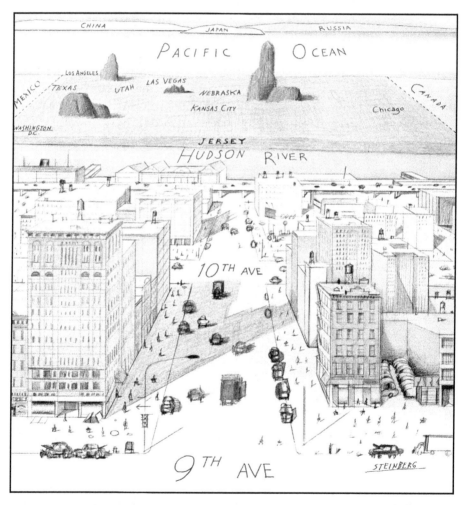

Figure 2. *View of the World from 9th Avenue.* Illustration by Saul Steinberg, published on the cover of *The New Yorker*, March 29, 1976. Reprinted by permission of the Saul Steinberg Foundation.

nothing to do with traditional, abstract maps. An example of this is Saul Steinberg's famous *New Yorker* cover (fig. 2), in which New York City looms large; the Hudson is a wide and definitive divide for the small strip of inconsequential land that separates the Hudson from the Pacific Ocean. We all have our homelands or desired spaces that distort the objective kilometers between cities or render our childhood homes larger in the mind than their actual metrics. Early Christians, too, had various spatial imaginaries, ones that sometimes imitated the mappings of the Roman Empire, as in the case of Acts, and ones with vertical mappings of the heavens in relation to the earth, as in Revelation or ascent literature such as the *Gospel of Mary*.[5]

Place matters, space matters, but as the phrase "the production of space" implies, mapping and power are intertwined; experiences of space as lived and perceived depend upon the power exercised by or impressed upon the viewer. The third goal of this chapter is to think about space and power in relation to New Testament studies. Immanuel Kant wrote about how the human body defines understandings of geography, and J. Z. Smith paraphrases him: "It is the relationship to the human body, and our experience of it, that orients us in space, that confers meaning to place. Human beings are not placed, they bring place into being. . . . Place is best understood as a locus of meaning."[6] If place, space, and power matter in the reading of New Testament texts, as I am arguing, then they can matter in multiple ways. As feminists often say, what you see depends upon where you stand. Feminist theoreticians have developed the idea of *standpoint epistemology*: the fact that we see and understand and interpret from a given vantage point can enrich our knowledge, rather than make it less objective. This insight allows us to perceive and to value how different human bodies—inflected as they are by gender, race, age, sexuality, and other rich experiences—and the particular bodies of others might interpret and experience place in various different ways. Who gets to produce a space? Whence are we barred, and where are we forced to go? Who finds a place safe and who finds it dangerous? Who experiences it, through what bodily differences, and who renovates it? (See the "Historical Approaches," "Feminist Approaches," and "African American Approaches" chapters.)

So, then, what you see depends upon where you stand, and where you stand depends in part on who you are and how you are formed socially, economically, politically by the culture that surrounds you. As you think about a biblical text in terms of place, you may want to consider the location from which you or others in our own time period read a text that is considered scripture. What you will see in the New Testament or in other ancient texts, for that matter, thus depends upon *your* place.[7] You might think about how the roles of women in evangelical Christian groups today are linked to certain kinds of biblical interpretation; you might study how New Testament texts are used to create a "prosperity gospel"; you might investigate the effects of Pauline thought in current churches in South Africa. From your place you might consider how passages from Paul's letters have been used to assert or to deny the rights of Christian worship and leadership to persons who are lesbian, gay, bisexual, transgendered; from your place, you might consider how Galatians 3:28's idea of "neither slave nor free" can inspire the eradication of global sex trafficking. These are several ways that place matters.

But ancient place also matters—the cities and communities to which Paul's letters were sent, for example. The reason I focus on the past is not because the ancient Mediterranean world and its spaces are any more important than, say, the world of nineteenth-century Tennessee or twentieth-century Pretoria or twenty-first-century Beirut. Yet attending to particularities, differences, to the details of what we can know about an ancient place from the archaeological and literary record forms or disciplines us. It helps us to attend to particularity, difference, and details of place today. In the rest of this chapter, I will use Paul's letter to the Philippians and the place of Roman Philippi to show some ways in which we might see New Testament texts differently or more deeply if we foreground place, space, and power.

PLACE: ROMAN PHILIPPI

How did the place of Philippi matter? If we think about space and place, and if we know something about the demographic, political, economic, and cultic realities of first- and second-century Philippi, we can reconstruct with more depth the many responses of the Philippian *ekklēsia* to Paul's letter. We can learn more about the spaces of empires, whether the Roman Empire or the kingdom of God. As we look at the earliest communities in Christ, a focus on particular cities or regions also forces us to avoid generalizations such as "it happened in the Roman Empire."

Philippi, with its nearby gold and silver mines in Mount Pangaion and its location thirteen kilometers to the northwest of the port of Neapolis (modern Kavala), had been a site of conflict long before Paul and his coworkers arrived there.[8] In the fourth century BCE, settlers from the nearby island of Thasos colonized the tribes that initially settled at Philippi, mainly Pieri and Edoni, whom we have come to call Thracians. The area was then taken over by Philip II, king of Macedonia, and in 167 BCE the Romans conquered the region. Nonetheless, even in the first through third centuries, reliefs carved on the bedrock to the west of the theater reveal an ongoing worship of a god in her local form: Artemis Bendis, a Thracian form of Artemis.[9]

As a colony Philippi's spatial organization is dictated by the Via Egnatia, an important Roman trade route (fig. 3). Running from the southeast to the northwest, it divides the three temples of the Capitolium from the forum to the south. We do not know much about Julio-Claudian Philippi—that is, Philippi at the time of Paul's writing of the letter—since the bulk of Roman-period archaeological remains in Philippi date to the second century.[10] Excavations of the Antonine forum

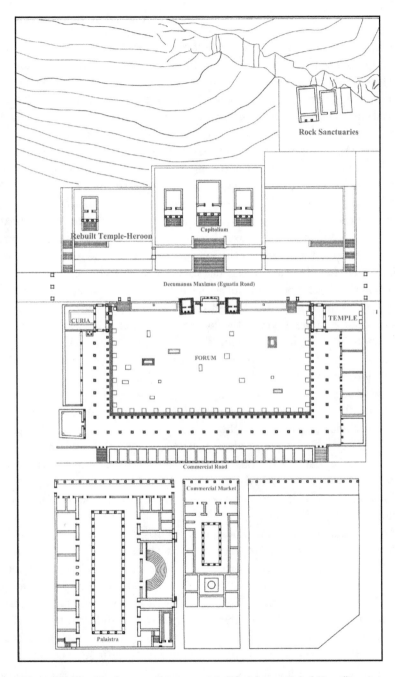

Figure 3. Plan of Philippi in the second century. Modified from Michel Sève, "Le côté nord du forum de Philippes," *Bulletin de correspondance hellénique* 110, no. 1 (1986). Thanks are due to Chaido Koukouli-Chrysanthaki and to the Presidential Information Technology Fellow program at Harvard University for modifications of the image.

(second century CE) revealed that the Julio-Claudian forum (first century CE) had the same general plan, although the Antonine forum had a larger central square. Two temple-shaped structures on the north side probably had the same function in the Julio-Claudian period as in the Antonine. The western structure was the *curia* of the Roman colony (its governmental center); the eastern was associated with imperial cult. Sculptural and epigraphic remains attest to the honoring of Augustus and his adopted sons Gaius and Lucius Caesar at Philippi both at the time of Paul and later.[11] The Antonine renovation included a large monument to priestesses of the empress Livia, reminding us of the ongoing power of Roman imperial cult and the intertwining of civic and religious space in antiquity.[12]

The second-century building boom also included renovations of the theater and evidence of open-air religious activity on the lower slopes of the acropolis to the west of the theater. Many rock-cut reliefs, likely from the late first century through the third century, dot the hill to the west of the theater. The majority of the over two hundred reliefs depicted or were dedicated to the goddess Diana (also known as Artemis in the Greek tradition, and associated with the Thracian goddess Bendis). On the same hill, incised into the bedrock of the acropolis, we find the founding and expansion of a sanctuary to the god Sylvanus. Higher up the slope and to the west of the Sylvanus cult, a temple for Isis and other Egyptian gods was established. Certainly, the Philippian community to which Paul wrote had many religious options dotting their city. Each had its ethnic affiliations: Sylvanus, a traditional agricultural god of the Romans; the Egyptian Isis; various forms of Artemis rooted in Thracian, Roman, and Greek iconographic and cultic traditions; none of these options precluded the other. Late third- or early fourth-century CE epigraphic evidence indicates a synagogue in Philippi, and surely a Jewish community existed there at an earlier date.[13] After all, those to whom Paul writes his letter did not live at a time when something called "Christianity" existed but rather were likely Gentiles interested in Judaism and in the peculiar Judaism in Christ that Paul discussed (see, for example, Phil. 3:2-3).

Like other Greek cities under Rome, Philippi may be considered a "contact zone" in which racial, ethnic, and imperial conflicts and negotiations occurred.[14] Like other cities, Philippi had in close proximity multiple gods of multiple "ethnic" origins, worshipped together, as we have just seen. In addition, Philippi was a contact zone of Thracians and Thasians, Greeks and Macedonians, Romans and those who had inhabited the area before Philippi's colonial status, and even Romans against Romans. It was the site of a major battle of the second triumvirate. In late 42 BCE, Octavian and Antony—soon and finally to war against each other at Actium (in 31 BCE, with Cleopatra supporting Antony)—triumphed over Cassius and Brutus on the low plains to the southwest of Philippi, marshes that, according to some scholars, had been reclaimed for farmland.[15] Afterward, the veterans who had served time wanted their due: to receive land in Italy. But that land was already settled.

As a result, some ancient literature depicts veterans as dispossessed, suffering from the lies and political machinations of the leaders they had served. Others, like the second-century writer Appian, represent a contestation over space and the chaos wreaked by soldiers and veterans upon the "ordinary" Italians whose lives the military disrupted:

> The task of assigning the soldiers to their colonies and dividing the land was one of exceeding difficulty. For the soldiers demanded the cities which had been selected for them before the war as prizes for their valour, and the cities demanded that the whole of Italy should share the burden or that the cities should cast lots with the other cities, and that those who gave the land should be paid the value of it; and there was no money. They came to Rome in crowds, young and old, women and children, to the forum and temples, uttering lamentations, saying that they had done no wrong for which they, Italians, should be driven from their fields and their hearthstones, like people conquered in war. . . . The soldiers encroached upon their neighbours in an insolent manner, seizing more than had been given to them and choosing the best lands; nor did they cease even when Octavian rebuked them and made them numerous other presents, since they were contemptuous of their rulers in the knowledge that they needed them to confirm their power (Appian, *Bell. Civ.* 5.12-13).[16]

But what does veteran settlement in Italy have to do with the battles at Philippi? According to Lawrence Keppie, "the only known overseas colony of this time was at Philippi itself."[17] Those veterans settled at Philippi were presumably even more disgruntled, disenfranchised, and ruthless than those sent back to their Italian homeland.[18] The descendants of these veterans may have been among those to whom Philippians was written. The veteran impact upon the city was certainly felt by those who had lived in the area before the Battle of Philippi, whose families also likely were recipients of the letter. In the first century, when Paul was writing and the Philippians were hearing this letter aloud in their assembly, space could be contested and imagined in various ways. The lines between "our space" and "their space" could be mapped not only in terms of those who were in Christ and those who were not, or in terms of Romans versus Greeks (or others whom they conquered), but also in terms of deep fissures within Roman society itself—fissures defined by war, by wealth, by loyalties.

New Testament scholars have recently shed light on how the battle and its social and political after-effects are a primary context in which to read Philippians. Edgar Krentz and Joseph Hellerman have shown the importance of the military to Roman Philippi and that Roman identity was on display in the *Colonia Julia Augusta Philippensis*.[19] Inscriptions come to be written primarily in Latin, the language of the

Roman rulers, rather than Greek; the theater was rebuilt in Roman style; the forum
too is in Roman style, framed by a curia and an imperial cult temple; and, by the
second century, a prominent monument to the priestesses of Livia was erected on
its northwest side. That is, this city, with its long history of settlement by the Pieri
and Edoni (whom we have come to call Thracians), then the Thasians in the fourth
century BCE, then Philip II of Macedon, becomes a more noticeably Roman space in
the Julio-Claudian period, although it had been conquered in 167 BCE. The impact
of such a cultural and social shift upon the peoples of the city is a significant context
for interpretation of Paul's letter. The Philippians experienced shifts in ethnicity and
politics in their own city. They were aware of the rise and fall of various powers, of
bowing the knee to various forms of glory, as they heard Paul's use of a text probably
known to them before Paul himself was:[20] "Every knee shall bow and tongue confess
that Jesus is Lord, to the glory of God the father" (2:11).

If Philippi was contested space between locals who had lived there and new imperial military colonists, it was also contested space between Romans. After his defeat
of Antony at the battle at Actium in 31 BCE, Augustus literally visualized the 42 BCE
victory at Philippi as his, with a series of bronze coins that associates the goddess
Victoria (Victory) with Augustus alone (fig. 4) (see also the "Visual Perspectives"
chapter). Yet, earlier numismatic evidence shows that Antony, not Octavian, was
the primary founder of Philippi, and that Antony used Philippi to settle not only
military personnel but also civilians. Later coinage tells a different story, depicting
the laurel-wreathed head of Augustus with the legend *COL(onia) AVG(usta) IVL(ia)*

Figure 4. Augustan coin from Philippi, 27 BCE—14 CE. Reverse (on left): three military standards
and the legend *COHOR(s) PRAE(toria)* ("Praetorian Cohort"). Obverse (on right): Victory holds
a wreath and palm branch; legend *VIC(toria) AVG(usti)* ("Victory of Augustus"). Courtesy of the
Bibliothèque Nationale de France, Paris.

Figure 5. Augustan coin from Philippi, 27 BCE—14 CE. Obverse (on left): august in profile facing right, legend *AVG(usti)*. Reverse (on right), two priests plowing a field. Courtesy of the Bibliothèque Nationale de France, Paris.

PHIL(ippensis) IVSSV AVG(usti). That is, the colony is named in relation to Augustus and the Julian family, and with the word *iussus*—an order, command, or decree—Octavian claims that it was *he* who founded the colony.[21]

Coinage both in Italy proper and in Philippi represents the realities of centuriation or land division that followed imperial occupation and, in these cases, veteran resettlement. Just as there were coins depicting military standards with a plough and a surveyor's rod in Italy, we find coinage in Philippi depicting the rituals of groove-making and the plow that marked the borders of the colony (fig. 5). One type of coin from Philippi represents an important act in the colony's foundation, when the founder, head ritually covered by a fold of the toga, traces a groove around the territory to divide it. At the same time a plough harnessed to a bull and a cow finishes the sacred rite. This is a common theme on colonial coinage, a *reductio* of religious ritual that reminds the money-bearer not only of the colony's origin but also of that origin as divinely sustained. Other coins represented surveyors (*agrimensores*) who divided the land into square parcels (*centuriae*) and then into lots (*sortes, acceptae*).[22]

Philippi lived on in legend and memory as a site that could confirm a man's power to become emperor. Second-century writers Dio (54.9) and Suetonius (14.3) tell of flames spontaneously blazing on the altars at Philippi when Tiberius passed through the region. Philippi becomes a space that affirms monarchy and authority even for the generation after the triumvirate, and after the *imperium* of Augustus.

Colonization and Romanization were not the only factors of importance to Paul's writing or the Philippians' hearing of his letter. Nonetheless, if we are to take up space and place as important categories that might deepen our interpretation

of Philippians, certainly a population influx of Roman soldiers and, more importantly, new divisions of land and the veterans' other impacts on the land and city
are important historical contexts within which to read the letter. So too are potential conflicts between veterans who owed their loyalties to Antony *versus* Augustus.
In addition, Paul refers once to the *praitōrion* and once to the household of Caesar
in Philippians (1:13; 4:22). Even though this *praitōrion* and the household of Caesar
are precisely *not* in Philippi, since Paul writes from his "bonds" elsewhere, his mention of them and the larger historical context of the *colonia* of Philippi means that
the effects of the Roman Empire are concretely in view in this epistle.[23]

SPACE MATTERS: PAUL'S AND OTHERS' BODIES

"At the heart of questions of resistance lie questions of spatiality—the politics of
lived space," writes critical geographer Steve Pile.[24] He argues:

> In a sense, this is a plea for recognising that the spatial technologies
> of domination—such as military occupation or, alternatively, urban
> planning—need to continually resolve specific spatial problems, such
> as distance and closeness, inclusion and exclusion, surveillance and
> position, movement and immobility, communication and knowledge,
> and so on. This is to say that authority produces space through, for
> example, cutting it up, differentiating between parcels of space, the use
> and abuse of borders and markers, the production of scales (from the
> body, through the region and the nation, to the globe), the control of
> movement within and across different kinds of boundaries and so on.[25]

In Pile's analysis of space, there is no simple binary of resister and empire, dominated and dominator. Pile's caution and his mention of surveillance and borders, of
parcels of space, reminds us of Roman imperial technologies of domination: to put
it more simply, of surveying, cutting up, and surveilling occupied territories. The
archaeology and spaces of country and city are not neutral; they can be manipu-
lated. They are walked, dwelt in, and, of course, transformed.

Place matters, but so too does space, and, indeed, the two are inseparable.[26]
Ancient writers constructed the spaces of the world through words and invited
their readers and hearers into a spatial imaginary. Mentions of cities, provinces, of
heaven and earth all evoke for the readers and hearers a spatial realm that has some
relationship with material place but which supersedes and reframes it, too. The
notion in Philippians 3:20 of *to politeuma en ouranois*, a citizenship in the heavens,
is not pie in the sky but is grounded by the real places of *politeia* and *polis* current

at the time. Or, to give another example, the *basileia tou theou*—usually translated the "kingdom of God" but equally the dominion or reign of God—is in the context of the real Roman empire and its claims. To those of us who have long heard New Testament texts used in classrooms or churches, such language may have lost its spatial (and political) edge and may seem "common sense." But we should be attentive to the spatial elements in Paul's letters, in order to understand more deeply the range of possible meanings and interpretations of such language to its first users and to recognize its strangeness to our conceptions of the world. Such attentiveness might also lead us to investigate spatial language used by religious communities in our age of "globalization."

Ancient texts, as well as more recent ones, theorize space, sometimes explicitly, sometimes less so. Writers of antiquity knew that the world was round and they mapped and projected its spaces based upon their observations of the stars. Vitruvius addresses his ideas about architecture to the ascendant ruler Octavian, someone on the cusp of his own form of globalization. For Vitruvius, Italy is the center of the world, and space and race/ethnicity coincide.

> Within the area of the entire earthly globe and all the regions at the center of the cosmos, the Roman People has its territories. The populations of Italy partake in equal measure of the qualities of both north and south, both with regard to their physiques and to the vigor of their minds, to produce the greatest strength. Just as the planet Jupiter is tempered by running its course between seething Mars and chilly Saturn, so, for the same reason, Italy, in between north and south, partaking of each in her composition, has balanced and invincible qualities. With her prudent counsel she smites the barbarians' strength; her strong hand does the same to the southerners' scheming. Thus the divine intelligence established the state of the Roman People as an outstanding and balanced region—so that it could take command over the earthly orb (*De arch.* 6.1.10-11).[27]

Vitruvius has mapped the globe and imputed to Nature the variegated mental and physical qualities of its inhabitants, as well as the varieties of architecture that emerge from these conditions.

Vitruvius is also wise to the ways in which urban planning and temple construction are rhetorically powerful: that is, space and buildings, too—not just words alone—have the power to persuade people (see the "Rhetorical Approaches" and "Visual Perspectives" chapters). Vitruvius states that the placement and architecture of such buildings should be responsive to the gods' tendencies and qualities and to the human body's interaction with space. The reason that temples and their cult statues should face the western regions of the heavens, states Vitruvius, is that "those who approach with offerings and sacrifices will look toward the image within the temple beneath the eastern part of the heavens; and thus when they are raising their prayers, they will view both the temple and the rising heaven, while the images themselves will seem to be rising as well" (4.6.5).

"Altars should face east," he emphasizes, "and should always be placed lower than the cult images that will be in the temple, so that those who make supplication and sacrifices may look up at the deity; the heights of these differ and should be designed to fit the dignity of each particular god" (4.9.1). The gods must be correctly placed in the spaces of the city so that, for example, more dangerous gods like Venus, Vulcan, and Mars—evoking lust, fire, and conflict—should be outside the city walls (1.7). Worshippers should be theologically persuaded, if you will, by the relative heights of the divinities over their altars and by the movement of their (human) bodies in procession toward those gods (with their imaged bodies) and their temples. Awe and theological convictions are spatially produced—or at least the architect can try.

Paul and Other Bodies in Space

We remember that Kant and others have emphasized the human body as the means from which we perceive space. We have just seen in Vitruvius's writing how an ancient architect articulates this explicitly. What if we bring the question of the human body and space to our case study of Philippi and Philippians? Paul's letter to the Philippians insists that hearers and readers focus on *Paul's* space and place. In 1:1 Paul identifies himself and Timothy as "slaves of Jesus Christ," and in verse 7, where his body appears again, he introduces key themes of the letter: "It is right for me to think thus concerning you, because I have you in my heart, since, in my bonds and in the defense and surety of the gospel, you all are partners with me of grace." I offer a clunky translation in order to highlight two things. First, early in the letter, Paul's own body is a specter, a ghostly presence—he is in bonds, even if we do not know where. Second, by using the term *synkoinōnoi*, or "partners," Paul insists upon proximity, a fellowship, even if he is distant. The intimacy is only reinforced by the metaphor of having people "in heart." Somehow, bodies merge in space.

The location of Paul in bonds is mentioned elsewhere in the letter, which both effaces and presents Paul's body. Paul's bodily absence and presence in the act of letter writing or in the future are themes he pursues in other letters. But in Philippians his absence from them has concrete effects: "What has happened to me has really served to advance the gospel, so that it has become known throughout the whole praetorian guard and to all the rest that my imprisonment is for Christ" (1:12-13). With this new disclosure, Paul's bonds and body are suddenly placed onto a larger map. The Philippians-in-Christ, given their recent history of war and veteran settlements, would likely notice mention of the praetorian guard. Paul's reference to his political bonds and to the *praitōrion* raises the issue of empire and where Paul (and, derivatively, the *ekklēsiai* that support him) belong within those spaces. Paul's bonds are the concrete cause of his absence, yet, paradoxically, this fixity of location and bodily absence at Philippi leads to the gospel's advancement. Philippians 1:14 goes on to say that "the majority of brothers and sisters in the Lord have been persuaded because of my bonds to dare even more fearlessly to speak the word of God" (my trans.). Paul's bonds, Paul's place, Paul's absence, Paul's for-the-moment fixed location in the spaces of empire make a difference to those who can move freely.

Paul may present his own body and its place as making a significant difference in the spread of those who are in Christ. But other bodies also transform space in Philippians.[28] Timothy and Epaphroditus become traveling lines that trace Paul's relation to this community and that enable continued contact across space. Philippians 2:19-24 expresses Paul's desire to send Timothy quickly to the Philippians and emphasizes Timothy's credentials, which include his being genuine and even *isopsychos* to Paul. We could translate this word as "of the same mind," but *isopsychos* implies an equivalency of soul, as if Paul could, through Timothy, bi-locate.[29]

Paul also presents Epaphroditus as a traveler who marks the distance and the connection between Paul and the Philippians. Epaphroditus is described as Paul's "brother and co-worker and co-soldier, but your apostle and servant (*leitourgos*) of my need" (2.25). This term arises again in verse 30 (here, *leitourgia*), where Epaphroditus brings together Paul and the Philippians through Epaphroditus' role as public servant (in a civic sense) and a minister (in a more religious cultic sense). In the case of both Timothy and Epaphroditus, the apostolic or ministering body becomes a means of transforming space and place: Timothy, a child and slave from Paul's own household (*oikos*; Phil. 2:22b), or Epaphroditus, from the *ekklēsia* at Philippi, become traveling lines that trace tense distance or joyful reunion between the fixed points of Paul (absent, in bonds) and Philippi.

The space of the *ekklēsiai* in Christ is also mapped through the flow of ancient capital—through what the bodies of those in Christ carry. David Harvey and other critical Marxist geographers insist that we notice the ways in which capital pools in and moves across space, forming a topographical map of goods and wealth.[30] In Paul's letters we find something similar, as he discusses donations, even if these are likely donations of the poor to the poor. The end of the letter to the Philippians provides one example (4:10-20): On the one hand, Paul emphasizes his lack of need (*autarkeia*, v. 11), a technical term that points to the philosophical goal of not being dependent upon external things. On the other, Paul maps *ekklēsiai* through regional competition: even if a gift was not necessary in the first place, Philippi does more than Thessalonikē (vv. 15-16). In other letters, too, the Philippians appear as part of the "Macedonians," and a situation of regional competition maps the spaces of in-Christ communities in three locations: Achaia, Macedonia, and Jerusalem (2 Cor. 8:1-5 and 9:1-4). Paul is making space, and placing the Philippians, among others, within it. Paul uses references to provinces and cities to produce a kind of topographical map of those who are in Christ.

In this passage Epaphroditus becomes the supplicant who brings not only "the things received," but things received that are described in ever more cultic tones: as a good aroma, as a *thysia* or sacrifice that is "well pleasing to God" (v. 18). In his ruminations on space, Vitruvius was concerned about the height of the altar that received offerings. In Philippians Paul becomes an altar or temple of a sort, receiving gifts which are a sacrifice; he also becomes the thing on the altar: "I am poured out upon the altar and religious duty of your faith" (2.17). The Philippians may see their gifts, tendered through Epaphroditus, as a payment in a patron-client relationship in which they are patrons of Paul's missionary endeavors, but Paul, both as a kind of priest and a kind of religious object, reframes space and transforms these gifts into offerings.

POWER: CHRIST'S BODY IN SPACE

Paul offers several examples in the letter to the Philippians to support his emphasis on oneness, particularly his emphasis on thinking the same thing or being like-minded (*to auto phronein*). Just as Paul and then Timothy and Epaphroditus have become examples of unity and fellowship, so too does Christ. And just as Paul and then Timothy and Epaphroditus become points in space, one stable, some moving, in Philippians 2:6-11 we find spatial language applied to Christ. Paul introduces the text with a variant of this phrase (*to auto phronein*) that he uses as a key concept and teaching in the letter (2:5): "think the same thing among yourselves, which also was in Christ Jesus." Paul then continues in 2:6-11, probably quoting traditional materials about Christ. In that passage, language of taking on the form of God (*morphē theou*, v. 6) and then the form of a slave (*morphē doulou*) and human likeness (*homoiōmati anthrōpōn*, v. 7) might remind the early hearers of this text of extant social hierarchies. There are slaves who are like and not like humans; there are gods who are represented as humans; there are those who are in the form of gods, like the imperial family members honored in cult, including in the forum at Philippi. The images of self-emptying (*ekenōsen*, v. 7) and self-humbling (*etapeinōsen heauton*, v. 8) similarly call to mind the hierarchal, or, in Elisabeth Schüssler Fiorenza's term, kyriarchal, structures of the ancient world, where the master stood above the slave in the social hierarchy, and the divine similarly above the human.[31] God's actions of "lifting him up" or "exalting him" (v. 9) and giving him a name "which is above every name" confirm the spatiality of this passage, as does the tripartite mapping of the spaces of the cosmos: the image of every knee whether in the heavens or upon earth or under the earth bowing (v. 10).

We can see a broader trend in Philippians to map vertically people's relations to each other.[32] Philippi was mapped not only as a significant capital of Macedonia, linked to the sea by Neapolis, but also, internally, according to vertical spatial organizations in which people knew where they stood on a social map. The Philippians who heard or read Paul's letter would have empire and its spatial expansion to Philippi in mind, as well as (likely) the empire's vertical spatial expansion in terms of the divinization of the imperial family (represented in the second-century monument in the Forum to the cult of Livia) (see the "Postcolonial Approaches" chapter). They may have been aware of the complex ranking of slaves even within the *oikia Kaisaros*, the household of Caesar mentioned at the end of the epistle (4:22). Those who heard and debated Paul's letter would not be ignorant of their city's own history as a site of contestation in the very late republican period, and then its site as the eventual triumph of one who would become emperor, and then its imagined status as a site of omen that confirmed Tiberius's rule.

To assert that someone has the form of a God and the form of a slave, or trades between these and between humility/humiliation and being lifted up/exaltation, is also to assert a queer thing.[33] In antiquity, the body of a slave was open to penetration, available, an *instrumentum* or *organon* for another's use (see the "Queer Approaches" chapter). To make this body into something before which others kneel and fall and to which others ascribe superiority was to transgress the normal order and hierarchical space of things. Philippians 2:6-11 presents a map in which Christ's form moves from God to slave, and in which the slave becomes lord (*kyrios*). Yet Paul inscribes that upside-down configuration within his own message of conformity. That is, he takes the queer idea of a slave lord and frames it in terms of his emphasis on conformity (Paul, his coworkers, and Christ are all "of the same mind," 2:5) and obedience (2:12), on the one hand, and his message of the importance of Christ's humiliation, not exaltation, on the other.[34]

CONCLUSIONS

Place matters. Where people lived in antiquity mattered, and their spatial imaginaries and their reactions to those of Paul and others are linked to significant theological and political debates. The spaces within which they moved imprinted them; they may have resisted and created their own pathways; there likely was tension between the rhetoric of architecture and the organizational attempts of town planning, on the one hand, and how various segments of the population *used* their spaces, on the other.

We receive the Pauline epistles within a "New Testament" within a "Bible" which looks very much like a unitary book, intended to go out to all places and times, as indeed it has and still does. But if we are interested in the historical specificities of the first communities that received Paul's letters, and if we are interested in specific historical and material conditions at all, we must understand that Paul's letters were *variously* received *in a particular place with its particular conditions*, not all of which Paul would have known, even if he had visited and dwelt among them. A focus on space and place may lead us to learn about Roman Philippi proper, as we did in one section of the chapter. It may lead us to ask questions about the traveling bodies of those early missionaries in Christ, and about the flow of capital and letters between them that created a kind of map of those in Christ within the spaces of the Roman Empire. A focus on space and place may lead us to consider the vertical spatial imaginaries of those who imagined themselves and their Christ as both slave and God.

Finally, to state that where people lived mattered—that the real spaces of their world had an impact on their theological, social, economic selves—is to make two larger methodological moves. First, it is to make a methodological turn away from Paul alone to many people of the earliest assemblies or *ekklēsiai*, of which Paul was one member. At the same time, a focus on place and space demands that we turn away from the idea of exegesis as reaching a singular conclusion. Instead, exegesis or close reading can open many possibilities for our understanding of the first reception of the letters of Paul and the spaces in which these letters were read and heard and discussed.

FURTHER READING

Theories of Space

de Certeau, Michel. *The Practice of Everyday Life*. Translated by Steven Rendall. Berkeley: University of California Press, 1984. Includes important ideas of tactics and strategies of walking the city—that is, of resistance to the rhetoric of persuasion attempted by civic organization and the built environment.

Lefebvre, Henri. *The Production of Space*. Translated by Donald Nicholson-Smith. Oxford: Blackwell, 1991. The very title shows him to be undoing the notion that space is an abstraction or mathematical concept. Sensitive to capitalism's effects on conceptions of space and on concrete productions of space, he develops a "trialectics" of space.

Pile, Steven. "Introduction: Opposition, Political Identities, and Spaces of Resistances," in *Geographies of Resistance*, edited by Steve Pile and Michael Keith, 1–32. London: Routledge, 1997. Argues that non-elite resistance takes place in variegated ways, demonstrates how geographies of resistance and domination are not equal and opposite, and foregrounds status and economic issues, as well as gender, in the analysis of space.

Halberstam, Judith. *In a Queer Time and Place: Transgender Bodies, Subcultural Lives*. New York: New York University Press, 2005. Insists that we take seriously how queer bodies experience space differently and map the human lifespan according to a different sense of time.

Tsing, Anna. "The Global Situation," in *The Anthropology of Globalization: A Reader*. Edited by Jonathan Xavier Inda and Renato Rosaldo, 2nd ed., 66–98. Malden, MA: Blackwell, 2008. Challenges readers to look beyond the binary of global and local. Tsing uses the metaphor of a flow within a creek: you cannot focus only on flow (in our case, the Roman Empire) or on creek bed (in our case, the city of Philippi), but on how each shifts in relation to the other.

Archaeology at Philippi

Bakirtzis, Charalambos and Helmut Koester, eds. *Philippi at the Time of Paul and after His Death*. Harrisburg: Trinity Press International, 1998. Includes several essays that give an overview of archaeological finds at Philippi in the Roman and early Christian periods.

Space in Antiquity

Nasrallah, Laura Salah. *Christian Responses to Roman Art and Architecture: The Second-Century Church amid the Spaces of Empire*. Cambridge: Cambridge University Press, 2010. Discusses how early Christian "apologists" crafted their theologies and polemic in relation to geographical spread and the built environment of the Roman Empire.

Ancient Writers Who Discuss Space

Strabo, *Geography*. This first-century writer shows the way in which geography and mapping are necessary for the expansion of empire.

Vitruvius, *On Architecture*. Dedicated to Octavian before he had become the emperor Augustus, these twelve books discuss topics like civic organization and how to place the temples of the gods safely within and without the city.

Claudius Ptolemy, *Almagest, Geography, Tetrabiblos*. This second-century CE writer uses astronomy to map the world in the *Almagest*, port stops to mark latitude and longitude in his *Geography*, and ideas of race, character, and regnant gods of various nations to map space in his *Tetrabiblos*.

NOTES

1. Steve Pile, "Introduction: Opposition, Political Identities, and Spaces of Resistances," in *Geographies of Resistance*, ed. Steve Pile and Michael Keith (London: Routledge, 1997), 27.

2. Michel de Certeau, *The Practice of Everyday Life*, trans. Steven Rendall (Berkeley: University of California Press, 1984).

3. Henri Lefebvre, *The Production of Space*, trans. Donald Nicholson-Smith (Oxford: Blackwell, 1991), 40. Recent critical geographers have taken the work of Lefebvre and others in several directions, with some emphasizing that we should attend not only to the human body's relation to space, but to the various spatial experiences of diverse human *bodies*— molded as they are by gender, race, sexuality, class. See, for example, Judith Halberstam, *In a Queer Time and Place: Transgender Bodies, Subcultural Lives* (New York: New York University Press, 2005); Anna Tsing, "The Global Situation," in *The Anthropology of Globalization: A Reader*, ed. Jonathan Xavier Inda and Renato Rosaldo, 2nd ed. (Malden: Blackwell, 2008), 66–98; Pile, "Introduction."

4. Edward W. Soja, *Postmetropolis: Critical Studies of Cities and Regions* (Oxford: Blackwell, 2000), 11; see also his *Thirdspace: Journeys to Los Angeles and Other Real-and-Imagined Places* (Oxford: Blackwell, 1996), 53–82.

5. On theorizing space and place in Paul, see Melanie Johnson-DeBaufre, "Flying, Cloud-Riding, and the God's Eye View: 1 Thessalonians 4:13-18 and the Production of Christian Space," from her work in progress *I'll Fly Away: Making Space in the Letters of Paul*; see also Laura Salah Nasrallah, *Christian Responses to Roman Art and Architecture: The Second-Century Church amid the Spaces of Empire* (Cambridge: Cambridge University Press, 2010), 51–84.

6. Jonathan Z. Smith, *To Take Place: Toward Theory in Ritual* (Chicago: Chicago University Press, 1987), 28.

7. A few examples of volumes that consider biblical interpretation in light of the interpreter's social location include: Elisabeth Schüssler Fiorenza, *Bread Not Stone: The Challenge of Feminist Biblical Interpretation*, 10th anniversary ed. (Boston: Beacon, 1995); Fernando Segovia and Mary Ann Tolbert, eds., *Reading from This Place*, 2 vols. (Minneapolis: Fortress Press, 1995); R. S. Sugirtharajah, *Postcolonial Criticism and Biblical Interpretation* (Oxford: Oxford University Press, 2002); Brian K. Blount, ed., *True to Our Native Land: An African American New Testament Commentary* (Minneapolis: Fortress Press, 2007).

8. For good general introductions of the history, topography, and archaeology of Philippi, see Paul Collart, *Philippes: Ville de Macédoine, depuis ses origines jusqu'à la fin de l'époque romaine*, 2 vols. (Paris, E. de Boccard, 1937); Peter S. Oakes, *Philippians: From People to Letter* (Cambridge: Cambridge University Press, 2001), esp. 1–54.

9. Valerie A. Abrahamsen, *Women and Worship at Philippi: Diana/Artemis and Other Cults in the Early Christian Era* (Portland: Astarte Shell, 1995).

10. Chaido Koukouli-Chrysantaki, "Colonia Iulia Augusta Philippensis," in *Philippi at the Time of Paul and after His Death*, ed. Charalambos Bakirtzis and Helmut Koester (Harrisburg: Trinity Press International, 1998), 5–35, 14–15; Michel Sève, "Le coté nord du forum de Philippes," *Bulletin de correspondance hellénique* 110, no. 1 (1986): 531–81.

11. Collart, *Philippes*, 1:353, plate LXXXIII.

12. Michel Sève and Patrick Weber, "Un monument honorifique au forum de Philippes," *Bulletin de correspondance hellénique* 112, no. 1 (1988): 467–479.

13. Koukouli-Chrysantaki, "Colonia Iulia Augusta Philippensis."

14. Joseph A. Marchal, *The Politics of Heaven: Women, Gender, and Empire in the Study of Paul* (Minneapolis: Fortress Press, 2008), 91–109. Other New Testament scholars who use the term are Tat-siong Benny Liew and Fernando Segovia ("Contact Zones and Zoning Contexts: From the Los Angeles 'Riot' to a New York Symposium," *Union Seminary Quarterly Review* 56 [2003]: 21–40); they borrow the term from Mary Louise Pratt's *Imperial Eyes: Travel Writing and Transculturation* (London: Routledge, 1992).

15. See Oakes, *Philippians*; Lawrence Keppie, *Colonisation and Veteran Settlement in Italy: 47–14 B.C.* (London: British School at Rome, 1983).

16. Translation is from *Appian's Roman History*, trans. Horace White, vol. 4, Loeb Classical Library (New York: The Macmillan Co., 1913), 396–97. Keppie depicts veterans as an unwelcome and politically dangerous force (68); Dio, *Rom. hist.* 48.4–14.

17. Keppie, relying on Collart, notes that "Philippi received veterans from a legion XXVIII . . . and of the Praetorian cohorts" (*Colonisation*, 60); see Collart, *Philippes*, 1:233–35.

18. Oakes hypothesizes that "Octavian and Antony's behaviour in settling colonists in Macedonia is likely to have been more ruthless than it was in Italy" (*Philippians*, 26).

19. See Edgar M. Krentz, "Military Language and Metaphors in Philippians," in *Origins and Method: Towards a New Understanding of Judaism and Christianity: Essays in Honour of John C. Hurd*, ed. Bradley H. McLean, (Sheffield: JSOT Press, 1993): 105–27; and Joseph H. Hellerman, *Reconstructing Honor in Roman Philippi: Carmen Christi as Cursus Pudorum* (New York: Cambridge University Press, 2005), 64-87.

20. Wolfgang Schenk, *Die Philipperbriefe des Paulus: Kommentar* (Stuttgart: W. Kohlhammer, 1984) for the idea that 2:6-11 may come from the Philippians themselves. Some argue, however, that this passage is Pauline. See, e.g., J. M. Furness, "The Authorship of Phil. 2:6-11," *The Expository Times* 70 (1959): 240–3.

21. Collart, *Philippes*, 1:232–33, 235–36; Krentz, "Military Language."

22. Collart, *Philippes*, 1:226–27.

23. Were Paul in Rome, the term *praitōrion* (a Greek loanword from the Latin *praetorium*) would likely mean the body of soldiers who guarded the emperor. Were Paul in a Roman imperial capital, the term would mean the governor's residence or palace, as the term is used, for example, in the Acts of the Apostles. See J. B. Lightfoot, *Saint Paul's Epistle to the Philippians: A Revised Text with Introduction, Notes, and Dissertations*, 6th ed. (London: Macmillan, 1881), 99–104.

24. Pile, "Introduction," 27.

25. Pile, "Introduction," 3.

26. Nasrallah, *Christian Responses*, 87–118.

27. All Vitruvius translations are from *Vitruvius: Ten Books on Architecture*, ed. Ingrid D. Rowland and Thomas Noble Howe, trans. Ingrid D. Rowland (New York: Cambridge University Press, 1999).

28. Paul puts forward his own body and those of others as exempla to persuade the Philippians to be like-minded; see Cynthia Briggs Kittredge, *Community and Authority: The Rhetoric of Obedience in the Pauline Tradition* (Harrisburg: Trinity Press International, 1998), 53–100; Johnson-DeBaufre, "Flying, Cloud-Riding, and the God's Eye View."

29. Yet while Timothy may have this sort of freedom of movement and authority to be a second Paul, he is also simultaneously located within a kind of *oikos Paulou* as slave and child: "as a child to a father, he slaved for me in the gospel" (2:22b).

30. David Harvey, *Spaces of Global Capitalism* (London: Verso, 2006), 119–48.

31. Elisabeth Schüssler Fiorenza defines *kyriarchy* as "a socio-political system of domination in which elite educated propertied men hold power over wo/men and other men. Kyriarchy is best theorized as a complex pyramidal system of intersecting multiplicative social structures of superordination and subordination, or ruling and oppression" in *Wisdom Ways: Introducing Feminist Biblical Interpretation* (Maryknoll: Orbis, 2001), 211.

32. On friendship relations, for example, see Stanley K. Stowers, "Friends and Enemies in the Politics of Heaven: Reading Theology in Philippians," in *Pauline Theology*, ed. Jouette

M. Bassler, vol. 1, *Thessalonians, Philippians, Galatians, Philemon* (Minneapolis: Fortress Press, 1991), 105–21; Marchal, *Hierarchy, Unity, and Imitation: A Feminist Rhetorical Analysis of Power Dynamics in Paul's Letter to the Philippians* (Atlanta: Society of Biblical Literature, 2006), 35–49.

33. Tyler Schwaller, "Jesus as Slave to Clement of Alexandria: How Clement Uses and Disposes the Slave Christ of Philippians 2," unpublished paper; Stephen Moore, "Sex and the Single Apostle," in *God's Beauty Parlor: And Other Queer Spaces in and around the Bible* (Stanford: Stanford University Press, 2001), 133–72.

34. Kittredge, *Community and Authority*, 53–100.

ECONOMIC APPROACHES

Scarce Resources and Interpretive Opportunities

PETER S. OAKES

The relevance of economics to the reading of Paul's letters goes far beyond discussing what he meant by instructing the Corinthians to gather money for his proposed collection for Jerusalem by putting aside, each week, "a sum of money in keeping with his[/her] income" (1 Cor. 16:2, NIV) or "whatever extra you earn" (NRSV). Not that this is without great interest in itself. Did the members of the house-assemblies have much surplus income? What about any slaves who were members—did they have income too? How was the money held? Did it go into a bank and earn interest? How was it to be transported to Jerusalem, given that it would all be coinage? Why was it needed there? Should we get the idea that the translators of NIV and NRSV were operating on differing assumptions about economics?!

In fact, our discussion is already opening up issues that have significant effects on the reading of all Paul's letters. To whom, in socio-economic terms, is he writing? Are they typically wage-earners? Do these assemblies include slaves or the very poor? On the other hand, are there members of the economic elite? Such questions about the socio-economic make-up of the communities can have far-reaching consequences. In a particularly influential study, Gerd Theissen concludes that the Corinthian assemblies included members of the elite. He then argues that the social tensions between the rich and the rest of the community members lie behind many of the problems that Paul is trying to deal with in 1 Corinthians. For instance, in chapters 8–10, Theissen argues, it was the social elite who had the attitudes and opportunities conducive to eating food offered to idols.[1] Andrew Clarke similarly sees the presence of the elite among the Corinthians as having led to problems because they continued to behave as the elite did everywhere in the Greco-Roman world, competing with each other for honor and precedence.[2]

More broadly, from an economic point of view, what is Paul doing when he writes? He asks for money for his collection to take to Jerusalem. How important a part of his relationship with the assemblies was this? More generally, how did the finances of Paul's life and mission work? Were his letters largely written to his financial supporters? What is going on in the texts where he talks of refusing money from certain communities (for example, 1 Cor. 9)? Thinking structurally, how did Paul's socio-economic position relate to that of his readers? Was he a member of the educated elite writing for the illiterate poor? Or did he, somehow, share the socio-economic position of many of the assembly members?

Economics has long had an involvement with Pauline studies, from Adolf Deissmann's study of the social structures of the earliest groups, via the work of Edwin Judge and others,[3] through to a substantial amount of economics-related recent work, whose authors range across a wide theological spectrum from, for instance, the evangelical Bruce Winter to the radical Richard Horsley.[4] Two major recent projects highlight the current interest. The People's History of Christianity series switches its focus of interest deliberately away from the prominent, often wealthy, Christian leaders and Christian secular rulers, who dominate traditional church histories, to turn towards the ordinary members of Christian groups, who tended to be far from wealthy.[5] A lecture series at St. Andrews University and the resulting book, *Engaging Economics*, edited by Bruce Longenecker and Kelly Liebengood, looks at economic issues in relation to a wide range of New Testament and other early Christian texts.[6]

The past decade has particularly seen a very vigorous debate on the socio-economic level of the members of the Pauline assemblies. The renewed discussion on this long-standing issue was triggered by Justin Meggitt's 1998 book, *Paul, Poverty and Survival*, in which he argued that all the Pauline community members were, broadly speaking, poor.[7] This was met by an exceptionally vigorous response in a review article by Dale Martin (alongside a less hostile one from Gerd Theissen).[8] In 2004, Steven Friesen supported Meggitt's view but articulated a range of economic levels among the poor by means of a poverty scale.[9] More recently, Bruce Longenecker has argued for the presence of a higher percentage than Friesen allowed of people some way above poverty.[10] The present author has also offered a model for the socio-economic make-up of a Pauline house-assembly, based on analysis of the range of housing in Pompeii.[11] These kinds of studies will continue to feed into discussion of whether we should be reading Paul's writings as letters to encourage mutual support within communities of the poor (as Meggitt would argue) or as letters which navigate their way through the complex issues raised by a wide social mix of people found in the early house-assemblies (Theissen, Clarke).

QUESTIONS OF DEFINITION AND SCOPE

Scholars who write on Paul and economic issues come at the subject from a wide range of angles and often use terminology in differing ways. In this field it is always worth looking carefully at the definitions that are being used. Words like "rich" and "poor" are notoriously difficult to define. The term "economics" is itself the subject of competing definitions. Most readers will not need to get too far into the technicalities of this but it is worth looking at a few prominent options.

I think that a classic kind of definition of "economics" works well for the first-century world: "the study of the allocation of scarce resources."[12] The word "scarce" is being used here in a technical sense, to mean anything that is not a free, unlimited resource. Air is not generally a scarce resource, although it would be so on a spacecraft. However, for biblical research, this idea of scarcity will usually be assumed, so it is probably safe to simplify the definition to "the study of the allocation of resources."

This kind of definition is not actually popular among current economics textbooks. They tend to prefer something that more closely matches what modern economists spend their time doing. So, for instance, a well-known current textbook by Michael Parkin gives a definition which focuses on "the *choices* that individuals, businesses . . . make."[13] I can see how that relates fairly well to the present day. However, it seems to me that it would sit awkwardly with first-century society because, in the first century, the exercise of choice was so restricted for so many that it seems unwise to make choice the key economic topic. Another kind of definition of "economics" is that of Marvin Harris, a cultural anthropologist. His definition focuses on "provisioning of a society with goods and services."[14] This is clearly related to the definition that I favor. However, Harris's phraseology seems to me to make the movement of resources sound too benignly purposeful to be ideal for the first century. The "allocation of resources" definition also has the advantage of fitting alright with the nature of ancient economies as "embedded economies."[15] This term refers to economies that are embedded in their context in such a way that financial factors are inseparable from many other factors such as family, patronal, or political ties. In the first century resources were not allocated by a free market.

Economics, on the above definition, deals with questions such as: Who allocates resources? Who receives resources, and how much? By what processes are resources allocated? More specifically, what material resources did the early assembly communities have? How did they interact with controllers of resources? How did assembly members allocate the resources that they did control?

I have discussed, elsewhere, issues in defining the terms "economic elite" ("rich" is a very vague term) and "poor." For "economic elite" a viable definition would seem to be "a wealthy group that controls a larger share of scarce resources than would be expected in a random distribution."[16] Many suggestions have been made for defining "poverty." The most persuasive seem to be behavioral ones such as "economically enforced lack of socially perceived necessities."[17] In particular, this draws in a more appropriate, wider range of people than definitions that see only those at or below food subsistence as poor. That loses sight of the many other economic pressures on people in the first century.

Recent theoretical work on "intersectionality" has rightly stressed that a person's experience of life relates to a wide range of variables—gender, ethnicity, and so on—which interact in varying ways (see also a number of the chapters to follow).[18] This means that a classic Marxist analysis, in which economic factors are substructure and all else is superstructure, is an over-simplification. However, insights on intersectionality do not do away with the fact that many identity variables, while important in their own right, are also important economic markers. For instance, if a first-century group was predominantly female they would, on average, tend to have less access to economic resources than would a predominantly male group of the same size. Gender is significant in its own right. However, it also needs consideration from an economic viewpoint. Many other identity markers that are found in New Testament texts also have economic implications: the nature of a person's work, geographical location (for example, urban/rural), ethnicity, religious practice, and status as slave, freed, or freeborn. The presence of all these in the New Testament texts, alongside more direct economic discourse about collections, wealth and poverty, and also alongside structural factors such as the socio-economic location of authors and audiences, invites us to engage in economic analysis of the texts.

THREE TYPES OF ECONOMIC APPROACH

Confusion easily arises between different ways in which economics can be involved in an approach to a text. Three types of approach can be distinguished. Economics can provide the *analytical framework* for interpretation, it can provide the *aim* of interpretation, or it can provide *resources* for interpretation.

In the first approach, *economics provides the analytical framework for interpretation*. This approach is based on assessing the socio-economic location of the writer, likely readers and other significant figures in the context. The text is then interpreted by analyzing which socio-economic groups' interests are promoted by the text and how this is done.

Frequently, such studies will focus on the interests of scribal groups since, inevitably, the producers of texts are very often, in some sense, scribes. This could be seen as true of Paul but most work so far has focused on the Gospels, maybe especially in studies of Q.[19] Gerhard Lenski offered an analysis of ancient social structure in which people such as scribes were part of a "retainer" group.[20] Retainers are a socio-economic group that, in terms of wealth, tends to sit between the elite and most of the non-elite. Although not elite themselves, retainers are closely dependent on the elite and may, to an extent, identify with elite interests. As well as scribes, priests would, in many societies, be classic instances of retainers (although Roman society was actually often an exception to this because many priestly roles were held by the elite).

To take a simple example of this approach: a religious text which greatly multiplied and complicated the religious laws that the hearer was expected to keep could be seen as serving the interests of the scribal class by increasing the number of occasions on which their services would be needed to explain the ramifications, and rule on the implications, of the complex legal system. The interpreter might seek to understand ways in which the elements of the text enmeshed the hearers in ever-increasing complexity, induced them to value careful compliance with the system, and encouraged recourse to scribal advice.

The word "class" slipped into the last paragraph and, indeed, this kind of use of economics in interpretation would, above all, be typical of a Marxist class-based analysis.[21] However, the issues go beyond purely Marxist ones. As Gerd Theissen has shown, the Synoptic Gospels can be analyzed as texts representing the interests of wandering charismatic preachers;[22] a socio-economic group indeed, but not one that would easily fit into a Marxist scheme.

The response of many to this approach will be skepticism as to its value. However, at some level, these questions must be considered. When Luke writes about Mary singing that God has "brought down the mighty from their seat and has exalted the humble and meek" (Luke 1:52), we surely have to ask whose interests are being served by Luke citing this in his tractate for the "most honored Theophilus."

In the second approach, *economics is the aim of interpretation*: the interpreter reads the text in order to discover economic information about the community members or the first-century world more broadly. Steven Friesen's article does this. He studies Paul's letters, looking for clues as to the economic situation of the named characters and groups. The conclusions of the article are economic descriptions. This approach is also characteristic of the People's History of Christianity series. Understanding the socio-economic circumstances of the Christian groups who are addressed or referred to in the texts is a key aim of the series. The analysis of the texts serves this end.

Anyone attempting this approach needs to be aware that there is an extra complexity to the task beyond the already-difficult problem of trying to find economic clues in the texts. The extra complication is that the interpreter may well need to consider the issues of the first approach alongside the second one. The interests that shape the production of the text will tend to prevent it being a repository of economic clues that can be interpreted in a straightforward way. The text's representation of the economic circumstances of the community members is itself part of the rhetoric of the text. For instance, when Paul, as part of a request for contributions to the Collection, tells the Corinthians that the Macedonian assembly members gave "out of their extreme poverty" (2 Cor. 8:2), the interpreter needs to consider how this description functions as part of the rhetoric of the passage.[23] Irrespective of the extent to which the interpreter buys into the value of analyzing economic interests, as the first approach does, the interpreter must still consider how the text functions rhetorically in a variety of ways that may make it less than straightforward to derive economic evidence from it (see the "Rhetorical Approaches" chapter).

In the third approach, *economics provides resources for interpretation*. At the detailed end this would relate to understanding the sums of money involved in Jesus' parables. At the broader end would be interpretative work such as that of Meggitt who uses his picture of first-century socio-economic structure and of the Pauline communities within it to argue that various texts in Paul's letters represent a strategy of mutual economic support among the poor.[24]

Economic evidence that can be drawn on for interpretation can be in various forms: archaeological, textual and comparative.[25] Archaeological evidence includes "loose finds" such as coinage—particularly interesting when found near a body in a particular domestic setting, as in some cases of people trapped by the eruption of Vesuvius (see also the "Visual Perspectives" and "Spatial Perspectives" chapters).[26] There are also large-scale fixed finds such as housing and associated wall decoration.[27] Textual evidence includes non-elite, non-literary texts such as ostraka (pieces of pottery reused as writing surfaces), most papyri and graffiti—for instance the list of wine prices on the wall of a bar in Herculaneum or ostraka carrying lists of goods delivered to the Roman fort of *Mons Claudianus* in Egypt. Other texts are elite, literary works. Again, the rhetoric of these texts needs careful interpretation but they carry a fair amount of economic evidence, even about non-elite life.[28] Comparative evidence draws on social situations more recent than the first century that operate within patterns having some comparability to first-century conditions. For instance, the yields of olives from trees farmed in a traditional manner are unlikely to have changed radically over the centuries.

Bringing economic evidence to bear on interpretation of a New Testament text can range from being fairly straightforward to very complex. We have a good idea of what the laborers' wages in the parable of Matthew could have bought for them.[29] On the other hand, Meggitt's task is, in principle, complex: to deploy his socio-economic profile of the Pauline assemblies in such a way as to understand the way in which quite a range of texts interact with that profile. A further level of challenge arises when we seek to use economic evidence as a resource for interpretation of New Testament texts that do not relate directly to financial issues. For instance, how does poverty relate to eschatology? Does Paul expect his hearers to be longing for a change in the world, or are they in economic circumstances that encourage them to be quite happy with matters as they are?

5) We will now turn to a passage that I have much engaged with recently, Romans 12.[30] How does this text look if studied using each of our three types of economic approach?

USING AN ECONOMIC ANALYTICAL FRAMEWORK: AN ITINERANT MISSIONARY WRITES TO A POTENTIAL SUPPORT BASE

A basic element of this approach is that Paul is not, in principle, considered as a unique individual. He is considered as representing a socio-economic group whose interests he is assumed to be promoting when he writes. The one sense in which this approach does see Paul as an individual is that, while promoting the value of his socio-economic group, he is also seen as promoting his own interests over against other members of that group. Putting this in concrete terms: Paul is seen not as a distinct personality but as representing the interests of itinerant missionaries and as competing with other itinerant missionaries.

In line with this type of reading, Paul can be seen as seeking to perform three functions in the chapter: first, promoting the value of itinerant missionaries and practical support for them; second, strengthening the potential support base, that is, the assembly groups at Rome; third, encouraging the groups to have allegiance to him.

Much of the evidence for the first and third points belongs together. Looking at the text, in the first instance, in relation to itinerant missionaries as a group, we can see the whole chapter as carrying the implicit message: You assembly members at Rome need guidance from outside—there are important things about the life of this community that you haven't figured out for yourself. This is, of course, true of all the teaching sections of Paul's letters, but it is important nonetheless. It is par-ticularly clear in a passage such as Romans 12, in which the external writer is giving advice about the mechanics of how the groups at Rome should organize their inter-nal affairs. It is also true notwithstanding Paul's disclaimer in 15:14-15. That text values the Roman assembly members' knowledge and insight, but it does not stop Paul thinking that they need his advice. Structurally, the New Testament letters represent a pattern of settled assembly groups in various towns, being resourced by a network of travelling teachers who visit them and write to them. A structural aspect of the rhetoric of the letters is that it reinforces dependence on the network of teachers.

More specifically, the way in which the opening of Romans 12 sits in the letter shows the itinerant missionary as the one with the insight (and education) to ground his practical instructions in a complex and compelling theological framework (chs. 1–11). This is a level of skill that is not likely to be available to a local house-assembly. Paul reinforces this more specifically with a reference to the missionary calling of the itinerant teacher: "through the gift that I have been given," which enables him to "say to each one among you . . . " (12:3). In verses 4-5, Paul uses the first person plural to talk about the body of Christ and ministries within it. As well as a rhetoric of solidarity, this switch to "we" tends maybe to draw attention to the element of experience that the itinerant missionary brings: "we" have seen what happens in house-assemblies all over the place. The itinerant missionary brings a breadth of experience that less-travelled community members lack. Among further specialist skills that Paul demonstrates in the chapter is knowledge of the Bible and of how to interpret it for their situation (12:19-20). Most house-assemblies would presumably not even possess a copy of the Septuagint. The itinerant missionary could know many key texts and would have a hermeneutical system for applying them to the present time.

Verse 13 probably presents the early Jesus movement as being more than local. Here, and explicitly in 15:25-28, there are seen to be financial links between assembly communities in different places. Paul's "one body in Christ" statement in 12:5 probably also includes some sense of translocal unity. A movement with translocal links, such as the early Jesus movement, needs people who move around, in order for the links to function. The translocal aspect of the early Jesus movement therefore validates the role of itinerants. More specifically, Paul, as an itinerant, acts as the person organizing financial support between these groups. Their financial support network depends on itinerant missionaries.

The second exhortation in 12:13 is about "pursuing hospitality." One can understand why the NRSV chose to render the Greek as "extend hospitality to strangers." The translators were presumably wanting to avoid the impression that Paul was referring to members of a house-assembly feeding each other. However, their introduction of the term "strangers" may miss a key application of the verse. It is likely to have related, among other things, to the prominent early practice of assembly communities welcoming and economically supporting itinerant missionaries. Paul effectively asks for such hospitality in 15:24 (cf. Phil. 22). Although itinerant missionaries might be "strangers" in the sense of being outsiders visiting a house-assembly, they must generally have arrived as people who were known of, and who often carried letters of recommendation, as Phoebe does in the text of 16:1-2.

This reading interprets Romans 12 in two further ways. The teaching of the chapter is seen as strengthening the group of recipients. It does so in terms of their organization (12:6-8), their cohesion (12:3-16) and their interactions with outsiders (12:14, 17-21). Economically, this can be seen as enhancing the stability of the potential support base for the itinerant missionary. A stronger group can offer fuller support. Finally, as indicated above, all the evidence in chapter 12 about Paul promoting the role of the itinerant missionary can also be read as Paul encouraging the group to have allegiance to him. Although they have not previously benefited from his ministry (except indirectly through people such as Prisca and Aquila), he has a particular gift from God that enables him to speak to each one of them (12:3). Paul makes this point at length in 15:15-19. Now he wants to come to them and have their support while he is with them and in his proposed mission to Spain.

AS AN ECONOMIC SOURCE TEXT: CONTRIBUTING TO A SOCIO-ECONOMIC PROFILING OF EARLY GROUPS

In this approach the text is being read with the aim of discovering economic data. There are two kinds of data that we could look for. First, we could look for evidence of existing economic circumstances among the hearers to whom Paul thinks he is writing. If Paul knows the situation of the Roman house-assemblies, the text could give evidence about that. If Paul knows little about them, we would need to view the text as more generally indicating the circumstances of house-assemblies that he had encountered. Second, we could look for evidence of the types of socio-economic relationships that Paul wanted his hearers to adopt. These relationships are unlikely to be purely aspirational. They are more likely to represent practices that, at least to an extent, are already in place in some assembly groups that Paul considers to be running well.

The first economic evidence that Romans 12 provides is a general indication of the sort of numbers in early groups. Group size is a basic factor in estimating the total amount of economic resources available to a group. The first indication of number is the word "many" in 12:5: "we who are many are one body in Christ." Although the "we" in that sentence suggests that Paul could be thinking of all who are "in Christ" everywhere, the list of ministries that follows suggests that he also has the local "in Christ" group in mind in his discussion of "members" and "the body." In that case, there would be "many" in an assembly community. Clearly, "many" is not a fixed number but it at least implies several, probably going beyond a single family. This point is supported by the list of "gifts" that Paul sees as providing forms of service in the house-assemblies (vv. 6-8). The degree of elaboration in these, and the types of gifts—leading, teaching, and so on—imply that the groups are reasonably large: say, twenty and upwards.

Economically, a key significance of group size is that the group, collectively, controls economic resources that are an order of magnitude (that is, more than ten times) greater than the resources that most of the individuals control. This provides the group with increased ability to withstand financial shocks. It also opens up possibilities for actions that most individuals could not undertake, such as providing money to external groups such as the recipients of Paul's collection.

As well as numbers, the system of gifts and ministries in 12:6-8 implies certain socio-economic structures. It may imply a structure in which some people dedicate part of their time to house-assembly activities rather than work that brings in money. Life for most of the first-century non-elite was economically so constrained that virtually all available time will normally have been used, when possible, for craftwork, and so on. Even meeting together regularly will have been financially difficult for some. The taking on of any roles that required time beyond the meetings must usually have meant some other person or people effectively contributing to their support, even if that was only in releasing them from expectation of work, rather than paying them as such, although we do know of financial support of leaders being an issue in other letters (Gal. 6:6).

The list of gifts in 12:6-8 includes "sharing," which is done "with generosity." Dunn argues that the association of "cheerfulness" with "showing mercy" implies that that too is likely to be an economic issue.[31] These gifts imply that some assembly members in particular are giving financial support either to outsiders or to others within their assembly community. Either possibility is economically interesting. My impression is that relationships with outsiders are more in focus from verse 13 onward so internal economic support is maybe more in view in verse 8. In either case, the first implication of these ministries in verse 8 is that there is not economic equality within the assembly community. Although, in theory, an economically equal group could exist in which some had the gift of sharing and others did not, that would make the rhetoric of v. 8 very strange. It is much more likely that some wealthier members of the group were feeling moved to share with poorer members. A second economic implication is that property was not held in common in the group (as in the Lukan picture of the early Jerusalem assembly).

A third piece of economically relevant information is that the house-assemblies have translocal links (interestingly, the chapter does not discuss links between house-assemblies in Rome, although that issue may be implicit in chapters 14–15). In principle, translocal links could be a further source of economic stability, especially when a crisis is caused by a local condition such as an earthquake. However, in Romans 12, the only economic effect of translocal links seems to be to place extra financial burdens on the Roman house-assemblies: "sharing in the needs of the holy ones, pursuing hospitality" (12:13). Locally, there may be a further economic outflow from the group implied by the enigmatic encouragement in verse 16 to "being carried away to lowly people."

The groups implied by Romans 12 have very difficult relationships with outsiders. They are persecuted (v. 14), have evil done to them (vv. 17, 21) and have enemies (v. 20). The rhetoric against taking revenge in these circumstances is so marked that Paul does seem to believe that persecution of the assembly communities is actually occurring. As I have discussed elsewhere, this need not be specifically religious persecution. It could be part of the typical negative group interaction that was common in the streets of Rome and elsewhere.[32] However, whatever kind of difficulty is implied by 12:14-21 (and by the "suffering" in v. 12) it will almost certainly have had negative economic consequences. In the "embedded economy" of the first century, almost any trouble ends up being economic trouble, whatever else it involves.

In the economic group context that we have been sketching so far, Paul's rhetoric evokes relationships within the group that have strong potential economic consequences. The group members are "parts of each other" (v. 5). They are called to unhypocritical love (v. 9), "brotherly love" (v. 10, see below), honoring one another (v. 10). What would be the economic consequences of such practices? They might be taken as implying that all the group members had control over the group's economic resources. However, my impression is that Paul is not calling for the kind of radical "sharing" that results in something like common ownership. "Sharing" looks more likely to be an ongoing activity within a setting that continues to include some structural inequality. On the other hand, the rhetoric of love would presumably imply a quite substantial degree of commitment to mutual economic support within the group. Paul's rhetoric projects a situation of some real rearrangement of access to resources but short of an abolition of existing socio-economic structures. This probably reflects his experience in at least some of the communities in other cities.

WITH THE HELP OF ECONOMIC EVIDENCE: ECCLESIOLOGY FOR CRAFTWORKERS

The previous section, as well as using Romans 12 as an economic source text, was in fact drawing on economic evidence to help interpret the text. For instance, the rhetoric about persecution gives us economically significant data, but we then need to draw in broader first-century evidence about the economic effects of suffering, in order to interpret what the persecution might involve. We can, however, go much further in using first-century economic evidence to construct a scenario for reading the chapter. A way of doing this is to construct a socio-economic model for a house-assembly in first-century Rome, then examine how the rhetoric of the chapter interacts with the model.

To construct our model we can begin by considering Roman apartment blocks and craftworkers. Let us follow the common scholarly assumption that typical first-century members of these communities were craftworkers. This is particularly pertinent for Paul's expected hearers in Rome because the house-based assembly that he refers to in 16:5 is hosted by tent-makers, Prisca and Aquila. In the urban landscape of Rome, the most common kind of location for craftworkers who might have space to host an assembly would be a ground-floor workshop in an apartment block. In the *Insula Aracoeli*, for instance, which dates from the Neronian period, we have the classic form of such a block with ground floor workshops, mezzanine apartments above the workshops, spacious apartments on the next floor up, then increasingly cramped apartments on the higher floors.[33]

A craftworker who rented a workshop and some living space could host a small house-assembly, meeting in the workshop. If there were, say, thirty people in the group, that would presumably mean the craftworker's household, a few other complete or partial households and, probably, a few individuals whose head of household was not a community member. The absolute numbers are not too important. What matters is the type of socio-economic structure that emerges.

The house/apartment-assembly consists of several components. First there is the host's family, entirely or almost complete. That usually means a male householder who has primary control of all the household's resources. There is then typically a wife, children (young or adult), maybe a couple of slaves and other dependents such as elderly relatives. There is a clear socio-economic hierarchy within such a household. The assembly also includes a few other partial or complete households. Each will replicate the kind of socio-economic structure in the host's household except that the other households will tend to be poorer and smaller. For instance, they are less likely to include slaves. Given that the difficulties of wives of husbands who were not also community members are discussed more than once in New Testament texts (1 Cor. 7:12; 1 Pet. 3:1), our model house-assembly should include some members from "non-Christian" households. Such people would occupy a curious socio-economic position: part of the house-assembly but with a primary location in an external socio-economic structure. All in all, the house-assembly is quite a complex socio-economic structure.

The socio-economic location of the house-assembly within Roman life is anchored by the position of the host who will tend to be the highest-status person belonging to the group. During analytical work on housing in Pompeii, drawing on earlier work by Andrew Wallace-Hadrill, Roger Ling and others,[34] I studied a craftworker's house, the *Casa del Fabbro* (I.10.7). This cabinet maker's house was 310 square meters in size, larger than 70 percent of other dwellings in Pompeii but less than a third of the size of the smallest elite houses. If the tenant occupying this house hosted an assembly, we could locate the probable socio-economic situations of members of this group as being spread across the bottom 70 percent of household income levels and across the range of slaves and other poor dependents. In Rome, although average sizes of accommodation would be smaller than Pompeii, it would seem reasonable to assume a roughly similar shape to the socio-economic structure. This could locate the wealthiest craftworker hosts, such as probably Prisca and Aquila, at a higher income level than more than half the population, although still a long way below the income of the elite. The community members would generally be at economic levels spread out from this point downward.

If we now use this socio-economic model of a Roman house-assembly to help us read Romans 12, it becomes apparent that the rhetoric of the chapter is constructing an idea of the assembly, an ecclesiology, that poses considerable potential challenges for life within the house-assembly's socio-economic structure.[35] At some points, the rhetoric also interacts interestingly with the group's socio-economic location.

The following points from the chapter look particularly pertinent. In verse 1, the assembly is a family: "brothers and sisters." Also in verse 1, it is a priesthood, offering "a living sacrifice." In verse 3, it is a community where faith is the measure of status. In verse 5, the assembly is "one body in Christ." Moreover, the members are "parts of each other." In verses 6-8, the ministries of the assembly are gifted by God. In verse 10, the assembly is a community of "brotherly love" and of mutual honoring. Finally, in verse 16, it is a community "thinking the same thing" and focused on the poor rather than on grandiose ideas.

If we think of the assembly as a family, as one body in Christ, as a community of love, this is attributing a oneness to the group that would be quite radical if even a single household adopted it as a pattern for relationships within it. However, the house-assembly goes beyond this. Several households are involved, as are people who do not belong to a "Christian" household at all. Economically, first-century craftworker households were primarily free-standing units competing with other households to bring in sufficient income to live and, if possible, to enhance the status of the householder. The ecclesiology of Romans 12 challenges the boundary of the household, presenting a new social structure in which the interests of a wider group take over from household interests.

Conversely, individual members from "non-Christian" households become part of this new trans-household structure, of which their own household heads are not a part. This must often have caused conflict within these kinds of families.

As well as togetherness, the ecclesiology of Romans 12 involves a reciprocity that challenges the assumptions of household socio-economic structures: "We are parts of one another" (v. 5); the members give honor, presumably to each other (v. 10). The assembly includes owners, slaves, men, women, adults, children, wealthier, poorer. First-century households might have a kind of unity but it was unity based on hierarchy. The slave honored the master but not vice versa. The reciprocity of Romans 12 poses quite a challenge to this. In line with that, self-evaluation within the group is not to be on the basis of status. In verse 3 after Paul warns against over-valuing yourself, he then ties true value somehow to faith, which is not a human achievement but something that "God has distributed."

The ministries of the assembly are organized charismatically (vv. 6-8). They too are gifts from God (v. 6). In principle, this cuts across the socio-economic order of the household. The householder controls the resources. He therefore gets to allocate the work. In the assembly the ministries depend on gifts from God. Having said this, we have already noticed that "sharing" is a gift that may well be linked to having economic resources at your disposal. It is not clear whether there would be assumptions about some of the other gifts too—for instance, whether teachers might be expected to be literate.

In the rather mysterious verse 16, the assembly is presented as having a socially downward focus, "not thinking high things but getting carried away to the humble." This is a curious contrast, but it probably makes more sense as a pair in the first century than now. In the first century, a contrast between intellectual activity and the lives of the "humble" is a contrast between wealth and poverty. Both high-level education and the leisure to discuss intellectual matters were attributes of the wealthy. The assembly is to be focused on action with the poor rather than academic reflection. All this rather inverts the normal order of the household. The household is primarily to serve the interests of the householder. The effort of the household is focused upwards, to benefit the person at the top. The assembly is focused the opposite way.

Finally, two elements in the ecclesiology of Romans 12 interact in interesting ways with the overall social location of the assembly community. The first is the characterization of the members as priests, each offering a living sacrifice, their own body (12:1). Much could be said about that but the point here is that, in Rome, priests generally belonged to socio-economic groups different from those of the house-assemblies. In particular, the prominent priesthoods at Rome were occupied by members of the elite. The characterizing of the assembly as a priesthood ascribes to the members a status they would not normally be seen as having.[36]

A second element in Romans 12 that may operate in a similar manner is a characterization of the assembly in terms that sound rather like the discourse of some types of elite male groups. This could be said of much of the language of love and mutuality. However, the issue is particularly raised by the term *philadelphia*, "brotherly love" (v. 10), and by the phrase, *to auto eis allēlous phronountes*, "thinking the same thing as one another" (v. 16). As Alan Mitchell argues in relation to Acts and Joseph Marchal in relation to Philippians, the latter phrase sounds particularly evocative of the interaction of elite male friends.[37] *Philadelphia* too, although it could evoke a range of ideas and is not even inherently male, could well give the impression of the assembly as the kind of society that might previously have been thought of as arising among men gathered in an association, and particularly among elite males.[38] If the ecclesiology of Romans 12 does evoke this kind of setting, its rhetoric is doing unexpected things in addressing a mixed-gender, mixed-status group, none of whom—or almost none of whom—had a socio-economic location that fitted the normal social setting of such language.

CONCLUSIONS

We have looked at three approaches to using economics in the study of Pauline texts and have tried out each of them in relation to Romans 12. The second and third approaches are ones that I draw on fairly regularly in my own work. The first approach is likely to evoke strong positive or negative reactions; however, it does raise important questions for consideration in analyzing what is going on in the rhetoric of New Testament texts. All three approaches deserve serious attention. Paul's letters handle a wide variety of issues, theological as well as social but, whatever the issue, we should keep in mind that the text is written in a context which, as all human contexts, inescapably involves economics.

FURTHER READING

Meeks, Wayne A. *The First Urban Christians: The Social World of the Apostle Paul.* New Haven: Yale University Press, 1983, 2003.

Theissen, Gerd. *The Social Setting of Pauline Christianity: Essays on Corinth*, translated by John H. Schütz. Philadelphia: Fortress Press, 1982.

These are two classics that sharply raised the profile of economic issues in the study of Paul's letters. On Meeks's book, now also see the collection of essays in *After the First Urban Christians*, edited by Todd Still and David Horrell (London: T&T Clark, 2009).

Friesen, Steven J. "Poverty in Pauline Studies: Beyond the So-Called New Consensus," in *Journal for the Study of the New Testament* 26, no. 3 (2004): 323–61. Builds on and refines Meggitt's analysis of the social structure of Pauline assemblies.

Horsley, Richard A., ed. *Christian Origins.* A People's History of Christianity I. Minneapolis: Fortress Press, 2005. Includes socio-economically focused essays such as by Neil Elliott on Romans.

Longenecker, Bruce W. and Kelly D. Liebengood, eds., *Engaging Economics: New Testament Scenarios and Early Christian Reception.* Grand Rapids: Eerdmans, 2009. Well-focused collection of essays.

Longenecker, Bruce W. *Remember the Poor: Paul, Poverty, and the Greco-Roman World* (Grand Rapids: Eerdmans, 2010). Modifies Meggitt and Friesen's approach as part of a wider study into financial relationships.

Meggitt, Justin J. *Paul, Poverty, and Survival.* Studies of the New Testament and Its World; Edinburgh: T&T Clark, 1998. Forcefully argues case for bringing poverty to the center of Pauline studies.

Oakes, Peter. *Reading Romans in Pompeii: Paul's Letter at Ground Level* (London: SPCK/Minneapolis: Fortress Press, 2009). Includes building a socio-economic model of a house-assembly and more on Romans 12.

Stegemann, Ekkehard W. and Wolfgang Stegemann. *The Jesus Movement: A Social History of Its First Century.* Translated by O. C. Dean Jr. Minneapolis: Fortress Press, 1999. Wide-ranging, detailed socio-economic survey.

NOTES

1. Gerd Theissen, *The Social Setting of Pauline Christianity: Essays on Corinth*, trans. John H. Schütz (Edinburgh: T&T Clark/Philadelphia: Fortress Press, 1982).

2. Andrew D. Clarke, *Secular and Christian Leadership in Corinth: A Socio-Historical and Exegetical Study of 1 Corinthians 1—6*, AGJU 18 (Leiden: Brill, 1993).

3. Adolf Deissmann, "Das Urchristentum und die unteren Schichten," in *Die Verhand-lungen des neunzehnten Evangelisch-sozialen Kongresses*, ed. Wilhelm Schneemelcher (Göttingen: Vandenhoeck & Ruprecht, 1908), 8–28; Edwin A. Judge, *The Social Pattern of the Christian Groups in the First Century: Some Prolegomena to the Study of New Testament Ideas of Social Obligation* (London: Tyndale, 1960).

4. Bruce W. Winter, *Seek the Welfare of the City: Christians as Benefactors and Citizens* (First-century Christians in the Graeco-Roman World; Carlisle: Paternoster/Grand Rapids: Eerdmans, 1994); Richard A. Horsley, *Covenant Economics: A Biblical Vision of Justice for All* (Louisville: Westminster John Knox, 2009).

5. Richard A. Horsley, ed., *Christian Origins*, vol. 1 of A People's History of Christianity: (Minneapolis: Fortress Press, 2005).

6. Bruce W. Longenecker and Kelly D. Liebengood, eds., *Engaging Economics: New Testament Scenarios and Early Christian Reception* (Grand Rapids: Eerdmans, 2009).

7. Justin J. Meggitt, *Paul, Poverty, and Survival*, SNTW (Edinburgh: T&T Clark, 1998).

8. Dale B. Martin, "Review Essay: Justin J. Meggitt, *Paul, Poverty and Survival*," *Journal for the Study of the New Testament* 84 (2001): 51–64; Gerd Theissen, "The Social Structure of Pauline Communities: Some Critical Remarks on J. J. Meggitt, *Paul, Poverty and Survival*," *JSNT* 84 (2001): 65–84.

9. Steven J. Friesen, "Poverty in Pauline Studies: Beyond the So-Called New Consensus," *JSNT* 26.3 (2004): 323–61, with responses from John Barclay and Peter Oakes.

10. Bruce W. Longenecker, "Exposing the Economic Middle: A Revised Economy Scale for the Study of Early Urban Christianity," *JSNT* 31 (2009): 243–78. See also, Bruce W. Longenecker, *Remember the Poor: Paul, Poverty, and the Greco-Roman World* (Grand Rapids: Eerdmans, 2010), 36–59, 220–58.

11. Peter Oakes, *Reading Romans in Pompeii: Paul's Letter at Ground Level* (London: SPCK/Minneapolis: Fortress Press, 2009), 46–97.

12. This often-repeated formulation generally continues, "among unlimited and competing uses." It relates to ideas in Lionel Robbins's 1932 "Essay on the Nature and Significance of Economic Science."

13. Michael Parkin, *Economics*, 7th ed. (Boston: Addison Wesley, 2005), 2.

14. Marvin Harris and Orna Johnson, *Cultural Anthropology*, 5th ed. (Boston: Allyn and Bacon, 2000), as cited (from an earlier edition) by Ekkehard W. Stegemann and Wolfgang Stegemann, *The Jesus Movement: A Social History of Its First Century*, trans. O. C. Dean Jr. (Minneapolis: Fortress Press, 1999), 16.

15. Karl Polanyi, et al., *Trade and Market in the Early Empires* (Chicago: Henry Regnery, 1971), 250.

16. Oakes, *Reading Romans in Pompeii*, 53–55, exemplifies this definition in relation to house sizes.

17. Peter Oakes, "Constructing Poverty Scales for Graeco-Roman Society: A Response to Steven Friesen's 'Poverty in Pauline Studies,'" *JSNT* 26:3 (2004): 367–71, here 369, adapted from Joanna Mack and Stewart Lansley, *Poor Britain* (London: Allen & Unwin, 1985), 39.

18. See Elisabeth Schüssler Fiorenza's helpful introduction to the subject in Laura Nasrallah and Elisabeth Schüssler Fiorenza, eds., *Prejudice and Christian Beginnings: Investigating Race, Gender, and Ethnicity* (Minneapolis: Fortress Press, 2009), 5–18.

19. For example, Douglas Oakman, "Jesus, Q, and Ancient Literacy in Social Perspective," *Jesus and the Peasants* (Eugene: Cascade, 2008).

20. Gerhard Lenski, *Power and Privilege: A Theory of Social Stratification* (New York: McGraw-Hill, 1966), 82.

21. See, e.g., Fernando Belo, *A Materialist Reading of the Gospel of Mark* (Maryknoll: Orbis, 1981).

22. Gerd Theissen, *Sociology of Early Palestinian Christianity* (Philadelphia: Fortress Press, 1978).

23. Wayne A. Meeks, *The First Urban Christians: The Social World of the Apostle Paul*, 2nd ed. (New Haven: Yale University Press, 2003), 66, although I think that this verse does actually give good evidence of poverty among the Macedonian assemblies: Peter Oakes, *Philippians: From People to Letter*, SNTSMS 110 (Cambridge: Cambridge University Press, 2001), 69.

24. Meggitt, *Paul, Poverty and Survival*, 155–78.

25. Peter Oakes, "Methodological Issues in Using Economic Evidence in Interpretation of Early Christian Texts," *Engaging Economics: New Testament Scenarios and Early Christian Reception*, eds. Bruce W. Longenecker and Kelly D. Liebengood (Grand Rapids: Eerdmans, 2009), 9–34.

26. For example, Penelope M. Allison, *The Insula of the Menander at Pompeii*, III. *The Finds: A Contextual Study* (Oxford: Clarendon, 2007), nos. 1241–46.

27. For a systematic survey of one location, see Roger Ling and Lesley Ling, *The Insula of the Menander at Pompeii*, II. *The Decorations* (Oxford: Clarendon Press, 2004).

28. For instance in the satirical works of Martial and Juvenal.

29. See, for instance, the calculation in Stegemann and Stegemann, *The Jesus Movement*, 81–85.

30. Oakes, *Reading Romans in Pompeii*, ch. 4.

31. James D. G. Dunn, *Romans 9–16*, Word Biblical Commentary (Dallas: Word, 1988), 732.

32. Oakes, *Reading Romans in Pompeii*, 123–26.

33. See, e.g., A. Wallace-Hadrill, "*Domus* and *Insulae* in Rome: Families and Housefuls," *Early Christian Families in Context: An Interdisciplinary Dialogue*, eds. David Balch and Carolyn Osiek (Grand Rapids: Eerdmans, 2003), 3–18, here 14–15.

34. Oakes, *Reading Romans*, chs. 1–2; Andrew Wallace-Hadrill, *Houses and Society in Pompeii and Herculaneum* (Princeton: Princeton University Press, 1994); Ling, *Insula of the Menander*, I; Allison, *Insula of the Menander*, III.

35. For a fuller discussion of these points see Oakes, *Reading Romans in Pompeii*, ch. 4.

36. Cf. Peter Oakes, "Made Holy by the Holy Spirit: Holiness and Ecclesiology in Romans," *Holiness and Ecclesiology in the New Testament*, eds. Kent E. Brower and Andy Johnson (Grand Rapids: Eerdmans, 2007), 167–83.

37. Alan C. Mitchell, "The Social Function of Friendship in Acts 2:44–47 and 4:32–37," *JBL* 111, no.2 (Summer 1992): 255–72; Joseph A. Marchal, "'With Friends Like These . . .': A Feminist Rhetorical Reconsideration of Scholarship and the Letter to the Philippians," *Journal for the Study of the New Testament* 29:1 (2006): 77–106.

38. See, e.g., the terminology of *adelphoi* in association inscriptions cited in Richard S. Ascough, *Paul's Macedonian Associations: The Social Context of Philippians and 1 Thessalonians* (Tübingen: Mohr Siebeck, 2003), 76–77.

VISUAL PERSPECTIVES

Imag(in)ing the Big Pauline Picture

DAVINA C. LOPEZ[1]

INTRODUCING PAUL AS SEEING OURSELVES:
THE BIG PICTURE(S)

It is often claimed that ours is an increasingly "visual environment"—that we are, more than ever, using and shaped by images and the technologies that fill our world with them—from "classic" media forms like art, film, and television, to evolving means of exposure to pictures such as smart phones and tablet computers. Moreover, the average American person can be exposed to thousands of advertising images daily. If we take seriously that we live in a world rapidly filling up with various pictures, and if the proliferation of images influences how, and on what terms, we communicate with one another, then how to interact with images ought to be a matter of concern for educated adults. Understanding the language of images is called "visual literacy." Such literacy, premised upon the ability to perceive, interpret, and learn from images, is becoming an essential tool for developing critical thinking skills in the present global context.[2]

The present is undoubtedly a moment when images reign, as you may observe if you take a moment to look up from the words you are reading and quickly survey the types of media with which you might be surrounded. However one might feel about the number and quality of images in our environment—whether this "visual world" represents an improvement upon or a decline of humanity—is beside the point. In order to understand and more effectively communicate in our world, we must learn the skills required for critically viewing, just as we learn to write and speak effectively. And while one might ultimately have to come to terms with living in a visual world, it is not the case that the proliferation of images is an innovation unique to our historical moment. Rather, the world has always been inclined toward "the visual." It is simply the mode of delivering images, and our ability to notice, which might have changed over time and across cultures. It is precisely because the world has always been visually inclined that it is imperative to recognize the essential role images play in shaping the material circumstances in every historical context, not just the one in which we happen to live.

One striking realization afforded by recent methodological studies of Pauline texts and contexts in relationship to pictures is that visual representations have been subordinated to literary representations. Because Paul's letters, indeed all New Testament texts, are collections of words, our historical reconstructions and interpretations of the ancient world in which these documents were produced, collected, and found their first hearers and readers have tended to focus on early Christianities as a product of an ancient culture fixated on reading and hearing words as a primary communicative mode. That is to say, most contemporary New Testament scholarship assumes that Paul's letters reflect a culture in which reading letters is prominent, or at least in which a sizeable number of people could read and understand words—despite studies that attempt to chart "ancient literacy" as a somewhat rare and complex phenomenon.[3]

Regardless of however else ancient peoples may have communicated with one another, modern interpreters have mapped the ancient world as if words were the *primary* means of communication and signification. By making such maps, New Testament scholarship has, in effect, naturalized a turn to ancient literary sources as the necessary methodological maneuver for comprehending "the world" of Paul, not to mention revealing the meaning of his letters. If and when images are discussed, they are often set apart and presented not as a communicative form in their own right but as a collection of pictures helping to confirm the historical reliability of the texts and illuminate the background of words.[4] In the end, though, it is still words and letters that convey ideas, meaning, and value, in both the ancient and contemporary worlds. Claiming that words are primary supports one of the basic assumptions of the study of biblical literature and, indeed, the study of religion: namely, that such studies should be methodologically delimited by locating authoritative sacred texts as objects of analysis, as focal points around which disciplinary boundaries are drawn, reinscribed, and reified, as the only representations of the "religious" that matter, as the only material of pedagogical value. Simply put, if one is a student of Paul, of the Bible, and of religion, one is a student of words.[5]

This essay aims to consider the ways in which Paul and his correspondence might be differently engaged, and what difference that might make in the contemporary world, if visual representations and landscapes were taken seriously as conveyers of ideas, meaning, and value. Herein methodological investment lies in identifying what is plausible for the study of Paul, and the New Testament as a whole, when images and texts are placed in conversation with, rather than in hierarchical relationship to, one another. Such a realignment of sources as the one we shall explore below could not only change our reading of Pauline literature—it could also challenge the conceptual framework in which the process of reading takes place. To that end, in what follows I will critically appraise the (non-)use of images in New Testament studies, asking what it could mean to position "Paul's letters" and "images" as interconnected sites from which to think about power relationships and constructions of knowledge. Raising these issues should result in opening a significant space for asking further critical questions of the Pauline corpus, early Christianities and early Jesus movements, and—most importantly— ourselves. For the study of Paul and the New Testament, in my estimation, might best be taught as an orientation toward investigating what it has meant, and can mean, to be human in this world, using sacred texts and traditions as an important site for doing so. This is not because such texts and traditions are more authoritative than other artifacts, or because they might have "the answers," but because sacred texts and traditions, and the various deployments thereof, serve as signifiers betraying various human discursive and performative responses to, and negotiations of, the world around us.

READING PAULINE WORDS:
A PRACTICE OF DISCIPLINING IMAGES

Whether or not one assents to a "religious" project where Paul is explicitly authoritative, his life, letters, and legacies are important to engage today. Paul's words have been used for various modern social purposes such as telling slaves to obey their masters, Jews that they are no longer God's chosen people, women that they should be subordinate to men, and homosexuals that their relationships are unnatural. And those same words have been used, at the same time, in favor of freedom for slaves, inter-religious dialogue, feminist spirituality, and gay rights (see also the "Feminist Approaches," "Jewish Perspectives," "African American Approaches," and "Queer Approaches" chapters). In light of such a controversial—and, some would say, radically inconsistent—heritage, it is imperative to be attentive to how we read Paul, Pauline representations, and Pauline inheritances. Some trends in New Testament studies propose that decentering Paul might lead to more just modes of relationship in our world, given how his words have been used to hurt the "others" throughout history. And some prefer to put interpretive energy toward retrieving Paul as an ancient hero who has been mis-read throughout the ages, or at least since Martin Luther's time. While there is value in each of those hermeneutical trajectories, such approaches do very little to advance a project that decenters an uncritical acceptance of textual authority or interrogates the type of relationship people have, and want to have, with texts—not to mention how, and why, people desire to cultivate or dismiss such relationships. In other words, using texts to blame or praise an ancient Paul for modern (in)justices does nothing but alleviate *our* responsibility for the state of *our* social relations and hierarchies. We therefore might ask how we could aim to nurture engagements of Pauline literature that emphasize a critical appraisal and reimagination of the apostle, his letters, their afterlives and interpretive histories, and, most of all, the politics and ethics of Pauline studies in the contemporary world. It is in this context that the methodological maneuvers engendered by realigning our sources, not to mention our assumptions about them, might be of assistance.

Paul is part of the world we have inherited and in which we live, inside and outside of institutionalized "religious" spheres of influence. Insofar as students have encountered the apostle in a classroom setting, they have done so through literary means and activities. Paul is ordinarily "introduced" through reading "his" undisputed canonical letters as the means to gain access to his theological orientation, as well as for documentary evidence of the "first urban Christians." During such initial encounters, the Acts of the Apostles is often implicitly or explicitly consulted for a roughly contemporary chronological overview and contextualization of the letters as the effects of several missionary journeys, as being written and delivered to house-church settings in eastern Greek cities under Roman imperial rule in the first century. In this way, the image of Paul as a writer, as an arbiter of words, and early Christianity as a word-focused phenomenon, is assumed from the moment one enters a learning environment where New Testament studies takes place.

This focus on reading words also manages how we interpret Paul's legacies. Some access to the effects of Paul's work among subsequent generations of Christians is thought to be possible through encountering canonical deutero-Pauline literature, extra-canonical legends about the apostle such as the *Acts of (Paul and) Thecla* and the *Apocalypse of Paul*, and other early Christian literature that scholars think represents a Pauline trajectory of sorts, or, alternatively, a repudiation of the apostle's work.[6] Paul's ancient religious background is often elaborated through readings of "his Bible," the Greek Septuagint, alongside other Jewish and Greco-Roman literature of the period. Finally and significantly, introductory pedagogical encounters with Paul tend to be mediated through reading modern scholarly writings about Paul, Pauline traditions, and Pauline theology such as introductory New Testament textbooks, the scholarly literature of Pauline studies, and books like the one in which this chapter appears. Regardless of how Paul is represented therein, it is through contemporary academic introductions to Paul that the discipline of reading Paul continues to be defined and naturalized.

That reading texts is now taken for granted as the preferred, and perhaps only, way to encounter Paul is not an accident. Even as it might seem as though biblical scholars or religious authorities are responsible for keeping texts and images in their place, that is not entirely the case either. That biblical texts function as the primary locus of sacred meaning and power is, rather, a product of several centuries of academic disciplinary formation alongside the historical reality that, since at least the Protestant Reformation of the sixteenth century, Paul has been constructed as a theologian—a theologian who writes—whose holy words are critical to authoritative articulations of the Christian faith. As biblical words replaced the rituals and ecclesiastical structures of the Catholic Church as a primary means of access to Christian beliefs and living, as the aftermath of the invention of the printing press in some sense contributed to the stabilization of the Bible as a "book" to be bought and read, and as "The Book" became an object used to support contact between cultures and peoples in processes of missionizing and colonization (as well as resistance to such dominating practices), so texts became normal as "the Way" to meaning-making. The words and "the Word," as mediating force through which Paul's ideas might be noticed, beckon approaches for unlocking their intrinsic meanings. And from the late nineteenth century to the present, the expansion of biblical scholarship as a distinct field of textually focused inquiry in Europe, the importation of such scholarly methods to the United States, the development of literalist approaches to reading biblical texts, and the persistence of questions like "what does the Bible say" on any number of contemporary issues thought to have social import, have served to keep texts authoritative and central to acts of the interpretive imagination.

As a product of this long trajectory, introducing Paul is now configured as an exercise in reading literary representations as reflective of, or challenging to, historical reality. This is not to say that images never make an appearance in the study of Paul. Reading Pauline texts is at times supported by approaches in New Testament studies that make use of material culture. Indeed, the discipline of archaeology prioritizes the location and identification of material remains, including visual representation—repackaged as "art" for consumption—as a way of fleshing out historical, social, and cultural realities behind phenomena already assumed to have existed and happened, simply because they are mentioned in texts. Items such as coins, inscriptions, architectural remains of relevant buildings like synagogues, temples, and houses, the decorative programs of these structures, mosaics, and representations of humans such as statues of emperors are used to illustrate the words under consideration.

A literary-focused discipline of studying Paul deploys material culture as irreducible data for historical reconstruction projects, particularly those attempting to articulate myths of Christian origins and those foregrounding the "social context" of the Pauline corpus. When discussed as part of introducing Paul, the reader-student has access to material culture through the medium of diagrams or photography, which lends a veneer of transparency and facticity. Such interactions between objects and words serve to reify theological commitments funneled through a quasi-social-scientific framework. Even as Paul's letters, according to the "rules" of New Testament studies, require layers of interpretation and all manner of reflection on the relationship between the text, context, and reading communities, it is still the case that the text ought to reflect an actual historical situation—and a theological orientation. And so it is with images: when confronted with a picture of material remains of one sort or another, we are taught to assume that the picture signifies the transparent raw data of the ancient world put before us to verify texts. If pictures do not obviously align with what is explicitly mentioned in texts, then they are deemed irrelevant. For instance, a scholar might contend that an image from an ancient city such as Aphrodisias, in western Asia Minor, is extraneous to Pauline studies because, according to the missionary journeys described in Acts, "Paul never went to Aphrodisias."

Let us entertain an example to illustrate this interpretive dilemma vis-à-vis encountering visual representation in the study of Paul. One popular image used for the purpose of teaching the New Testament in its Roman imperial context is that of an emperor such as the statue called "Augustus of Prima Porta" (fig. 1), which is perhaps safer than an image from Aphrodisias to explore in relationship to Paul. Visual representations of this emperor are handy for New Testament studies because many copies of his likeness have been excavated across the Roman empire. Furthermore, the only extant copies of his *Res Gestae*, itself an image and text used in New Testament studies, were excavated in central Turkey, the ancient Roman province of Galatia, to whom Paul is supposed to have sent his famous letter in the 50s CE.

Augustus of Prima Porta is a vital visual representative of the "Augustan age," the ancient historical epoch thought to account for the political and social context of Paul's writings. Images like this one are suitable support for arguments about New Testament theology because, according to Roman literary and visual tradition, Augustus was represented as the ruler chosen to fulfill Roman destiny during his lifetime, and after his death he was represented as a divine being. It is also thought that images of emperors were worshipped in ancient "imperial cult" complexes all over the Empire, including the cities mentioned in the New Testament. Thus, the image of Augustus, as a "son of God," "father of the fatherland," and "savior" who promoted "faith" among the people and "peace" for the whole world, is appealing for the study of Paul (see, for example, the "Postcolonial Approaches" chapter).[7] Indeed, Augustus is one of the few emperors mentioned by name in the New Testament canon, so his image can be invoked to illustrate the name in the text. As attractive as these links are, we must ask: is the image only interesting or relevant because Augustus is mentioned in the New Testament? Or because Paul mentions some terms associated with his likeness in his letters? Is Augustus pictured as a god to be encountered solely as visual confirmation for theological concepts like "idolatry"? Once we position the image of Augustus as a resource for the study of Paul, what comes next, and why

Figure 1. Statue of Augustus of Prima Porta. Found in Livia's Villa in 1863. This statue may have been a popular way the emperor was represented, as similar types have been found across the empire. Braccio Nuovo, Vatican Museums, Rome. Photo by Davina C. Lopez.

does it matter? How could looking at Augustus help us understand Paul?

Maintaining that images cannot be relevant to studies of literature unless they are explicitly referenced in texts effectively reveals the persistent methodological dilemma engendered by the use of images in the study of Paul and the New Testament: whether encountering pictures should change how readers encounter words. It is not adequate to insist that looking at images remain secondary to exegesis, or that interpreters should only do one or the other. If students of Paul are to engage (t)his world, if interpreters desire to take seriously that the world has always been visually inclined, and if we are going to work with images, how should we best do so? If pictures are couched simply as a subset of archaeological investigation subordinated to textual study, if they are nothing but reinforcement for ideas thought to be already inside words, if they are seen as "other" and opposite to words, then how might we proceed? If "reading Paul" needs to signify "rehearsing Pauline studies," which in turn means dismissing visual representation in favor of words, or deploying images to further stabilize and naturalize texts and their theologies, how might those interested in a different way respond? Where might we make a room for both Augustus's images and Paul's letters? What would that room look like?

"READING IMAGES": A PRACTICE OF PAULINE REALIGNMENT AND REIMAGINATION

I raise multiple questions at this juncture because such inquiry points to the live, unsettled, and contested methodological issues in the discipline of New Testament studies at the moment. Such unsettlement might be disorienting or frustrating, and yet I submit that we should be honest about such difficulties in discussions of how to introduce methodologies in the study of Paul. Just because the use of visual culture is becoming fairly fashionable in New Testament scholarship does not mean it is actually helpful or innovative for understanding Paul and his epistolary corpus, not to mention what the process of understanding Paul and his corpus says about the people committed to such ventures. In other words, it is not so much *that* images are used: it is, rather, *how* they are used and what such use says about the users that makes the difference in interpretive projects.

As far as what images like Augustus might have to do with Paul, it is crucial to recall that the predominance and naturalness of thinking with and through words and letters as though they have been the primary mode of communication since ancient times is not accidental. All studies of the ancient world are ultimately also about how we might relate to that world. In introductory pedagogical contexts, practitioners of New Testament scholarship do the work of constructing the world in which these texts were produced, the "ancientness" of which is manufactured and presented according to the standards of the manufacturers. It would seem to be no coincidence that people who read a lot of books in a highly literate culture would map bookishness onto an ancient context in order to render it more intelligible, as well as to justify modern obsession with words as the principal and preferred means of expressing human relationship. While scholars might acknowledge that the world in which *we* live is visually inclined, this premise is somehow more difficult to accept for Paul's world. And when it is acknowledged that the ancient world was as, or perhaps more, inclined toward images than words, the assumption that engaging images cannot have been the same as reading texts perseveres.

Even if a photograph of the Prima Porta Augustus statue might be expedient for introducing Paul, it also stands that, insofar as such images are exploited for the purpose of illustration, and the premises and assumptions about the ancient world and its visual inclinations remain, so the word/image hierarchy remains. What would it look like to turn things around? What it would do for introducing Paul were we to use Paul to think with from the vantage point of visual literacy? Herein I suggest taking seriously the reality that images are not just to be looked at or used but are readable in their own right as a form of language—after all, what are words but strings of symbols, small images about which we are trained, from an early age, to make sense? While the case has been made that both words and images should be seen as reflective of historical and social realities, I maintain, along with scholars of language and art, that words and images are not mere reflections but rather constructions and naturalizations of human relationships. Images, like words, are products of social relations—they in turn suggest and produce social relations and hierarchies. They serve an ideological function by rendering the social relations and hierarchies they produce, and from which they are made, natural, inevitable, universal, and eternal. Even—perhaps especially—when an image like the statue of Augustus is thought to be a suggestion of divinity or an object of worship, the point is that the image is made with human hands, and therefore must be located as an articulation of human relationships and reality.

As long as we uncritically accept that the utility of visual representation is limited to exegetical support for texts, we will not be able to move beyond justifying why we might look at images of Augustus, or Aphrodisias, or any other pictures in relation to the ideas we think Paul had because we can read letters. One way to negotiate this interpretive dilemma is to consider this chapter's proposal that it is entirely possible to see images as constituting a complementary semantic system to literary remains. Doing so requires a sustained effort of realigning the sources available for the study of Paul—which may in turn require venturing into territory and resources considered "irrelevant" by the discipline in its most ordinary discourses.

Engaging in a realignment of sources available for introducing Paul allows us to make some methodological moves that working solely with words, and the categories interpreters use words to invoke, might deny. Foregrounding images in the study of Paul can afford opportunities to critically examine what it means to engage in the process of reading in the first place. Such a maneuver should open a space to complicate the question of ancient literacy. We would do well, for example, to think about the following: just because a select number of people like Paul could read and write words, we cannot assume that his audiences could, or desired to, do likewise. Further, even if it was that Paul's communities "heard" the letters read aloud in whatever setting we imagine them to have done so—house church, synagogue, ancient classroom, gymnasium, forum—it still does not follow that Paul's audience understood what they were hearing as a letter, or received it in terms of abstract concepts that scholars have insisted on associating with reading literary representations, never mind what Paul might have "meant to say" in his epistles.

A practice of realigning the sources available for the study of Paul must further consider the possibility that reading images might be the principal means of how ancient people negotiated their world. This is an assumption that art historians and other interpreters of visual media have carried for some time, and it is worth noting in New Testament studies desiring to undertake the examination of visual representation. If we rethink what it means to read, we can assess whether our definitions are too limited, for the ability to make sense of images as means of communication comprises a powerful and overlooked form of literacy in its own right. Should we do this, we might ask, then, whether Paul might be using words not as a means to explain a doctrine or to build a sustained textual argument, but as a response to and interaction with a visual environment in which images were primary sites for the articulation of power relationships and hierarchies. This realization should give pause to contemporary readers of Paul, for it means that we must at least entertain the prospect that ancient Pauline texts do not harbor stable meanings, nor are the words reflections of rather narrow semantic ranges that always somehow are circumscribed by theological vocabulary and literary parallels.

THESE THINGS ARE ALLEGORIZED!
IMAG(IN)ING AUGUSTUS, PAUL, AND US

Let us now experiment with our proposed practice of realignment by attempting to place images and an exemplary Pauline text, Galatians 4:21–5:1, in the same space. Looking again at the picture of the statue of Augustus, we recall that reading images as products of social relations does not take for granted that said images simply reflect reality. If we are interested in fostering visual literacy, then we are invested in understanding what and how pictures communicate, as well as what visions of social relations they construct and promote. To that end, consider an image that might be more familiar than Augustus's likeness and yet is structurally similar to that of the emperor despite its difference in provenance: a 2003 photo of President George W. Bush arriving to deliver his "Mission Accomplished" speech (fig. 2). This is a picture of the then-sitting President of the United States, dressed in a flight suit, walking on the *USS Abraham Lincoln* aircraft carrier among other military service personnel. A few hours later, and in a different outfit, he delivered a speech on the aircraft carrier underneath a banner reading "Mission Accomplished" that announced the end of formal military operations in Iraq, stating that the United States and their allies had prevailed.

Such images of President Bush are notable because they record the first time that a sitting President boarded an aircraft carrier in an airplane and not a helicopter. They also constitute an attempt to communicate a set of circumstances, a reality, to viewers: the President flew a plane onto the aircraft carrier, he is dressed as a military pilot, his military has won the war. Most remarkable is the disjunction between the content of the images and the actual historical circumstances appearing to be managed, which have not gone without comment in the news media and political scene since this photo was produced and disseminated. For the President did not fly the plane onto the aircraft carrier, as his flight suit would seem to suggest; nor did the war end on that date. One might say that these images, attractive as they seem, are evidence that President Bush participated in efforts to control public perception

Figure 2. President George W. Bush boards the *USS Abraham Lincoln* and passes through the "side boys" saluting him on May 1, 2003. United States Navy Photo by Photographer's Mate Third Class Tyler J. Clements. Public Domain.

through elaborate photo opportunities like this one. Moreover, when "Mission Accomplished" photos are placed alongside depictions of the torture of prisoners at Abu Ghraib prison by United States military personnel (released in 2006), the juxtaposition of two seemingly different visual messages suggests that there are two conflicting realities about how the War on Terror is being conducted and handled.

It might be easy to resonate with sentiments that President Bush's administration used images to create and naturalize a reality that is contrary to the "truth." The point about how images work, however, is that pictures are not transparently about "truth" but serve to construct reality as far as social relations are concerned. As art historian Peter Stewart proposes, there is likely less systematic intentionality behind images on the part of their manufacturers and viewers than we might think—rather, the creation of images is likely more indebted to a network of production than to a single impulse, "author," or audience.[8] The same broad apparatus of production that we are assuming lies behind a literary product, therefore, also lies behind a picture. What we take to be a relatively stable snapshot with a clear message of a moment with enormous subsequent social import—a President wearing a flight suit, standing under a "Mission Accomplished" banner—also suggests a random process of "coming into being" that reveals something of both the fundamental instability of value and multiplicity of meanings inherent in that snapshot. With pictures, then, what we see is not necessarily what we get.

Keeping this framework in mind, we turn to Paul's visual world, wherein we can see that Augustus of Prima Porta is not transparently depicting a ruler that ancient people may have worshipped but is an image worth noting as one (among many) betraying a complex narrative. More than high-quality sculpture, this statue is similarly a product of a random process of "coming into being" that includes its rediscovery as an archaeological artifact in the nineteenth century, its deposit into the Vatican Museums for viewing as "art" by a consuming public, and its photographic reproduction in numerous scholarly volumes, including this one. There could be a particular rationale behind the production of this image of the emperor depicted this way. As archaeologists and art historians have shown, there are numerous types and examples. It is safe to say, then, that images like this one would have been seen throughout the empire in antiquity—even if this particular statue was found in what is thought to be a private garden in his wife Livia's villa outside of the Roman city center, and even if Paul and his addressees never set foot in that villa. Augustus is here wearing an elaborate military cuirass and a victory cloak, and has his arm extended as if addressing an audience or announcing "Mission Accomplished." Such a statement of victory is bolstered by the baby Eros riding a dolphin next to his right leg, which the Romans understood as a symbol of the winner. Further, he is not just any winner but a divine one, as his bare feet signify.

When reading visual representation, it is important to identify the various elements of the whole—bare feet, military dress, hand gestures—that might appear

Figure 3. Statue of Augustus of Prima Porta. Detail of the cuirass showing divine favor for Roman victory over the Parthians and two other defeated nations. Braccio Nuovo, Vatican Museums, Rome. Photo by Davina C. Lopez.

over and over again in the images under consideration. Whatever else we might (not) be able to assert about the ancient world Paul inhabited in terms of reading and literacy, we can state that it is a culture of repetition, or *mimesis*, that helps us to understand how the language of images works. Engaging the language of images, we can see that, as with words, certain symbols, figures, and poses appear often and indicate a certain range of possible significations that assist in constructions of social relations. Taking the Prima Porta statue as an image that is linked to others through its relative consistency in elements, we notice that the visual program on the breastplate, an image in its own right, provides further information about the "reality" of divinely condoned military victory this likeness of Augustus attempts to construct and naturalize. The emperor's torso (fig. 3) features a "barbarian" Parthian man declaring defeat by handing over the Roman standard to a military character. The scene of military success is a signal motif in Roman visual representation of the early imperial period, bolstered here by personifications of the Sun, Moon, and Dawn offering godly approval draped across the top of Augustus's chest as well as the depiction of Tellus or Terra Mater, "mother earth," offering her cornucopia of fertility in his groin area.

Aside from the exchange of arms on Augustus's abdomen, the emperor's apparel features two crouching female figures sitting near his armpits, each dressed in different clothing and surrounded by weapons. These two women are common in Roman imperial visual representation as personifications of lands and peoples, or "nations," defeated in battle. In fact, the defeated "other non-Roman woman" is one of the most popular visual tropes in ancient Roman representation. This trope has two main types: allegorical representations of specific lands—for example, Galatia, Judea, Britannia, Hispania—that are identifiable by dress, posture, and setting, and the anonymous barbarian, usually shown in groups showing deference to, and enslavement by, Roman captors. Looking for similar images reveals that such women make their appearance in a variety of media, including coins, domestic items such as cups, jewelry, and public sculpture. A few sculptural examples include monumental reliefs from the Temple of Hadrian (one of whom, thought to be "Hispania," is shown in figure 4), a keystone thought to be "Dacia" (fig. 5), and a relief believed to tell the story about the defeat of Germania under the emperor Domitian that once adorned a building in Rome (fig. 6).

Just as it does not matter what President George W. Bush intended when he was photographed in a flight suit on an aircraft carrier, it matters very little if Augustus "really" wore the military costume, had the approval of the gods (or became one himself), had the standards taken from the Parthians, or conquered the cowering barbarian nations. It does not matter if he intended to be portrayed in the likeness of the Prima Porta statue. What matters for the type of methodological inquiry we are exploring here is that this portrait incorporates a series of visual elements that, together, participate in the construction of a reality and vision of social relations

Figure 4. Relief of an allegorical personification thought to be the nation of Hispania (Spain), Hadrianeum. One of a series of at least a dozen nations found as part of this complex. Hadrian preferred to represent the nations in standing position, often shaking hands with him in "friendship." Capitoline Museum, Rome. Photo by Davina C. Lopez.

which, given its constancy, ancient viewers would have confronted on a daily basis. It could be said that this reality centers on the portrayal of a Roman "Mission Accomplished" in relation to a variety of peoples and lands—again, depicted as ethnically "other" female bodies—who eventually became adopted foreign step-children of an emperor-father or, as Tacitus would have it in his *Agricola*, "fellow slaves . . . in this world-wide, age-old slave-gang" (31.2). The ideological configuration that the Prima Porta Augustus renders natural, inevitable, and divinely inspired can be interpreted as one that includes a hierarchical vision of international social relationships, represented allegorically in the visual language of male and female bodies

Figure 5. Keystone depicting a crouching woman, perhaps the personification of Dacia, from the Trajanic period. Capitoline Museum, Rome. Photo by Davina C. Lopez.

interacting with one another. There seem to be options for negotiating such representations, that one can read this constructed reality as evidence of Roman foreign policy in terms of "positive" familial relations or "negative" slavery connotations, is itself an indication that this particular reality was negotiated and responded to in contemporaneous literature.

By now it should be clear that Paul's letters can be seen as "contemporaneous literature" negotiating the reality constructed and naturalized by visual media examples like the ones under consideration here. We have been noticing a single visual trope—the representation of Roman imperial social relations through allegorized male and female bodies, where male Romans are victorious and foreign

Figure 6. Relief depicting the defeat of Germania (Germany) under the emperor Domitian, found at Ostia. The female figure is shown in a crouching, "mourning" pose at the foot of a military trophy adorned with the weapons of the conquered, and a male figure is depicted with his hands bound behind his back. National Museum of Rome at the Baths of Diocletian. Photo by Davina C. Lopez.

women captured—as part of a readable ancient landscape that, through a realignment of available sources, can be seen as a part of the ancient world in which the apostle Paul builds his own epistolary reality, not to mention that to which he and his addressees belonged and negotiated. We (re)introduce Paul here from the position that images are texts, and a Pauline letter interacts with images to articulate particular visions of social relations that may be consistent with those portrayed visually, resistant to such visions, or somewhere in between. In this schema Augustus and Paul can occupy the room together with us, and perhaps President Bush can come along as well.

In order to further a practice of realignment toward a reimagination of Pauline texts and traditions, let us keep in mind the aspects of the ancient visual environment described here as we raise questions about another portrayal of social relations using similar imagery: that of Galatians 4:21–5:1, the so-called "Allegory of Hagar and Sarah." Endeavoring to read, or rather *see*, this particular passage through the lens of visual culture and literacy affords an opportunity to revisit what is at stake in introducing the study of Paul. Galatians 4:21–5:1 involves a comparison of two well-known female characters from Israelite tradition, both of which are mentioned in Genesis: Abraham's childbearers, Hagar and Sarah. Paul is quick to point out, near the start of this passage, that Abraham, having two sons, one of the "slave woman" and one of the "free woman," is allegorical, that the women and sons represent what he calls "two covenants" (4:24). He identifies Hagar with two places, Mount Sinai in Arabia and "Jerusalem now," who is further linked to being in slavery with her children (4:25). By contrast, the female figure we presume to be Sarah (she remains unnamed) is called "Jerusalem above," who is "free" and formerly barren but now has many children (4:26-27). The children of the free woman, according to Paul, are the Galatians, who are also "brothers" (4:28, 31).

In the context of this image-laden passage, who one's mother is—or which Jerusalem one calls an ancestral home, Jerusalem "now" or Jerusalem "above"—matters because, Paul states, the children of the free woman will receive an inheritance whilst the children of the slave woman get nothing. Paul exhorts toward "casting out" the slave woman, for she and her children "of the flesh" were persecuting the children of "the spirit." Paul also connects this to his current rhetorical situation by writing "so also now" (4:29), perhaps as a reference to a current round of persecutions between different people with the same "father" and different "mothers." At the end of this section, Paul reminds his addressees that Christ has set them free, and they should not submit again to a yoke of slavery (5:1).

The history of interpretation of Galatians 4:21–5:1 has taken Paul's declaration of allegory seriously, particularly when seeking to establish justification for an emergent Christianity over and against Judaism. This passage is used to support Christian supersessionist claims, where Hagar is identified not just with "Jerusalem now" but also with the Jewish synagogue—and Sarah with a triumphant

Christian church. This is the literary reference for a whole host of visual representations in Europe's classic Christian cathedrals, depicting two women at war with one another. At the famous Strasbourg Cathedral in France (ca. 1230 CE), Sarah is cast in dramatic sculptural relief as a victorious "Ecclesia"/Church—complete with military standards and crown—opposite a defeated "Synagoga"/Synagogue with her rejected law book, broken weapons, and captured posture. During the Protestant Reformation, these women were again allegorized to imagine Hagar as Catholicism and Sarah as Protestantism, where the Mother "according to flesh" would not receive the inheritance from God. In the modern era, Hagar and Sarah have operated as allegories for how white and "ethnically other" women relate to one another in racist, patriarchal societies: white women are "free" and "cast out" their slaves when they are finished with them—even as their sons might share the same father. Such trajectories serve to create realities that Paul likely did not intend—the defeat of Judaism by Christian prowess; the legitimation of Protestantism as that which supersedes Catholicism; and a legacy of ethnocentrism that forces modern women against one another in hierarchical relationship.

Whatever else we might make of Galatians 4:21–5:1, the imagery of a free woman and an enslaved woman in conflict with one another, and the victory of one over the other, can be read as a Pauline "Mission Accomplished" vision of social relations. Given what we have been discussing in terms of a visual environment to which literary representations might respond, this passage could look different when we acknowledge the pervasive kind of visual representation that might be behind this text, and not just an unfortunate result of its subsequent reception history in the development of Christian theology, ethics, and liturgical practices. The correspondence between female bodies and geographical places is a trope in biblical literature—and when coupled with the personification of lands and peoples as female "nations" as powerfully present in Roman visual culture, it becomes almost impossible to avoid noticing such a narrative pattern. Paul and his addressees would have been exposed to such visual language regularly, whether they intended to be or not. Whilst walking down a street or to a market, using coins to pay for goods and services, gathering in public places, or spending time in houses and synagogues, images of the conquered and conquerors permeated the Pauline visual environment. While it takes a lot of speculative interpretive legwork to demonstrate that Paul and his audiences were readers of certain kinds of literature such as "Hellenistic philosophers" or "Greek medical texts," a visual environment is, in the end, much easier to defend than a literary one. It may well be that Paul's audience could not follow his arguments "from scripture."[9] In their environment, they may have more readily connected with the visual rhetoric Paul constantly evokes in his letters.

Given the visual environment we have been exploring, I briefly offer two options for preliminary engagement with this passage. In doing so the aim is not to "make sense" of Paul's letter, for outside of rehearsing pat theological categories and other such religious justifications, such a task might be impossible. I offer this world full of pictures that structure meaning and relationships as a means of freeing up Pauline discourses for additional exploration and experimentation. To that end, it is not difficult to link the image of an enslaved "Jerusalem now" with captured and cowering female figures on display as casualties of battle in Augustus's armpits and all over the Roman world. Using the image of a conquered nation could be an indication that Paul is attempting to offer his audience a "way out" by advocating for a family relationship not with the enslavement to a conquering world order that Hagar represents but with the freedom suggested by a genealogical alignment with "Jerusalem above." This woman, the mother of the children of the promise, emerges as the restored Jerusalem that welcomes the people among whom Paul has been laboring—perhaps toward liberation from unjust enslaving visions of Roman imperial social relationships. In this schema, of course, Paul subverts the Roman imperial tendency to conquer, enslave, and assimilate the "national other," envisioning a new space of freedom when the children of Abraham will not be unduly subjected to a "law" that has been captured and defeated. Galatians, through this allegory, becomes a rallying cry for liberation among those who, like the women in Augustus's armpit and other images shown here, are mourning for their loss of freedom at the hands of their ancient colonizers.

The image of an anti-imperial ancient Paul working among the defeated on behalf of their freedom might seem attractive to those of us in the contemporary world who long for a different vision of social relations, particularly when less-than-stellar interpretive legacies of the apostle's work as oppressive on any number of fronts are taken into account. This kind of reimagined—or perhaps just repackaged—Paul, as an "apostle to the conquered," could be incredibly useful for contemporary liberation projects hungry for scriptural support. Perhaps I should just stop here with such a portrait, thus stabilizing such a reimagined Paul. However, exploring how visual representation and literary representation interact if a practice of realignment is taken seriously should give us pause, for the instability of the range of significations expands considerably as a fuller range of sources is taken into account when encountering the Pauline corpus. A "Jerusalem above" who "casts out the slave woman and her children" need not necessarily call up a picture of the safe haven for all people who wish to be liberated from empire. After all, another popular Roman image contributing to the construction of conquest as social reality is that of the winged Roman goddess Victory (fig. 7), who often appears as a woman "above" defeated personifications, declaring the Romans the winners of war and divine favor. Victory, as the "woman above" who appears at the conclusion of public visual narratives celebrating the "casting out" of the slaves, helps affirm the inevitability of empire, of an eternal hierarchy between those who conquer and those who are conquered. It would not be outlandish to say that this image is, in effect, a depiction of Roman freedom. Victory might be rather inconvenient for those of us interested in the stability of an anti-imperial Paul, as she represents a visual option that he could appropriate, that "Jerusalem above" could very well express, and that an audience might "see" as they hear, read, or otherwise encounter Paul's rhetoric.

CONCLUSION

A practice of realignment in the study of Paul highlights the notion that the ancient world is much larger, more complex, and less like the modern world than the narrow and abstract religious setting that the history of New Testament scholarship informing contemporary introductions to Paul might suggest. Any engagement of the ancient world starts not in and with the past but in and with the present. Therefore, introducing Paul in light of images and visual literacy is not actually about Paul, his letters, his (or our) ancient world, or the images. Such introductory overtures are always and already about us, insofar as endeavoring to understand

Figure 7. Relief featuring a winged figure, perhaps the goddess Victory, flying in to announce the end of war with a Roman standard in her arms. She is pictured here approaching the miniaturized captured national "others" who are bound and placed near their weapons at the base of a tree. Found at Ostia. National Museum of Rome at the Baths of Diocletian. Photo by Davina C. Lopez.

Paul and his letters is about understanding the relationships we have, and desire to cultivate, with this material and, ultimately, with each other as human beings. The human relationships we use Paul's letters to support, though, say more about our own visions and inclinations than those of Paul. For some, it is tempting to gravitate toward the "Paul above" who "casts out" the "victory paradigm" in favor of liberation and mutuality among "brothers." For others, the portrait of Paul who casts out the "others" in favor of maintaining a hierarchy of oppressions is more preferable. However, the point in engaging images is not that we must choose one option or the other, or that one is more historically accurate or viable—but that we recognize that it is we, and not texts, who do the ethical work of signifying toward meaning for ourselves and each other.

Finally, in this respect, an identification of the personified Jerusalem above with the image of Roman Victory, even if inconvenient and provisional, could point to a series of questions about social relations that is thoroughly biblical, not to mention humanistic, in nature: should the conquered, in their quest for freedom, become the conquerors? What would be the (dis)advantages of doing so? Can freedom ever be achieved without the enslavement of another? How can we know which option is best, if we, as heirs to this world of slavery and freedom, share a common father? As Paul would have it, these things are allegorized! This means we have interpretive choices. It is not so much the evaluation and judgment of the choices that matters but rather that we ought to be honest about the choices we make, how we make them, and why. In the end, it is we, not Paul, who would do well to see the difference, as well as depict what is at stake for visions of social relations in whatever image(ry) we choose to embrace, eschew, and/or deploy.

FURTHER READING

Butler, Judith. *Frames of War: When Is Life Grievable?* New York: Verso, 2010. Analyzes contemporary visual representations of war and terrorism to propose a critical response to the discourses and publics manufactured by such mediating images.

Elliott, Neil and Mark Reasoner, eds. *Documents and Images for the Study of Paul.* Minneapolis: Fortress Press, 2010. A collection of primary literary and non-literary sources assembled in the service of assisting alignments of Pauline literature with Jewish, Greek, and Roman representations.

Lopez, Davina C. *Apostle to the Conquered: Reimagining Paul's Mission.* Paul in Critical Contexts. Minneapolis: Fortress Press, 2008. Attempts to take Roman imperial visual representation seriously as a "complementary semantic system" to literary texts, applying this methodological shift to Paul's life, letters, and legacy.

Olson, Lester C., Cara A. Finnegan, and Diane S. Hope, eds. *Visual Rhetoric: A Reader in Communication and American Culture.* London: Sage, 2008. Focusing on the United States, this reader outlines methodological perspectives on the interconnectedness of visuality and rhetoric.

Stewart, Peter. *The Social History of Roman Art*. Key Themes in Ancient History. New York: Cambridge University Press, 2008. A critical introduction to Roman art emphasizing the ubiquity of images as a means of communication in the ancient world, as well as the methodological difficulties and contemporary myths surrounding their interpretation in the modern world.

Sturken, Marita and Lisa Cartwright. *The Practices of Looking: An Introduction to Visual Culture*. New York: Oxford University Press, 2009. Appraises the frameworks used to understand the pervasiveness of visual communication in a global context.

NOTES

1. I thank Joseph Marchal for seeing visual representation as a methodological trajectory worth introducing in Pauline studies, along with Kelsi Morrison-Atkins for her keen critical eye. This piece was completed during my 2011 tenure as a Scholar-in-Residence at Columbia University's Burke Theological Library. I am grateful to Todd Penner, my comrade at the Burke and in much else, for encouraging me to come to terms with the rhetorical aspects of visuality that effectively decenter textual fetishism, and for his reading multiple versions and fragments of an essay that is now, unfortunately, mostly words. As efforts to engage Paul and the ancient world, however introductory, are ultimately about engaging ourselves through a different lens, I dedicate this essay to the memory of my grandmother, Dorothy "Dolly" Casperino (1920–2011), who taught me, above all else, to fearlessly question the transparency and naturalness of what our world wants us to see.

2. For an elaboration and discussion of "visual literacy," see Marita Sturken and Lisa Cartwright, *The Practices of Looking: An Introduction to Visual Culture* (New York: Oxford University Press, 2009).

3. See William V. Harris, *Ancient Literacy* (Cambridge: Harvard University Press, 1989), as well as the broader views on what it meant to read and write in antiquity in *Ancient Literacies: The Culture of Reading in Greece and Rome*, ed. William A. Johnson and Holt N. Parker (New York: Oxford University Press, 2009).

4. See, for example, the full-color insert on images in Bart D. Ehrman, *The New Testament: A Historical Introduction to the Early Christian Writings*, 3rd ed. (New York: Oxford University Press, 2004).

5. Vincent Wimbush proposes that a shift in methodological focus should move from "scriptures" to "scripturalizing," which asks questions of what exactly it is humans think "scriptures" are, and what exactly they think they are doing when they interact with "scriptures." Such maneuvers require seeing texts not solely as artifacts, but as sites for articulations of power relationships and hierarchies. See Wimbush, "Introduction: TEXTureS, Gestures, Power: Orientation to Radical Excavation," in *Theorizing Scriptures: New Critical Orientations to a Cultural Phenomenon*, ed. Vincent L. Wimbush, Signifying [on] Scriptures, vol. 1 (New Brunswick: Rutgers University Press), 1–22.

6. For a collection of primary sources on Pauline traditions in early Christian literature, see Richard I. Pervo, *The Making of Paul: Constructions of the Apostle in Early Christianity* (Minneapolis: Fortress Press, 2010).

7. For a summary of approaches emphasizing the dialectical relationship between Roman and Pauline "gospels," see *Paul and Empire: Religion and Power in Roman Imperial Society*, ed. Richard A. Horsley (Harrisburg: Trinity Press International, 1997).

8. Peter Stewart, *The Social History of Roman Art*, Key Themes in Ancient History (New York: Cambridge University Press, 2008), 10–39.

9. For a development of this point throughout the Pauline corpus see Christopher D. Stanley, *Arguing with Scripture: The Rhetoric of Quotations in the Letters of Paul* (New York: T&T Clark, 2004).

6

FEMINIST APPROACHES

Rethinking History and Resisting Ideologies

CYNTHIA BRIGGS KITTREDGE

For the past fifty years, biblical scholars, historians, and theologians have engaged in vigorous and productive work on Paul's letters from a feminist perspective, using various methods and with a range of different goals. This chapter will present (1) the commitments and assumptions of feminist approaches to Paul's letters; (2) a narrative of the Jesus movement and the communities at the time of Paul, which draws on the major insights of feminist scholarship and highlights the texts on which the narrative is based; (3) the contribution of historical and ideological criticism of Paul's world view from a feminist perspective; (4) attention to Romans 8:14-39, illustrating how the strategies of historical reconstruction and ideological criticism engage this text and the questions feminist interpreters address to this text; and (5) conclusions and directions.

COMMITMENTS AND ASSUMPTIONS

Feminism is a movement to end sexism, sexual exploitation, and oppression.[1] A feminist approach to the study of the Bible seeks to critique patterns of thought that define women as inferior to men and to find resources within it to construct a vision of equality and flourishing for all. A feminist approach to the study of Paul's letters takes as its starting point a commitment to the well-being of all wo/men. The term *wo/men* indicates that women are not a unitary group but are diverse in class, race, and ethnicity. "Wo/men" may be read inclusively. Just as the word "men" customarily is used to include women, so "wo/men" may include men who are marginalized and exploited.[2] Beginning with an explicit advocacy stance, a feminist approach does not claim to be ethically neutral, but names its ethical and political commitments at the outset. While it names its "bias," feminist criticism continues to conform to the general norms of biblical criticism: the citing of evidence, close readings of texts, attention to genre, and interpreting cultural codes in historical context.[3] A feminist critical approach recognizes its own role in presenting convincing portraits of Paul and his colleagues, of telling the story of early missionaries, and of raising critical questions about Paul's rhetoric and theology. Thus, feminist criticism takes seriously its own rhetoric and persuasive role in the public and ecclesial space of debates about the Bible. In its concern for the flourishing of all, feminist criticism does not consider itself as representing a "special interest" but contributes insights to the study of Paul's letters that benefit and change the field of biblical studies.

The current political context in which Paul's letters are read is important to feminist criticism. The epistles are read publically in churches weekly, preached on, taught about, and heard and received as authoritative sacred texts in Christian contexts. Different denominations regard Paul's letters differently—some giving them more weight and others less, but still they are significant as scripture in these communities. Beyond their role in churches, Paul's letters have shaped ideas about gender in Western culture, and the letters continue to operate as an authority in political debates about women's roles, the legitimacy of same-sex relationships, and the shape of the family. For both theologians and scholars of religion, in ecclesial and public contexts, feminist criticism of Paul is important and relevant.

For centuries Paul's letters have been used to silence and to subordinate women. As interpreted by Augustine and the church fathers, passages in Paul's letters, particularly 1 Timothy 2:11-15 and 1 Corinthians 14:34 and 11:2-16, have undergirded the ideology of women's inferiority and sinfulness.[4] These texts have given divine legitimation to women's inferiority and necessary subordination to husband and father. These authors justify this order in marriage by the creation story in Genesis 2 and ground female inferiority and subordination in "nature." Because of the role of Paul's letters in constructing this worldview that has been destructive to wo/men's flourishing, feminist interpreters have read these texts with particular urgency. They have chosen different strategies and methods for dealing with the ongoing legacy of Paul's letters for human communities.

This chapter will focus on two major strategies—historical reconstruction and ideological criticism. Because of the powerful role of Paul as a "person" in religious imagination and of the role of the texts in constructing worlds of meaning, feminists have wanted to use biblical criticism either to position themselves in opposition to Paul or to claim him as an ally for liberation. This presentation will sketch out an approach to Paul's letters that does not depend on a theologically appealing or useful reconstruction of Paul's person or position, but broadens the inquiry to describe and assess the wider conversation around contested issues in the assemblies. The goal of this approach is not to reconstruct "what Paul thought," but for the interpreter to engage with the conversation within the community.

Feminist criticism recognizes that the biblical texts in general and letters of Paul in particular are androcentric texts, that is, they are written from the perspective of men, with women being seen as "other," as derivative or marginal. Many are written by men, but women also can write androcentric texts. An example of an androcentric text from the Bible is the tenth commandment, "You shall not covet your neighbor's house; you shall not covet your neighbor's wife, or male or female slave, or ox, or donkey, or anything that belongs to your neighbor" (Exod. 20:17). The text does not include "husband"—"you shall not covet your neighbor's husband"— because the commandments are written from the perspective of males, speaking to other males, who have wives, not husbands, and who would wish to steal or take for themselves another man's property, his "wife." The androcentric nature of texts is in plain sight, but usually overlooked, because as modern readers, we "translate" such a commandment into a mutual or inclusive version, and thus read "you shall not covet your neighbor's wife or husband." Androcentric texts are limited in that they can only say certain things and they make some things visible and render others invisible. For example, in the commandment, a woman who covets another woman's husband is invisible.

Not only are the texts of Paul's letters androcentric, but the tradition of commentary and interpretation is also biased toward erasing the evidence of women's activity and agency in history. Evidence of women's leadership is rendered invisible by the assumption of women's absence. An example of this erasure in the textual tradition is the name of Junia in Romans 16:7. Because the scribes who copied the manuscripts were part of a tradition that thought it was impossible for a woman's name to be modified by the epithet, "apostle," the name was changed to "Junias," a male name, and passed down in that amended form.[5] Scholarship on the manuscript tradition and the attestation of the name Junia and Junias has shown that the original name was the woman's name, Junia. Feminist criticism uses methods of analysis that account for the biases of androcentric texts, translations, and commentaries to resist or get "underneath" them. Sometimes this technique is called "reading against the grain" of the androcentric text.[6]

Feminist criticism of Paul recognizes that the letters of Paul are not neutral descriptions of history but rhetorical texts intended to persuade, to motivate action, and to create particular understandings of reality. Therefore, rhetorical criticism—analysis of the situation, audience, and exigence—is an important part of a feminist approach to Paul's letters (see the "Rhetorical Approaches" chapter). Feminist analysis seeks to reconstruct the theological positions of other members of the communities through analyzing Paul's rhetoric. An influential example of this approach is Antoinette Clark Wire's analysis of the Corinthian women prophets.[7] Through an analysis of Paul's rhetoric in 1 Corinthians, Wire reconstructs the self-understanding of the prophets in Corinth who uncover their heads and whom Paul seeks to silence. She shows how their theological perspective arises out of their understanding of baptism. They see the resurrection of Jesus as effecting a rearrangement of power and implying radical change in social relationships in the community. Paul censures their enactment of the implications of their baptism, through prophetic speech and removing their head coverings.

HISTORICAL RECONSTRUCTION
AND A NARRATIVE OF THE EARLY JESUS MOVEMENT

Scholars of Paul have employed insights from the field of women's history to reconstruct the history of women in the assemblies and to understand women within the wider social historical context of the Greco-Roman world. Women's history for this period of Christian origins is of more than academic interest, because of the power of narratives of origin for Christian self-understanding in the present. Because of the huge influence of Paul's letters throughout history and in present ecclesial and public contexts, how one tells the story of these early generations is very significant.

The following brief narrative will tell the story of the early communities that we glimpse in Paul's letters. This account acknowledges that all historical accounts are impartial and imperfect, shaped by the lenses of those who tell it (see the "Historical Approaches" chapter). The lens through which this narrative views the story reads against the grain in one very significant way. While the letters depict Paul at the center, this account decenters Paul, directs its attention to the vibrant post-Easter communities and the vigorous missionary movement of many women and men who worked as apostles, prophets, evangelists, teachers, overseers, patrons, and coworkers. When he taught the letters of Paul, Krister Stendahl had an expression that he insisted that his students keep in mind when studying Paul: "There were other people."[8] It is difficult to maintain the perspective of a movement of people, because of the emphasis in the Christian tradition on Paul's singularity and lone genius.

How one tells the story of the assemblies depends largely on what Pauline texts one foregrounds. If one begins with the account of Paul's conversion in Galatians 1:11-24, for example, the way most introductions do, Paul's biography becomes the focus of the story. If, on the other hand, one begins with Romans 16:1-16 and 1 Corinthians 14 and 15, the story becomes an account of a corporate movement of people preaching the gospel of Jesus Christ, working to establish communities of solidarity, risking censure and danger in the culture of the Greco-Roman world. Paul is an important contributor to that movement, but he is not the only leader or only source of authority for the development of the community's ethics and teaching.

In Romans 16:1-16, Paul commends to the congregation in Rome "our sister, Phoebe, a deacon of the church at Cenchreae" (16:1). In the opening verses, Paul asks the congregation to welcome her and to help her, "for she has been a benefactor to many and of myself as well" (16:2). Following this commendation there is a list of greetings to congregation leaders with epithets that explain their role and relationship with Paul. The tradition of commentary and scholarship has marginalized this passage because of questions of its originality in the manuscript of Romans.[9] Although this question has been definitively resolved in favor of its having been part of the original letter, the passage is rarely foregrounded in the study of Romans. Yet, because of the number and prominence of women's names in the passage, it is considered a source for the history of women in the early assembly communities. From a feminist perspective, however, the passage is a source for history of the early congregations and of the missionary movement in general. It is a key passage in understanding the multiple leadership roles in the communities and for putting Paul's activity in the context of other community activity. While Paul's own rhetoric elsewhere positions himself as the center and head of the missionary movement, and his rhetoric is amplified by the history of interpretation that sees him as sole leader of "Pauline churches," the evidence of Romans 16:1-16 provides a more nuanced picture.

For example, all introductions to the letter to the Romans point out that Romans is the only letter written to a congregation that Paul had not visited. This fact is stated with an assumption of Paul's centrality, and that preconception prevents inquiry into who did establish it, who were its leaders, or how authority operated within the congregation/s in Rome. The letter to the Romans has been called "Paul's last will and testament" and the summary of his theology, but the direct address to the audience in Romans 16:1 gives strong grounds for it to be named "Paul's commendation of Phoebe." The greetings in Romans 16:1-16 convey a vivid sense of inter-dependence between Paul and his patron, Phoebe, with his coworkers, Prisca and Aquila, who endangered themselves on his behalf, and with Epaenetus and with Mary. Paul also says that Andronicus and Junia, who are prominent among the apostles, were in Christ before him (16:7). Through the catalogue of names— men and women, male-female pairs (Andronicus and Junia), and pairs of women (Trypheana and Tryphosa) —and its repetition of family language, the passage conveys the vitality and diversity of the holy ones, the "saints" in Rome, and belies the familiar image of Paul's singularity and dominance.

The energy unleashed by the experience of presence of the risen Christ appears, by all evidence in the letter, to be understood as an outpouring of the spirit after the model of Joel 2:28-32, the messianic age.[10] This activity of the Spirit by all accounts did not discriminate between women and men or between Jew and Gentile. Unpredictability was a hallmark of the Spirit's action. Paul's instructions about worship in the congregation in Corinth in 1 Corinthians 14:1-33 present a picture of the corporate worship that is overflowing with spiritual gifts, of prophecy, tongues, interpretations, prayer, and singing. While Paul is counseling order and arguing for the superiority of some gifts over others for the building up of the body, the sense conveyed by the passage of the generous gifts of the spirit and their representation in the members of the congregation is striking and bears emphasis in a feminist retelling of the story.

In order to reconstruct these assemblies and the theological and practical ferment within and among them, it is necessary to recognize the significance of the corporate ethical and liturgical practices around which the communities were organized. The eucharistic meal and baptism were central and issued in practices of mutual support, such as the collection for Jerusalem, patronage of missionaries, and care for the weaker members of the *ekklēsia*. Both the eucharist and baptism retold and reenacted the story of Jesus' passion and death, his resurrection and vindication by God, and the reordering of power that Jesus' resurrection effected. The reading and rereading of scripture was an integral part of these liturgical practices. The proclamation of the remembered words of Jesus and prophetic utterances of the risen Christ were also important. Through all these practices the early congregations "remembered" Jesus' words, received commands, were commissioned, and given the Spirit to heal, teach, prophesy, speak in tongues, and so on. The leaders whose names are recorded in the letters of Paul, as well as many others who are anonymous, participated in all these activities. To recognize the centrality of these corporate practices is to bring to mind the multiple sources of authority within the early communities. While many reconstructions of the missionary movement attribute authority to Paul as founder of churches and to his ongoing correspondence, it is clear that the Spirit granted vision and prophecy to individuals and to the body itself. Authority was highly decentralized. During the first century, some leaders tried to channel and organize this authority into a body of apostolic teaching, passed down through authoritative male figures, and rites of succession and offices, while others resisted the circumscription of Spirit and prophecy.

Authorship became a very important aspect in the development of orthodoxy, but the earliest gospel, the Gospel of Mark, is anonymous. John, also, in its earlier version, may have been anonymous. Ancient liturgical traditions had their origins in the ritual, prayer, and song of the community, and therefore could claim no individual "authorship." These texts are some of the most revered and important in the canon of Paul's letters, the functional canon within the canon, and they are usually called "pre-Pauline" traditions or formulae. A feminist approach to historical reconstruction that focuses on the communities rather than Paul understands authorship in a broader, more communal way. Early traditions that assemblies sung and recited and proclaimed are "owned" by the body of Christ rather than "authored" by one person.

Three important communal texts are preserved in 1 Corinthians 15:3-5, a primitive narrative outline of the gospel, Philippians 2:6-11, a song of Christ, and Galatians 3:28, a fragment of a prayer used at baptism. All these texts have liturgical, communal origins and continue as powerful traditions cited in Paul's letters in his communication with the congregations. These texts function as evidence of living traditions of Christ belief and practice that flourished independently of Paul. They provide access to women's "authorship" and participation as agents in the formation of early Christian creeds and ground belief in the ritual life of the early assemblies.[11]

The earliest creedal account in the New Testament, 1 Corinthians 15:1-8, describes how the "gospel," the *euangelion*, is a tradition that is received by Paul, and proclaimed to others. What Paul "hands over" is a creedal formula that matches the outline of the passion narrative in the Gospels and was likely the pattern the evangelists followed. Introduced with *hoti*, "that," the creed reads:

Christ died for our sins
in accordance with the scriptures,
and that he was buried,
and that he was raised on the third day
in accordance with the scriptures (15:3-4).

Then, as in all the Gospels, a sequence of appearances is narrated. The sequence here may be part of the creed or may be Paul's particular version of appearances of Christ that authorizes leadership for the one receiving the appearance. An appearance to Cephas, Peter, is first, then to the "twelve," and then to "more than five hundred brothers and sisters at one time" (15:6). The magnitude of the appearance is an important piece of evidence for the explosive energy of the risen Christ. The Gospels record nine appearance stories, and the Gospel of John indicates that there are many more not recorded in the book (John 20:30). The fact of the variety of the appearance stories in the Gospels, the testimony in 1 Corinthians of a mass appearance, and the active presence of the Spirit, testify to the likelihood that many claimed ongoing relationship with the risen Christ as authorization for their ministry and speech.[12] The NRSV translation, "brothers and sisters" is more accurate than previous translations (KJV, RSV) that read "brothers" or "brethren."

It is significant that Mary Magdalene is absent from the list of witnesses to Jesus' appearances here in 1 Corinthians 15: 5-8. All of the canonical Gospels include her among the women at the empty tomb who witness to the resurrection of Jesus; and in the Gospel of John, she is the first to receive an appearance of the risen Christ. She is a prominent witness in the longer ending of Mark, and in the *Gospel of Mary Magdalene*, she is depicted as a leader among the disciples. The evidence indicates that there was controversy around her role and a rivalry between those who identified with her and those who claimed Peter as their connection with Jesus.[13] The arrangement of this early list highlights Peter and the twelve and concludes with Paul. Although Mary may be included among "more than five hundred brothers and sisters" or among "all the apostles," she is not explicitly named in this tradition that Paul hands over to the Corinthians.

The baptismal prayer of Galatians 3:27-28 is another key communal tradition that gives evidence of what the early members of these communities proclaimed in the *ekklēsia*: "As many of you as were baptized into Christ have clothed your-selves with Christ. There is no longer Jew or Greek, there is no longer slave or free, there is no longer male and female; for all of you are one in Christ Jesus." Baptism into Christ transforms the major categories that divided up the world in the first century: the distinction between the people of God and those without the law, the relationship of ownership between slave and free, and the separation into male and female described in Genesis 1.[14] As is clear in the other essays in this volume, the meaning and implications of this proclamation for social relations in the assem-blies and beyond are ambiguous and complex. What is evident in the collection of Paul's letters is that the disputes around the relationship between Jew and Gen-tile, between slaves and masters, and between male and female remained contested issues for a long period of time.

The "Christ hymn" in Philippians 2:6-11 proclaims Christ's exaltation over the powers in heaven and on earth and under the earth. The narrative describes one who shares the form of God and who empties himself, takes on slave form, human likeness, including death and crucifixion. This reversal of status from God to slave causes a corresponding transformation from dead on a cross to exalted above all. While the hymn was sung to proclaim liberation and victory by those who were saved by Christ's death, when Paul quotes the hymn, the exhortation draws not on the motif of reversal and transformation but upon the necessity of obedience (2:12-13). The tension between the hymn and its context indicates the different ways of inter-preting the significance of Christ's death in this period and its implications for social relationships in the *ekklēsia* and society.

Feminist reconstruction of the early assemblies tries to imagine what this Spirit-inspired movement of people, trying to live out the resurrection life, was like. The letters give ample evidence about the questions of practice and observance that arose in the communities and that they had to work out by trial and error, argu-ment and consensus. The communities asked: "Who is holy?" They tried to work out what happens to the physical and symbolic markers that distinguish people in this world, *ethnē* or *Ioudaios*, slave and free, male and female. They asked, "What are now boundaries of the community? What is God doing now, and how does it change who we are and what we do?" Feminist reconstruction describes the com-plexity of the conversation about these questions rather than conceiving it as a conflict between Paul and his opponents. It does not equate Paul with orthodoxy and others with heresy by reading back later formulations into the disputes of the letters. As it reconstructs the conversation, feminist reading of Paul recognizes that the controversies around racial, national, and religious divisions, about the relationship of male and female in sexuality and marriage, and around domination of one human being by another in slavery remain unresolved in the present. These powerful texts are drawn into these arguments in contemporary controversies in an effort to persuade, motivate action, and resolve them.

The story of Christian origins has power for many people in the present who identify with it as the founding story of their community. The preceding narrative about this early missionary movement and the establishment and organization of congregations that reflected the values of the gospel emphasizes the presence and agency of women not as objects of instruction but as subjects. Rather than being passive recipients of teaching, women share in the communal authorship of tradition. By foregrounding Romans 16 and 1 Corinthians 14 and 15, feminist reconstruction highlights the corporate missionary movement rather than "Paul's churches." After the death and resurrection of Jesus, communities experienced the Spirit doing deeds of power, provoking prophecy, and bestowing a variety of gifts. Through baptism the Spirit transformed relationships of Jew and Greek, slave and free, male and female. The practical implications of this transformation were contested, and there is evidence of disagreement in the letters of Paul and elsewhere in the New Testament.

The letters of Paul show him in active partnership with his coworkers, both women and men. These women participate in shaping the vision of the gospel. Free women, slave women, Jewish and Gentile women all receive the gospel and interpret it for themselves and their communities. These women, Junia, the apostle, Phoebe, the deacon, Prisca, head of a house assembly, and others, provide models for contemporary Christian women who hear and tell this history. The women prophets in Corinth, who unveil themselves in order to be one in Christ, offer models of resistance to theologies which subordinate and silence them. By adapting feminist practices and putting wo/men at the center of the analysis and reading against the grain of androcentric texts, the task of historical reconstruction creates a new "story."

IDEOLOGICAL CRITICISM

A second important branch of feminist criticism of Paul's letters is not focused on reconstructing history, the events lying behind the text, but on making visible the symbolic and ideological structure of the texts themselves and their effects in the history of reception and interpretation. "Ideology" refers to the system of ideas, values, and symbols that provides a framework in which people understand themselves within the social order. In the history of interpretation of texts about women, for example, readers took for granted the ideology of gender shaping the texts and understood it as "reality" or as divinely given order.

Developing from the observation about the androcentric language of biblical texts mentioned at the beginning of the chapter, this approach shows how the culture and society of the first century gave to the texts their language and metaphors, and these in turn influenced the ways in which readers were able to think and to see. The texts both describe relationships, between husbands and wives, masters and slaves, fathers and sons, Jews and Gentiles, and reflect these relationships in society. They prescribe and envision these relationships in the assemblies in the period of those who read them. It is not simply that the letters in the Pauline tradition advise slaves to obey their masters and wives to obey their husbands. The ideologies of patriarchal marriage and of slavery thoroughly saturate these texts. They are the structural girders of the letters. Rather than being occasional references, patriarchal marriage and slavery are so thoroughly inscribed in the texts that they cannot be simply removed. The authors of the letters assume slave-owning and male domination in marriage, unquestioned features of their culture—they do not need to argue for it. For example, the story of "Adam and Eve" in Genesis 2:15-24 narrates the origin of marriage customs in the society of its time, how it came to be that a man would leave father and mother and cling to his wife. In the history of interpretation and reception, that biblical text gave that relationship between husband, parents, and wife universal significance and embedded it in the structure of divine and human reality. Paul exegetes and applies the Genesis story in 1 Corinthians 11:3-11 when he describes the arrangement of Christ and God, wife and husband: "But I want you to understand that Christ is the head of every man, and the husband is the head of his wife, and God is the head of Christ" (1 Cor. 11:3).

Patriarchal marriage gives Paul categories to "think with" as in the analogy of marriage, death, and remarriage in Romans 7:1-4:[15]

> Do you not know, brothers and sisters—for I am speaking to those who know the law—that the law is binding on a person only during that person's lifetime?

Thus a married woman is bound by the law to her husband as long as he lives; but if her husband dies, she is discharged from the law concerning the husband. Accordingly, she will be called an adulteress if she lives with another man while her husband is alive. But if her husband dies, she is free from that law, and if she marries another man, she is not an adulteress.

> In the same way, my friends, you have died to the law through the body of Christ, so that you may belong to another, to him who has been raised from the dead in order that we may bear fruit for God.

In this passage the obligation of a woman who is married, *hypandros* (literally "under the man"), to her husband is made parallel to the relationship of a person to the law. Death allows her to marry again without censure. The comparison assumes and elaborates upon this particular construction of marriage, adultery, and freedom.

The arrangement of hierarchical subjection of superior to inferior in marriage and in slavery is reflected in the relationship between God and the Son in the final eschatological vision: "When all things are subjected to him, then the Son himself will also be subjected to the one who put all things in subjection under him, so that God may be all in all" (1 Cor. 15:28). In their repetition of such terminologies of subjection, the letters of Paul reinscribe and do not critique this order and are silent on key questions about the role of slaves in the assemblies.[16]

The history of interpretation and commentary on Paul's letters reinforces the power of this symbolic structure in a number of ways. The first is by ignoring it, by making no critique of it whatsoever. The rhetoric of the text is so successful in "naturalizing" the hierarchies of slave and master and wife and husband that the relationships require no comment. Many commentators recognize it but offer an apologetic defense—that modern commentators cannot require first century writers to reflect the enlightened ideals of the present. Commentators who read the text as the direct dictated word of God read such texts positively as prescriptive texts giving women's subordination the status of divine commandment. I will provide a more involved demonstration of a feminist kind of ideological criticism in the section to follow. By making visible the ideology of gender and slavery in the biblical text, the biblical interpreter is able to analyze how it operates in the text and its interpretations, raise critical questions about it, and envision ways to resist or transform it.

FREEDOM PROCLAIMED AND IDEOLOGIES INSCRIBED (ROMANS 8:14-39)

In the following section attention will be given to Romans 8:14-39 in order to illustrate how the feminist strategies of ideological criticism and historical reconstruction would engage the text and to indicate some of the important questions addressed to this text by feminist interpreters. Feminist approaches attempt to be explicit about their own interests and purposes in exegesis and interpretation and to make their commitments visible rather than hiding them. I choose to illustrate a feminist approach with this passage in particular because of the high esteem in which Paul's letter to the Romans is held in Christian history and its primacy within the canon of Paul's letters. Rather than advocating "special interests" and being restricted to particular texts about women, a feminist perspective can be fruitfully integrated into all interpretive approaches and used with the reading of any and all biblical texts. This text affected its ancient readers and moves and shapes the experience of those who read it in the present.

Because of the legacy of silence and subordination of women supported by Paul's letters, I engage this passage because it does not directly address women or slaves, and it is not "about" women and how they should act. Rather it is an ecstatic text that proclaims the liberation of those in Christ and their adoption as children of God. Paul uses the imagery of becoming a free child of God instead of a slave to describe the effects of baptism in Christ. The dramatic contrast between being a "son" and a slave and the image of adoption as children has become a central dynamic in constructions of Pauline theology. Sociologist and public intellectual Orlando Patterson has claimed that Paul gave the West its concept of freedom, and Romans 8:14-25 plays a critical role in his argument.[17] The concluding hymnic passage of Romans 8:31-39 functions as comfort and challenge and as affirmation of life out of death in the funeral and burial liturgies in Catholic, Protestant, Evangelical and Pentecostal churches. For feminist interpreters who read this text as members of faith communities, it is a familiar and significant text. It is important as well for those feminists who study this text in its ancient context and its role in the shaping of Western culture and politics. Using the methods of ideological and cultural criticism, these scholars analyze the way this text and its interpretations continue to shape ideas of gender, family, and society.

In the rhetorical context of Paul's letter to the Romans, Romans 8:14-39 is the climax of the section of the letter that describes life in the Spirit that runs in a series of linked arguments in Romans 5–8, beginning and ending with the motif of hope. The power of sin over the human being is overcome by the gospel of Jesus Christ. The dynamic opposition of life and death is the central contrast of the letter to the Romans and the language of this passage reflects this central opposition. Death defines the old aeon before Christ, and Christ brings life where there was only death. The image of slavery and freedom is mapped onto this central dynamic. The movement of redemption is from death to life, from slavery to freedom. The contrast is shown in the following verses:

> For the law of the Spirit of life in Christ Jesus has set you free from the law of sin and of death (8:2).

> But if Christ is in you, though the body is dead because of sin, the Spirit is life because of righteousness (8:10).

> So then, brothers and sisters, we are debtors, not to the flesh, to live according to the flesh—for if you live according to the flesh, you will die; but if by the Spirit you put to death the deeds of the body, you will live (8:12-13).

Feminist criticism places this text within the historical narrative of the mission-ary movement in the mid first century. The repeated emphasis on the Spirit, the phrase "receiving the Spirit," the images of transformation, including adoption and divine sonship, all suggest baptism as the context of this passage (like Gal. 3:28, above). The center of gravity in the passage is the contrast between the spirit of slavery and the spirit of adoption as children:

> For you did not receive a spirit of slavery to fall back into fear, but you have received a spirit of adoption. When we cry, "Abba! Father!" it is that very Spirit bearing witness with our spirit that we are children of God, and if children, then heirs, heirs of God and joint heirs with Christ—if, in fact, we suffer with him so that we may also be glorified with him (8:15-17).

Commentators debate whether in the language of slavery and freedom in Paul's letters the emphasis lies on freedom or on obedience and subjection. Many see Paul's statement in Romans 8:14-15 as a climactic exclamation in which slave status is replaced with the status of an adopted child. Thus, the freedom asserted in this passage, then, would be harmonious with the freedom from slavery expressed in Galatians 3:28: "no longer slave and free." However, in Romans 6:12-23 the notion of slavery is used to describe sin, and this slavery to sin is opposed to slavery to God or to righteousness. Many assert on the basis of Romans 6:18 that early members of this movement saw no alternative to enslavement—that the human being was always enslaved to one master or another.[18] They use this view to argue against notions of liberation that are unlimited by social responsibility. A feminist approach that reconstructs the diverse positions within the early assemblies dis-putes this view. The controversy around the interpretations of baptism for the rela-tionship of slaves and masters and women and men in the assemblies was debated in the first and second century. Although in developing orthodoxy the argument was resolved to restrict the freedom of wives and of slaves, many maintained the vision of baptismal equality.

The strategy of ideological criticism notes the thoroughgoing kyriarchal imag-ery of sons and slaves, adoption and heirs in this passage. "Kyriarchal" imagery derives from the relationships of ruling and domination of elite men/masters over wo/men. The tapestry of imagery is based on the power of a superior over an inferior and reflects the patriarchal culture of the Roman Empire. Even when it opposed "son" with "slave," the symbol system of slavery and patriar-chy remained unchallenged. The power of this language remains in force and offers potent imagery and rhetoric to those who would use slavery and subordi-nation as the hermeneutical key to the letters, rather than freedom, equality, and democracy.

Feminist scholars debate whether the "sons" who receive "adoption" by God should be interpreted inclusively, as the translation "children" (NRSV) implies, or as a term referring only to male children. Elizabeth Castelli argues in Greco-Roman society it was not the custom for daughters to be adopted and receive rights of inheritance. Therefore Paul's use of "adoption" and "sons" to describe redemption and freedom is androcentric and exclusive language.[19] Sheila McGinn argues in response that for Paul to use "daughters" to speak of those adopted would replicate the same inequity of the society's adoption practices. She argues for an inclusive reading of adoption that is reinforced by the letters' use of the Greek word *tekna*, children, in 8:21.[20] In her analysis of the role of Jesus' sacrifice in Paul's understanding of the relationship of Jews and Gentiles, Pamela Eisenbaum argues that through the sacrifice of God's Son, Jesus, the Gentiles receive the adoption as God's children that the Jews already possess (see also the "Jewish Perspectives" chapter). The adoption as children of God makes sense in a patrilineal system in which the father has the power to incorporate or reject a child into the family.[21] As Paul "uses women to think with" in Romans 7:1-6, so he uses the patrilineal system of inheritance, and the slave-master system.

A feminist approach to this passage notes the dualistic discourses of flesh and spirit in Romans 8:1-13 and the association of life with spirit and death with flesh and the impact of this flesh/spirit dualism on the view of women in Western culture.[22] At the same time Paul's understanding of the interdependence of nature and humanity in the description of the whole cosmos awaiting liberation has been used as a resource for feminist theology of creation.[23] The use of the female experience of labor pains as a metaphor of struggle to describe the groaning of creation (8:22) is also an aspect of Paul's rhetoric that is engaged by feminist interpreters. Beverly Gaventa connects this occurrence of the labor motif with Paul's description of himself as "in labor" in Galatians 4:19 and his reference to himself as a nurse with her children (1 Thess. 2:7) to note Paul's understanding of himself not only as father to the assemblies but also as mother (see also the "Queer Approaches" chapter).[24] Feminist criticism does not simply accept and seek to translate the thought of Paul in Romans 8:14-39, but asks exegetical, literary, social, and theological questions of the text from a feminist perspective. Whatever "authority" the text is to have will be achieved by an energetic process of reading with the text and also reading against the grain.

The strategy of historical reconstruction engages Romans 8:14-39 by foregrounding the agency and leadership of women in the community that produced this text and in the practices in which this text was proclaimed and embodied. As described in the first part of this chapter, the greetings to prominent women and men in Romans 16 indicate the diverse community of the congregation(s) in Rome. Women in the assemblies own and author the exultant acclamation of freedom in crying "Abba" and the assertion that no power can separate them from the love of

God in 8:39. As they sang hymns and prayed in the liturgy of baptism, women were not simply recipients of this text but contributed to creating and proclaiming it. The voices of Junia and Phoebe, Tryphaena and Tryphosa, speak and pray in "sighs too deep for words" (8:26). Those who are suffering and being "killed all day long" (8:36) include Junia, imprisoned with Paul (16:7). A feminist reading of this text, or any in the letters of Paul, chooses lenses for reading that recover the presence and participation of women that are erased by perspectives that assume women's passivity, marginality, or invisibility.

In feminist historical reconstructions and theological accounts, baptism and the prayer in Galatians 3:28 are put in the center of the frame. It is the abolition and transformation of relationships of Jew and Gentile, slave and free, and male and female effected by Jesus' death and resurrection and proclaimed in baptism that provides the prototype for visions of equality and democracy (see also the "African American Approaches" chapter). Feminists exercise imagination and reproclamation in reading Romans 8:14-39. Those who read the text within a faith community ask what a text like this does, what kind of community might it create, and how those who claim this text as their own can reclaim it to work for justice and well-being for all.

CONCLUSIONS AND DIRECTIONS

A feminist critical approach to Paul's letters takes seriously the impact of these texts on the lives of women and men throughout their history of reception in Christian communities and cultures. Because these texts and their readings figure prominently in contemporary political debates, critical engagement with these texts is an urgent ethical matter. Acknowledging the powerful tradition that views the person of Paul as the central authority and focus of debate, the feminist approach sketched here refocuses attention on the variety of metaphors for redemption and for Christian life that people proclaimed in the assemblies, the different impact of the gospel on slave women and men, free women and men, Jewish and Gentile women and men, and the ongoing contestation around the practical way that the gospel would be lived out by these believers.

Analysis of the androcentric language and kyriarchal worldview of Romans and other Pauline letters makes visible the gulf between the hierarchical society assumed by the text and the ideals of equality and mutuality valued by most contemporary interpreters including feminists. Traditional arguments deal with whether Paul preached subordination or equality or whether his rhetoric reflected, inscribed, mimicked, overturned, or subverted imperial language of subjection and conquest (see also the "Postcolonial Approaches" chapter). The feminist approach sketched here does not try to enlist Paul as an ally but recognizes the complex ways that communities negotiate with empire and sees the variety of possible stances of resistance and compromise in the early assemblies. Just as there were multiple sources of authority in the first century assemblies —corporate worship and prayer, ecstatic prophecy, scripture, tradition, apostles and teachers—so there are many elements that contribute to the interpretation of Paul's letters besides a reconstruction of Paul's position. To cross the gulf between Paul's worldview and ours requires an honest encounter and engagement between the democratic ideals of the present and the kyriarchal language and perspectives of the texts. This is the work of a feminist critical approach to Paul.

FURTHER READING

Castelli, Elizabeth A. *Imitating Paul: A Discourse of Power*. Louisville: Westminster John Knox, 1991. Ideological analysis and criticism of Paul's language of imitation.

hooks, bell. *Feminism Is for Everybody: Passionate Politics*. Cambridge: Pluto, 2000. An accessible, but broad introduction to feminisms.

Johnson-DeBaufre, Melanie and Laura S. Nasrallah. "Beyond the Heroic Paul: Toward a Feminist and Decolonizing Approach to the Letters of Paul," in *The Colonized Apostle: Paul Through Postcolonial Eyes*. Edited by Christopher Stanley, 161–74. Minneapolis: Fortress Press, 2011. A recent, but key argument demonstrating why de-centering Paul is vital for feminist and other emancipatory efforts in biblical studies.

Kittredge, Cynthia Briggs. "Rethinking Authorship in the Letters of Paul," in *Walk in the Ways of Wisdom: Essays in Honor of Elisabeth Schüssler Fiorenza*. Edited by Shelly Matthews, Cynthia Briggs Kittredge, and Melanie Johnson-DeBaufre, 318–33. Harrisburg: Trinity Press International, 2003. A proposal to understand early traditions quoted in Paul's letters as authored by women.

Kraemer, Ross Shepard and Mary Rose D'Angelo. *Women and Christian Origins*. New York: Oxford University Press, 1999. A useful collection gathering the research on the roles of women in both historical reconstructions and textual representations, includes several chapters on the ancient contexts and Pauline traditions.

Levine, Amy-Jill and Marianne Blinkenstaff, eds. *A Feminist Companion to Paul*. Cleveland: Pilgrim, 2004. A selection of essays by authors using different feminist perspectives.

Schüssler Fiorenza, Elisabeth. *In Memory of Her: A Feminist Reconstruction of Christian Origins*. London: SCM, 1995. Classic rereading of the evidence and reconstruction of the story of Christian origins.

———. *Wisdom Ways: Introducing Feminist Biblical Interpretation* (Maryknoll: Orbis, 2006). An elaboration of Schüssler Fiorenza's feminist method.

Wire, Antoinette Clark. *The Corinthian Women Prophets: A Reconstruction through Paul's Rhetoric*. Minneapolis: Fortress Press, 1990. A reconstruction of the theology, practice, and self-understanding of women in the community of Corinth.

NOTES

1. bell hooks, *Feminism Is for Everybody: Passionate Politics* (Cambridge: Pluto, 2000), 1.

2. Elisabeth Schüssler Fiorenza, *Wisdom Ways: Introducing Feminist Biblical Interpretation* (Maryknoll: Orbis, 2001), 58.

3. John Barton, *The Nature of Biblical Criticism* (Louisville: Westminster John Knox, 2007).

4. Elizabeth Clark, ed., *Women in the Early Church* (Wilmington: Glazier, 1983).

5. Bernadette J. Brooten, "Junia . . . Outstanding among the Apostles (Romans 16:17)," in *Women Priests*, ed. Leonard S. Swidler and Arlene Swidler (New York: Paulist, 1977), 141-44.

6. See Schüssler Fiorenza, *Wisdom Ways*.

7. Antoinette Clark Wire, *The Corinthian Women Prophets: A Reconstruction through Paul's Rhetoric* (Minneapolis: Fortress Press, 1990).

8. Krister Stendahl, lecture notes, "Biblical Preaching," Harvard Divinity School, 1983.

9. Harry Y. Gamble, *The Textual History of the Letter to the Romans: A Study in Textual and Literary Criticism* (Grand Rapids: Eerdmans, 1977).

10. Elisabeth Schüssler Fiorenza, *In Memory of Her: A Feminist Reconstruction of Christian Origins* (New York: Crossroad, 1983), 160–204.

11. Cynthia Briggs Kittredge, "Rethinking Authorship in the Letters of Paul," in *Walk in the Ways of Wisdom: Essays in Honor of Elisabeth Schüssler Fiorenza*, ed. Shelly Matthews, Cynthia Briggs Kittredge, and Melanie Johnson-DeBaufre (New York: Continuum, 2003), 318–33.

12. Dieter Georgi, *Theocracy in Paul's Practice and Theology* (Minneapolis: Fortress Press, 1991).

13. Jane Schaberg, with Melanie Johnson-Debaufre, *Mary Magdalene Understood* (New York: Continuum, 2008).

14. Wayne A. Meeks, "The Image of the Androgyne: Some Uses of a Symbol in Earliest Christianity," *History of Religions* 13 (1972): 165–208.

15. Elizabeth Castelli, "Romans," in *Searching the Scriptures: A Feminist Commentary*, volume II, ed. Schüssler Fiorenza (New York: Crossroad, 1994), 280–84.

16. Jennifer Glancy, *Slavery in Early Christianity* (Minneapolis: Fortress Press, 2007).

17. Orlando Patterson, *Freedom in the Making of Western Culture* (New York: Basic, 1991), 325–44.

18. For instance, Victor Paul Furnish, *Theology and Ethics in Paul* (Nashville, Abingdon, 1968), 177. See a critique of historicist arguments in Sheila Briggs, "Slavery and Gender," in *On the Cutting Edge: The Study of Women in the Biblical Worlds*, ed. Jane Schaberg, Alice Bach, and Esther Fuchs (New York: Continuum, 2004), 171–92.

19. Elizabeth Castelli, "Romans," 290–291.

20. Sheila E. McGinn, "Feminists and Paul in Romans 8:18-23: Toward a Theology of Creation," in *Gender, Tradition and Romans: Shared Ground, Uncertain Borders*, ed. Cristina Grenholm and Daniel Patte, in Romans through History and Cultures series (New York: T&T Clark, 2005), 32.

21. Pamela Eisenbaum, "A Remedy for Having been Born a Woman," in *Gender, Tradition and Romans*, 123.

22. Castelli, "Romans," 285–86.

23. McGinn, "Feminists and Paul in Romans 8:18-23," 26.

24. Beverly Roberts Gaventa, "Romans," in *The Women's Bible Commentary*, ed. Carol A. Newsom and Sharon H. Ringe (Louisville: Westminster John Knox, 1992), 318.

7

JEWISH PERSPECTIVES

A Jewish *Apostle to the Gentiles*

PAMELA EISENBAUM

Over the last generation, there has been a revolution in Pauline scholarship. Whereas once Paul's letters were seen to contain the signature statement of Christianity's superiority to Judaism, many now read Paul as representing an ongoing attachment to Judaism and thus as displaying no condemnation of his native religion. Whereas once he was perceived to be a convert from Judaism to Christianity, now many see Paul's religious transformation more along the lines of a prophetic call rather than a conversion. If Paul understood himself to be as fully Jewish after his Damascus road experience as before, then presumably he did not reject Judaism as an inferior religion.

The significance of this new trend in Pauline scholarship is profound. Some would argue that Paul is the father of Christian anti-Judaism and, by extension, modern anti-Semitism. No less a thinker than Frederick Nietzsche claimed that Paul, in direct opposition to Jesus' message of love, preached a message of hatred, and furthermore that he "falsified the history of Israel, so as to make it appear a prologue to his mission."[1] More recently, Rosemary Radford Ruether argued that anti-Judaism was inextricably embedded in Paul's proclamation about Jesus.[2] From a post-Holocaust perspective this situation is troubling, to say the least. Therefore, a reading of Paul capable of demonstrating that he did not condemn Judaism, and that he did not reject Jews and replace them with Gentiles, would be welcome to many Christians and perhaps others. As Lloyd Gaston has said, "a Christian church with an anti-Semitic New Testament is abominable."[3]

COMMITMENTS AND GUIDELINES

It is important to understand that reading Paul from a Jewish perspective does not mean the reader must be Jewish. Rather, it first and foremost means the reader is sensitive to the issue of anti-Judaism that has been linked to the interpretation of Paul. Secondly, it means the reader is interested in taking Paul's Jewish identity seriously and perceiving the ways in which Paul thought like a Hellenistic Jew. Thus, anyone with these commitments can read Paul from a Jewish perspective.

In order to gain an understanding of this new orientation to Paul and utilize it in exegeting Paul, one needs to be aware of several starting assumptions:

> *Paul did not convert from Judaism to Christianity; he is as Jewish after his Damascus road experience as before.*

> *Interpretation of Paul's letters must be predicated on a fair and histori-cally plausible picture of ancient Judaism.*

> *Paul's rhetoric is directed to Gentiles. Most of Paul's seeming condemna-tions of Jewish law are really admonitions specifically to Gentiles not to feel compelled to observe Jewish law.*

> *Paul has an apocalyptic orientation, and that is why he is adamant that Gentiles must not practice Jewish law.*

> *Jesus saves, but he only saves Gentiles.*

Following the order enumerated above, I will briefly address each of these.

Paul Is as Jewish after His Damascus Road Experience as Before

Although it may seem obvious to many, it still needs to be stated: Paul is Jewish—that is his religious identity. Christianity had not yet been invented. The term "Christianity" does not appear until a generation after Paul, and Christianity was not yet its own religion. Obviously, there were those who followed Jesus, but things had not yet institutionalized into a distinctive religion. Paul refers to himself as a Jew, not as description of his past but as description of his present (Gal. 2:15; Phil. 3:4-6; 2 Cor. 11:22). Some have said that Paul regards himself as ethnically but not religiously Jewish. In antiquity, however, there really is no such clear distinc-tion. [4] To be sure, Judaism at this time is becoming a religion one can convert to—one need not be born Jewish to become Jewish—but becoming Jewish also meant becoming part of the lineage of Abraham and, therefore, the Jewish people. Ancient Judaism may be best thought of as an ethno-religion.[5]

Because they have seen Paul as a convert who rejected Judaism and embraced Christianity, Christian interpreters have read Paul's letters, especially Romans and Galatians, as if their primary message were to offer a critique of Judaism per se, and thus provide an explanation of Paul's conversion. But if the starting assumption is that Paul is as Jewish after his encounter with the resurrected Jesus as before, and that he is not some sort of "marginal Jew,"[6] then by definition rejection of Judaism cannot be the message of the letters. Paul neither rejected his Judaism nor did he think Christianity was a replacement for Judaism, and his teachings do not constitute a wholesale critique of Jewish faith and practice.

Interpretation of Paul's Letters Must Be Predicated on a Fair and Historically Plausible Picture of Ancient Judaism

The traditional understanding of Paul is predicated on a fundamental misunderstanding of Judaism. In particular there are two characterizations of Judaism that have pervaded the study of Paul and caused the distortion of his writings: that Judaism was legalistic and that Jews were extremely insular and exclusive in the conception of their religion.

Judaism was presumed to be a religion of "works," which meant that Jews believed they had to earn God's grace by doing various "works"—fulfilling commandments of the Torah. The whole religion was structured on doing these works, regardless of any intention and seemingly devoid of any spiritual dimension. Pharisaic Judaism in particular did indeed proliferate legal obligations, going beyond the written Torah, and developing something that became known as the "Oral Torah," considered to be virtually as binding as the written Torah. But in the Christian imagination, these laws constituted minor preoccupations with technical rituals that distracted people from what was truly important. (To a large degree, the portrayal of the Pharisees in the Gospels reflects this view. See Mark 7:1-13; Matt. 15:1-9 and 23:23-26.) Moreover, according to Christian perception, Jews must keep each and every law perfectly in order to win God's approval. Jewish tradition was seen to be a merit system in which the object was to "score points" with God. This form of religion was seen to be oppressive. No less an influential figure than Rudolf Bultmann described Judaism this way: "that sanctity was an entirely negative affair, since most of the regulations were negative and prohibitive in character. . . . To take them seriously meant making life an intolerable burden. It was almost impossible to know the rules, let alone put them into practice."[7] Pauline Christianity was then seen to be the liberation from this oppressive religion, because Christianity was the religion of pure faith.

In addition to legalism, Judaism was seen to suffer from another problem: particularity and exclusivism. While Christianity was (apparently) a universal religion because it transcended people's regional and ethnic identity and reached out to everyone in a broadly spiritual way, Judaism was particular in that it was very inward looking, even xenophobic, with a tendency toward maintaining strict ethnic boundaries, making it an exclusive club. Its rituals were seen to be specifically Jewish, while Christianity required little beyond having faith in Christ, and thus it could transcend all cultural specificity, at least theoretically. (That is why many Protestant theologians historically have seen Christianity as the most evolved form of religion.) Torah observance was understood as creating a barrier between Jews and Gentiles. Dietary laws, for example, keep Jews from sharing meals with non-Jews, and are thus a way of restricting social intercourse. Circumcision creates an indelible mark on the body that distinguishes Jew (at least Jewish men) from Gentile. Baptism, by contrast, was seen to be a universal and easily accessible ritual. Presumably, when Paul was a Pharisee he had virtually no contact with Gentiles and would have even considered them impure. Along with his conversion to Christianity, however, came his realization that all people are equal before God and this caused him to open up and reach out to Gentiles. Paul could never have achieved this realization while still within the bounds of Judaism, because, so the thinking goes, Jews understood themselves to be specially elected, enjoying a special covenant with God which could never be extended to others.

Both of these features of Judaism are greatly exaggerated, and they constitute gross distortions. They are due to Christian stereotyping and have little to do with historical reality. In general, ancient Jews did not understand being Torah-observant to mean that they were to attend to every jot and tittle, as if every individual prescription represented a divine imperative of the highest order. Unfortunately, there is not space here to lead the reader through a tour of Judaism in the first century; I have offered an overview of Judaism elsewhere,[8] and there are many good introductions to ancient Judaism (see, for instance, the Further Reading list). Jewish practices are the ways in which Jews believed they were enacting the will of God—Torah observance is in fact the way in which Jews expressed their faith in God. To be sure, there were some small groups of Jews who did display a special devotion to fulfilling the commandments—like the Pharisees—but their motivation was not fear that God would punish them for breaking each individual commandment no matter how small. Their motivation was the desire to sanctify their everyday life so as to live in the presence of God. In fact, the Pharisees took on the practice of many purity laws as an implicit critique of the Jewish priesthood and temple establishment. By observing all the purity laws, including those originally reserved exclusively for priests, the Pharisees were democratizing Judaism—anyone who observed these laws had the same access to God as the priest who served in the temple. Although Protestant theology, based on an interpretation of Paul, came to see faith and works as opposites of one another, that binary division would not have been conceivable to ancient Jews (or, for that matter, modern Jews). Faithfulness to the covenant, which meant faithfulness to the commandments laid out in the covenant, was the way in which God had instructed the children of Israel to demonstrate their faithfulness to God.

Moreover, with a few small exceptions, Jews had the same kinds of interactions with non-Jews that most other ethnic groups had during the Greco-Roman period. Jews of the diaspora spoke Greek, had Greek names, did business with Gentiles, and many of them seem to have intermarried. Conversion to Judaism also came to be a relatively common practice—many different ancient Jewish texts speak of converts favorably, including Philo and Josephus. The Pharisees, too, accepted converts, and several passages in the Mishnah, the first codified work of rabbinic law, prescribe rules for how to treat converts to Judaism, providing ample evidence that non-Jews were not excluded from becoming a member of Israel if they chose to worship the God of Abraham.

Paul's Rhetoric Is Directed toward Gentiles

This may be the single most important aspect in order to avoid reading Paul as anti-Jewish. Paul's primary identity is as apostle to the Gentiles. As he says at the opening of Romans: "Paul, a servant of Jesus Christ, called to be an apostle, set apart for the gospel of God . . . to bring about the obedience of faith among all the Gentiles for the sake of his name, including you yourselves, who are called to belong to Jesus Christ" (Rom. 1:1-6). There are many other texts to which we could point where Paul explicitly indicates that his mission is to Gentiles (like Rom. 11:13; 15:18; and Gal. 2:9).

The reason this is important is because it means that whatever Paul says applies specifically to Gentiles. For example, in Galatians, Paul says "if you let yourselves be circumcised, Christ will be of no benefit to you" (Gal. 5:2). If we take this to be a generic statement applicable to everyone, the claim is that circumcision and Christ are mutually exclusive. Traditional Christian interpretation of this statement and others similar to it in the Pauline corpus were taken to mean that Paul condemns not only circumcision but Torah observance in general. Observance of any kind of ritual commandments from the Torah has become obsolete. Put another way, the covenant between God and Israel has now been abrogated, and whatever privileges Jews enjoyed as party to the covenant have now been revoked. As Paul says in Romans 10:4 (according to the NRSV translation), "Christ is the end of the law." Furthermore, circumcision is regarded as a "work," and Paul's message is understood to be that one is justified *by faith*, not by works. Thus, to practice Jewish law constitutes an act of faithlessness in what God has done in Christ, according to the traditional understanding. Circumcision no longer serves as the rite that makes one a child of God; it has been replaced with baptism.

If we keep in mind, however, that Paul is speaking to Gentiles, then Paul's claim applies only to Gentiles. Paul is saying that *Gentiles* should not be circumcised, not that circumcision is an inherently defective or obsolete practice. Christ has provided an alternative to Torah observance for Gentiles. Paul's remarks in Galatians 5 do not address the observance of Torah by Jews. Although he never explicitly directs Jewish followers of Jesus to continue observing Jewish law, implicit in his letters is the assumption that Jews would continue circumcising their sons and observing the law. Paul certainly never condemns Jews' observation of Torah, never advocates their abstaining from circumcision.

Indeed, in 1 Corinthians 7:19-20, Paul says, "Circumcision is nothing, and uncircumcision is nothing; but obeying the commandments of God is everything. Let each of you remain in the condition in which you were called." This verse has puzzled many interpreters. Why would Paul say that circumcision is irrelevant and then say that the commandments of God mean everything? Is not circumcision a commandment? By reading this text from a Jewish perspective, it is really quite simple: Paul understands that Jews are commanded to be circumcised (see Gen. 17:10-12), but Gentiles are not commanded to be circumcised. Therefore, by circumcising their sons, Jews are obeying Torah, and by not circumcising their sons, Gentiles are also obeying Torah.

Most negative statements Paul makes about Jewish law can be explained simply by being aware of Paul's Gentile audience, as I demonstrated above with Galatians 5:2. Another instance appears in Galatians 2:21: "I do not nullify the grace of God; for if justification comes through the law, then Christ died for nothing." If we assume that he is addressing the justification of Gentiles, then Paul is not claiming that the law is inherently useless for achieving justification before God. He is claiming that the death and resurrection of Jesus have achieved justification specifically for Gentiles, thus there is no reason that they must live a Torah-observant life; in fact, to observe the commandments of the Torah is a denial of what has been accomplished in the Christ event—that's why it is a problem; that's why Paul describes Gentile Torah-observance as faithlessness.

The important thing to understand is that Paul's negative statements about the law can be explained as being admonitions specifically against Gentiles undertaking circumcision or other practices in which they are attempting to become Jews or are acting like Jews.[9] It is not the case that Paul is condemning Jewish practice or arguing against the legitimacy of Judaism per se.

In addition, one should be aware that Paul's opponents—those Paul is often arguing against in his letters—are most likely other Jewish followers of Jesus or perhaps Gentile followers who are advocating Jewish practice. They are not simply Jews trying to convert Paul's congregants to Judaism, which is traditionally how interpreters perceived the rhetorical situation. Thus, the argument Paul is having, especially in his letter to the Galatians, is with a different vision of what it means to follow Jesus. It is not an argument between Judaism and Christianity. It is an argument with those who have a different vision of the role of the law for Gentile Jesus followers.

Paul Has an Apocalyptic Orientation, and That Is Why He Is Adamant That Gentiles Must Not Practice Jewish Law

Paul believes that the world is in the process of being redeemed. Christ's resurrection signaled to him that the end was near. Resurrection was not something that happened to one person at a time; it was envisioned as a collective experience, one that preceded the final judgment. In any case, the apostle believes he is living at the end of history, and he understands the end of history in terms of traditions found in the prophets, specifically the tradition commonly known as the ingathering of the nations. The vision of the end time found in Isaiah, Micah, Zechariah, and others is of the nations streaming to Jerusalem to worship the one God, the God of Israel. The very texts in Isaiah and Micah that speak of beating swords into plowshares and the age of eternal peace envision all the nations streaming to the "house of the God of Jacob; that he may teach us his ways and that we may walk in his paths" (Isa. 2:2-4; Mic. 4:1-3).

Paul, in other words, understands that he is at the beginning of this culminating moment in history. Indeed, he believes his mission is to help inaugurate this event by drawing the Gentiles in—not literally going to Jerusalem but turning them from their worship of idols to a recognition of the one, true God, and thus integrating them into the family of God. Furthermore, Paul believes that the ingathering of the nations constitutes the fulfillment of the promise to Abraham that all the nations would be blessed through him (Gen. 12:3; 18:18). In order to achieve the realization of this promise, Gentiles cannot become Jews. Undergoing circumcision, which is the signature mark of Jewish identity, would effectively turn Gentiles into Jews, and would not, therefore, constitute a fulfillment of God's promise to Abraham and the prophetic vision of the ingathering of the nations.

Paul believes he is helping God fulfill these eschatological (or end times) promises. This is why he is reaching out to Gentiles, and drawing them to God, but self-consciously not turning them into Jews. It is not because he hates or rejects Judaism or any such thing. It is, rather, because Paul is drawing on a classical Jewish vision of the end times, in which Gentiles are redeemed—*as Gentiles.*[10] To be sure, other Jews might not agree with Paul that it is the end of time, time for the Gentiles to be redeemed, but they would not necessarily argue with the legitimacy of the vision itself.

Jesus Saves, but He Saves Only Gentiles

This is the most controversial feature on the list. There are interpreters who would support the claims about Paul's ongoing Jewish identity, that he did not see Jesus as a replacement for Judaism, that his negative comments about law are really exclusively directed at Gentiles, and so on, but who would adamantly oppose the claim that Paul thinks Jews have no need of the saving power of Jesus' death.

Nevertheless, there is a growing number of scholars, myself among them, who would argue that what was accomplished by Jesus' death was the reconciliation of *Gentiles* to God, and that that is all Paul ever claimed Jesus accomplished. In other words, Jesus' death is not intended for the salvation of the whole world but rather just for the salvation of Gentiles. The thinking goes something like this: Jews enjoyed a long-standing covenant with God, a covenant embodied in the Torah. If we follow this new paradigm of a fully Jewish Paul who never rejected Judaism or found it lacking, then it cannot be that Paul views Jesus as having come to "fix" something that was wrong with Judaism. Paul did not have a problem with Jews, Judaism, or Jewish law. Rather, his problem was what to do about the Gentiles who had not had the benefit of Jewish law.

As already mentioned, the observance of Torah was not thought of by Jews as a burden but a privilege. The performance of commandments was regarded as an expression of the people Israel's faithful participation in the covenant. God's covenant with Israel was everlasting. Even if Israel was disobedient, God would not withdraw from the covenant—God would discipline Israel but not abandon her. The point here is that Jews did not exist in a state of alienation from God. The covenant between God and Israel ensured that Jews were always in a relationship with their God. And perfect performance of commandments was not necessary—in fact, it was not even assumed. A good portion of the Torah addresses transgressions. What's to be done when someone defrauds her neighbor? Or commits adultery? Or doesn't render an appropriate sacrifice? Many prescriptions in the Torah, in other words, are prescriptions about how to atone for one's sins. For sins against God, certain kinds of sacrifices are required. For sins against one's neighbor, compensation may be required or in some cases punishment. The Torah as a whole is viewed as the complete expression of God's law. Thus, the observance of Torah meant that Israel enjoyed a special status as a holy nation, set apart from the other nations.

Precisely because Gentiles did not have the benefit of Torah, they are not in relationship with God—that is why they are in need of redemption. The problem is Gentiles have been worshipping other Gods and have not been part of the covenant, and therefore they have not known God. Moreover, because Gentiles have not been part of the covenant, they have not had any means to atone for the their sin. Hence it has accumulated.[11]

Jesus is the answer to the accumulated debt of sin that Gentiles suffer. Paul believes the end of the world as we know it is imminent, which means the final judgment is imminent. That final moment of accountability spells certain doom for Gentiles. They will be condemned as wicked. But Jesus is the answer to this problem. Jesus' death vicariously and in one fell swoop atones for their accumulated sin. In Paul's theology, Jesus' death is surely a saving event, but it is not everyone that needs saving, only Gentiles.

GOD'S PROMISE TO ABRAHAM TO SAVE THE GENTILES (GALATIANS 3:6-14)

Paul's letter to the Galatians, where the famous doctrine of justification by faith is prominent, is also widely considered to contain the most anti-Jewish rhetoric of his writings. Because Paul contrasts justification by faith with justification by works of the law, and because the latter is usually understood as a shorthand way of speaking of Jewish practice, Galatians has often been read as an attack on Judaism. Moreover, it is in Galatians that Paul tells us about his religious transformation when he encountered the risen Jesus, which is taken to be the story of Paul's conversion. And the story of Paul's conversion is the story of his rejection of Judaism.

But as many scholars have shown in recent years, Galatians is not some sort of attack on Judaism, certainly not Judaism in general. The primary argument Paul makes in Galatians is that the Galatians, who are Gentiles, should not undergo circumcision. The situation that prompted Paul writing seems to be that other traveling, Jesus-following missionaries had come through Galatia sometime after Paul had missionized them (apparently successfully), and taught them that, in order to be fully "in Christ," they would need to be circumcised.[12] Circumcision is the sign of the covenant between God and Abraham, and if they wanted to become part of the people who enjoy this special covenant with God, they would have to be circumcised.[13] Paul argues vehemently against this position. He calls the teaching of these other missionaries "another gospel" (1:6-7). For Paul, Christ has rendered circumcision unnecessary for Gentiles.

For traditional interpreters, Paul's argument was taken to mean that circumcision for anyone is no longer necessary since the coming of Jesus. (Indeed, Christian interpreters from Justin Martyr to Martin Luther argued that the practice of circumcision by Jews was in direct defiance of God's will, precisely because of Paul's teachings, or at least how they understood his teaching to his followers in Galatia. The church fathers argued that baptism into Christ had replaced circumcision.) For modern interpreters sensitive to a Jewish perspective on Paul, the apostle's argument is understood as directed specifically to Gentiles. In other words, Paul has no "beef" with Jews who continue to circumcise their sons; his only concern is with Gentiles who, even after having accepted Jesus, wish to undertake circumcision.

In chapters 1–2, Paul lays the groundwork for the case he wants to make, but in chapter 3 he really gets going, and one could justifiably claim that 3:6-14 is the heart of Paul's argument. It is in this section that Paul takes up the figure of Abraham. The apostle's argument here is complicated—as is often the case—so it is worth going through it with some care. I will initially cite each section from the NRSV, but, because the NRSV itself is so embedded in the traditional paradigm for interpreting Paul, I will sometimes offer my own translation as part of my analysis.

> *"Just as Abraham 'believed God, and it was reckoned to him as righteousness,' so you see, those who believe are the descendents of Abraham"*
> *(vv. 6-7).*

Just as he mentions Abraham for the first time in the letter, he quotes scripture, specifically Genesis 15:6. This is a very important verse for Paul; it plays a key role not only in this letter, but also in Romans (ch. 4). Like most any Jew of his day, scripture is absolutely central for Paul, and so it is no surprise that he frequently appeals to it for evidence in making his case; in this section of Galatians, though, he relies on it heavily. For Jewish interpreters, including Paul, each and every word of scripture matters; nothing is superfluous. Thus it is no surprise that Paul highlights this verse precisely because of two words, "believed" and "righteousness." Both of these words are significant for Paul.

The English word rendered "believed" in this verse is a translation of the Greek verb *pisteuō*. In Greek there is an etymological relationship between the verb *pisteuō* and the noun *pistis*—they are in fact the same word, one is in the form of a verb and the other in the form of a noun. But in English the word *pistis* is typically translated as "faith," while the verb *pisteuō* is typically translated "to believe," since there is no verbal form of the word "faith." Paul's interest in this very word (in both its nominal and verbal form) will become clear in the verses that follow. For now, I simply want to point out that one could translate the verb *pisteuō* as "to have faith"—"faith" in the sense of "trust"—rather than "to believe." As I said earlier, Jews of the first century did not think that having faith and doing works were two wholly different things in which one was good and one was bad. Instead of assuming that Paul speaks from a Christian perspective, rather than a Jewish one—let us start with the assumption that he is a typical Jew.[14] There is nothing in these verses that would lead us to believe that Paul is contrasting faith or belief with works.

The word translated in this passage as "righteousness" is the same word as appears in Galatians 2:21, *dikaiosynē*, where it is translated "justification." The importance of Genesis 15:6 to Paul is that the verse links the word "faith" (*pistis/pisteuō*) with righteousness/justification (*dikaiosynē*), and links both of these to Abraham. Paul will subsequently claim that Abraham is the ancestor of Gentiles as well as Jews (Gal. 3:14, 29), and that this connection to Abraham benefits Gentiles, just like it does Jews. The benefit Paul is concerned with here is that God will reckon righteous Gentiles by virtue of their participation in the lineage of Abraham, and that participation gets "activated" by Jesus, as we shall see later in the passage.

> *"And the scripture, foreseeing that God would justify the Gentiles by faith, declared the gospel beforehand to Abraham, saying 'All the Gentiles shall be blessed in you.' For this reason, those who believe are blessed with Abraham who believed" (vv. 8-9).*

Now Paul appeals to another verse from the Abraham story, Genesis 12:3 (see also Gen. 18:18, 22:18), sometimes translated as "All the *nations* shall be blessed in you," because the Greek word *ethnē* can mean either Gentiles or nations. It is variously translated depending on the context, not just in Paul but in Greco-Jewish writings broadly speaking, including the Septuagint. Here "Gentiles" is a good choice because Paul's concern is specifically with Gentiles. No one would argue about whether or not Jews are the heirs of their ancestral patriarch, Abraham. The question is whether Gentiles, by becoming followers of Jesus, are now also heirs of the promises to Abraham, because the quotation, "All the Gentiles shall be blessed in you," is one of the promises God makes to Abraham. Paul will come back to this promise in verse 14, the culmination of our section, so this verse is in some ways the core of Paul's argument in this passage. Indeed, Paul introduces this verse by saying "scripture . . . declared the gospel beforehand," implying that this verse contains the gospel. We will see why at the end of the passage.

Verse 9 offers an interpretation of the scripture. Again, the NRSV translates the verb *pisteuō* as "believe," rather than "have faith," implying the contrast between "faith" and "works" is operative here, even though Paul does not explicitly make that opposition here. The NRSV rendering of this verse is a freer translation than is typical. A more literal translation would be "So that those from faith are blessed with the faithful Abraham." The words I have translated "those from faith" have been a matter of some debate. In Greek it looks like this: *hoi ek pisteōs*. Some scholars have argued that what Paul means here is really "those descended from faith."[15] Prepositions are notoriously difficult to translate because they function very flexibly, but one common usage of *ek* is as a marker of genealogical descent, especially when the word before it refers to a person or group of people. In Philippians 3:5, where Paul describes his identity as being "a member of the people of Israel . . .

a Hebrew born of Hebrews" (*ek genous Israēl Hebraios ex Hebraiōn*),[16] the construction is similar to what we have in Galatians 3:9. Therefore, what Paul most likely means in v. 9 is that those who are counted as descendants of Abraham are blessed because of the faith of Abraham. In other words, Abraham's heirs enjoy God's favor not because they did anything to earn it, but because they benefit from Abraham's faithful actions, which resulted in a covenant with God, a covenant that scripture says explicitly extends to Abraham's descendants (see Gal. 3:16). Perhaps the best reason to understand this text in terms of genealogical descent is that Paul has, in fact, already used the expression "those descended from faith" in verse 7, and there he explicitly uses it genealogically to say that "those descended from faith" *are the sons of Abraham.* (This is masked in the NRSV which reads "those who believe are the descendants of Abraham.")

The quotation from Genesis 12:3, which claims that Gentiles are blessed because of Abraham, is scriptural proof that it is not just Jews who are descended from Abraham but Gentiles as well. Elsewhere in Genesis, God's promise to Abraham takes a slightly different form: "You shall be the father of many nations" (Gen. 17:4). Jews and Gentiles are kin through Abraham, so both are part of the family of Abraham, and that means both share the benefit of God's promises. As we shall see, it is Christ who enabled the realization of the promise that the Gentiles would be blessed through Abraham.

The rest of the passage is best taken as a unit.

> "For all who rely on works of the law are under a curse; for it is written, 'Cursed is everyone who does not observe and obey all things written in the book of the law.' Now it is evident that no one is justified before God by the law; for 'The one who is righteous will live by faith.' But the law does not rest on faith; on the contrary, 'Whoever does the works of the law will live by them.' Christ redeemed us from the curse of the law by becoming a curse for us—for it is written, 'Cursed is everyone who hangs on a tree'—in order that in Christ Jesus the blessing of Abraham might come to the Gentiles, so that we might receive the promise of the Spirit through faith" (vv. 10-14).

The first thing that must be observed in verse 10 is that, where the NRSV translates "all who rely on the works of the law," the Greek uses the same expression as verse 9 discussed above, *hoi ek pisteōs*, only instead of "those descended from faith" we have "those descended from works of the law." Paul could mean Jews, because all Jews are presumably part of the Mosaic covenant—this is how the phrase has traditionally been understood. But I suspect Paul is speaking more theoretically. With "those descended from works of the law" he creates an expression parallel to "those descended from faith" for rhetorical purposes. This group is a kind of fiction—it is what the Galatians will become if they undergo circumcision, because, if even after accepting Christ they feel the need to become circumcised, then they have not realized the significance of Christ. They would be putting more faith in the laws given at Sinai than in the promise to Abraham and its fulfillment in the death and resurrection of Jesus, which is exactly what Paul says in the next passage (see Gal. 3:17-18).

Paul is adamant that Gentiles not undergo circumcision, that they not take on the mantle of the Torah (see 5:2-4). The reasons for this are more easily seen in other texts besides this one. Suffice to say here that the reason lies with Paul's apocalyptic perspective. Since Paul believes he is seeing the end of history, he is guided by the prophetic tradition that all the nations (=Gentiles) will turn from their idols and worship the one true God, the God of Israel, a tradition commonly known as the ingathering of the nations.[17] The apostle believes this vision is coming to fruition. Although he does not cite from the prophets in this passage (as he does in another ingathering passage in Romans 9–10), Paul understands the prophecy about the ingathering of the nations as closely connected with the promise to Abraham that all the nations will be blessed through him, which he has just cited in verse 8.

Now then, in these few verses, Paul cites four different scriptural quotations (Deut. 27:26; Lev. 18:5; Hab. 2:4; Deut. 21:23) and weaves them together to form an argument. The first is from Deuteronomy 27:26; in its original context it appears in a long string of curses and blessings that are part of the covenant between Israel and God. It is obviously a curse upon any member of the covenant who does not observe the commandments. One needs to note that Paul is not claiming that the Torah itself is a curse; the curse is upon those who do *not* follow the command-ments.[18] As already discussed, the context of the letter to the Galatians is that other missionaries have taught the Galatians that they need to undergo circumcision, just like Abraham did when he accepted God's covenant. Paul says later in the letter that undergoing circumcision means that one is then obligated to keep the whole Torah, for circumcision is the mark of conversion to Judaism, and taking on that identity means taking on the obligation to observe the Torah (Gal. 5:3). This is a typical Jewish view. Gentiles are not obligated to observe the Torah—that is what Jews do. Jews believed it was a privilege to observe the Torah, but such observance did not "earn" one salvation. Thus, the apostle is telling the Galatians that, if they circumcise themselves, they commit themselves to live by an entirely different set of rules and must be prepared for the consequences if they don't. The law contains the threat of curses for disobedience, and that is disadvantageous compared to the unconditional blessing they have in Christ.[19]

Verse 11 is a tricky one. When he says "no one is justified" by the law, it sounds as though Paul is making a critique of the law *in general*. He seems to be saying that Torah is inadequate for justification—for anyone, Jew or Gentile. If we wish to remain consistent with the Jewish perspective adopted here, there are two possible ways to explain what Paul is saying here. One possibility is that when Paul says "no one," he means "no Gentile." In other words, he is not speaking generically of the whole human race but speaking only of the group to which his audience belongs: Gentiles. People frequently speak in general terms when they in fact mean them to apply only within the specific context. If a parent, angry at her two children, says "No one is leaving this house tonight," she no doubt means the children, not everyone in the world.

Another possibility is that Paul literally does mean this to be a categorical statement—*no one* is justified. . . . But the claim that no one is justified by the law is probably not as radical as it sounds. While performing God's commandments was understood as part of being a righteous person, and not doing them meant you were a wicked person, the commandments do not lead to moral perfection. Some claim that what is wrong with the law for Paul is that no one can ever keep every single commandment perfectly all the time, and therefore if one is only "under the law," one can never be anything more than a sinner, not justified in the eyes of God and destined for divine condemnation.[20] But the special status Israelites enjoyed derived not from their own meritorious deeds in observing Torah. Rather it is the other way around. God makes a covenant with Israel, bestowing upon her divine favor, and, as a result, the Israelites serve God by performing the commandments.[21] They do not get "kicked out" of the covenant by failing to keep each and every commandment; they may get punished, but not banished. The curses of Deuteronomy entail drought, infertility, and so on, but not complete dissolution of the covenant. And in no sense is there an expectation that the slightest slip-up results in eternal damnation. Wickedness means repeated, willful acts of disobedience. As discussed earlier, the covenant itself includes processes for atonement, the assumption being that people make mistakes.

The point here is that when Paul says "no one is justified before God by the law," Paul means justification in the sense of having a special relationship with God, which in turn will lead to eternal life. But that special relationship with God is one God initiates, whether it was through the initiation of the covenant with Israel or with the death and resurrection of Jesus. In either case it is a gift from God, an act of grace, not a reward or a wage paid for services rendered.[22] This theology of grace Paul advocates is not, however, a deviation from the mainstream Jewish view at the time, but a reflection of it. So when Paul quotes Habakkuk 2:4, "The one who is righteous shall live by faith," he is claiming that what matters is being faithful in the sense of trusting God, that God will deliver on God's promises.

Paul appears to be contrasting the quotation from Habakkuk with the terse statement in verse 12: "But the law does not rest on faith."[23] What does Paul mean by this remark? It is likely that the word "faith" here is a shorthand way to speak of Jesus or at least what Jesus has accomplished through his faith, that is, his faithful obedience in going to his death (see Phil. 2). In other words, it is not that the law is bad because it has nothing to do with faith per se. Rather, he is saying that what Jesus accomplished through faith renders it unnecessary for Gentiles to follow. So when Paul quotes Leviticus 18:5 ("Whoever does the works of the law will live by them"), he is articulating the mutual exclusivity of Christ and Torah *for Gentiles.* The Jew lives through the covenant of Torah; the Gentile has no need of Torah because of Jesus.

In verse 13, Paul hooks back in with where he began this section of the letter. Jesus has taken on "the curse of the law" by becoming accursed.[24] In Deuteronomy 21:23, Paul finds a text that connects the "curse" to crucifixion. Recall that in verse 10 Paul quoted Deuteronomy 27:26, which says that those who do not observe the law are cursed. Gentiles are by definition those who do not observe the law, so they are threatened by the curse. Technically, the curse was intended for those who had signed on to the Mosaic covenant, namely, Jews. But the Galatians are considering doing just that by circumcising themselves.

Paul comes to his ultimate point in verse 14 when he says that the blessing of Abraham has come to the Gentiles. Paul wants his audience to realize that they became part of the family of Abraham when they were baptized in Christ. As he says later in the same chapter, "If you belong to Christ, then you are Abraham's offspring, heirs according to the promise" (3:29). Just as Abraham's descendants reap the benefits of Abraham's faithfulness by virtue of simply being part of the Abrahamic family, so Jesus' faithfulness on the cross benefits those who are in Christ. In ancient Judaism, just as in Judaism today, there is something called "the merit of the fathers." The merit of the fathers is the idea that the people Israel enjoy God's favor because of the faithfulness of the patriarchs, especially Abraham, with whom God had a very special relationship. The primary reason the covenant was understood to be everlasting was because it was not dependent on the present and future performance of Israel, but on the merit of Abraham.[25] The people might be disobedient, sometimes egregiously so, but God promised that the covenant would be everlasting.

As we discussed earlier, Paul believes he lives at the end of history, the time for the ingathering of the nations. Abraham was widely regarded as the founding patriarch of the Jews. But God had also promised that the patriarch would be the father of *many nations* (Gen. 17:4-5; 22:18). Since God always fulfills God's promises, that promise must be fulfilled before the end of time. Paul thinks that fulfillment is happening because Christ has initiated the process. Paul, the apostle to the Gentiles, understands his mission as bringing the Gentiles into the family of Abraham through Christ. In verse 8, when Paul quoted Genesis 12:3—God's promise that all the nations would be blessed in Abraham—he introduced the citation by saying "the scripture . . . declared the gospel beforehand to Abraham." In other words, Abraham received "the gospel" that "announced the full inclusion of all people in the people of God."[26]

CONCLUSION

Paul did not reject his Judaism; he embraced a form of apocalyptic Judaism, triggered by an experience of the resurrected Jesus. Since resurrection was not something that happened one person at a time but, rather, collectively at the end of time, Paul thinks Jesus is just the "first fruits" of the general resurrection—that is why he is expecting the end of the world. Paul did not convert from Judaism to Christianity, but he *did change his mind about what time it was in history.* And once he made that change, certain associations connected with classical Jewish eschatology came to the fore, one of which was the tradition of the ingathering of the nations (an inclusive, not exclusive, tradition). Whatever else it was, the apostle's experience of Jesus was a commissioning for him to assist in bringing about this momentous event. Hence, Paul turned his attention to Gentiles to gather them into the bosom of Abraham and help God realize God's promises to the patriarch.

There are at least two distinct benefits to reading Paul from a Jewish perspective. First, a reading that attends to the "Jewishness" at the heart of the apostle's teachings deconstructs the centuries-long bias against the validity of Judaism and Torah observance that has pervaded Christian biblical interpretation and theology—a bias that to a large degree is rooted in the interpretation of Paul. Second, the prophetic tradition of the ingathering of the nations, and the way Paul employed the tradition, is one that can speak to the issue of religious pluralism in constructive ways. Paul's message is not only one of inclusion, it is a vision of inclusion that recognizes the legitimacy of difference. When we read Paul's (rather strident) admonitions against the practice of Jewish law, and we realize that his position is only against Gentiles observing Jewish law, then a text that was once read as an attack on Judaism now becomes a text about respecting difference! Gentiles should not be compelled, or feel compelled, to "become Jews" in order to become part of Abraham's family. At the same time, Jews can continue being Jews. Yet, both groups nevertheless share the same community. Although Paul addressed only relations between Jews and Gentiles, Paul's teachings can hopefully become a model for thinking about religious pluralism in the broader, more complex world in which we find ourselves.

FURTHER READING

Ancient Judaism

Barclay, John M. G. *Jews in the Mediterranean Diaspora: From Alexander to Trajan (323 BCE—117 CE)*. Edinburgh, T&T Clark, 1996. A study of the qualities and features that characterized Judaism specifically in Diaspora communities.

Cohen, Shaye D. *From the Maccabees to the Mishnah*, 2nd ed. (Louisville: Westminster John Knox, 2006). A very readable historical introduction to ancient Judaism from 200 BCE to 200 CE.

Nickelsburg, George. *Ancient Judaism and Christian Origins: Diversity, Continuity, and Transformation* (Minneapolis: Fortress Press, 2003). A thematic overview of ancient Judaism with special sensitivity to correcting the anti-Jewish bias that has characterized much Christian scholarship on the subject.

Paul and Judaism

Eisenbaum, Pamela. *Paul Was Not a Christian: The Original Message of a Misunderstood Apostle.* San Francisco: HarperOne, 2009. A portrait of Paul that critiques the traditional view and reinterprets the apostle's writings in light of a thoroughly Jewish perspective.

Gager, John. *Reinventing Paul.* New York: Oxford University Press, 2000. An introduction to the radically Jewish reading of Paul that focuses on Romans and Galatians.

Gaston, Lloyd. *Paul and the Torah.* Vancouver: University of British Columbia Press, 1997. One of the seminal Pauline scholars who advocated a radically Jewish reading.

Langton, Daniel. *The Apostle Paul in the Jewish Imagination: A Study in Modern Jewish-Christian Relations.* New York: Cambridge University Press, 2010. A study of Jewish scholarship on Paul covering a range of figures in the modern period.

Roetzel, Calvin J. *Paul: A Jew on the Margins.* Louisville: Westminster John Knox, 2003. A slim but very helpful introduction to Paul's basic theological orientation.

Sanders, E. P. *Paul and Palestinian Judaism: A Comparison of Patterns of Religion.* Philadelphia: Fortress Press, 1977. The book that ignited the "new perspective" on Paul. It constitutes one of the most thorough-going studies of how ancient Judaism was viewed in the twentieth century; only a small portion of the book attends to Paul directly.

Jewish Perspectives on Galatians

Fredriksen, Paula. "Judaism, the Circumcision of Gentiles, and Apocalyptic Hope: Another Look at Galatians 1 and 2," *Journal of Theological Studies* New Series 42:2 (1991): 532–64. An influential article arguing that the circumcision of Gentiles, which Paul attacks vehemently in Galatians, was an intra-Christian issue motivated by the fading of apocalyptic anticipation.

Nanos, Mark. *The Irony of Galatians: Paul's Letter in First-Century Context.* Minneapolis: Fortress Press, 2002. A highly original study that argues that the problem for the Galatians was a desire to become fully integrated with the local Jewish community.

Williams, Sam K. *Galatians.* Abingdon New Testament Commentaries. Nashville: Abingdon, 1997. An accessible yet deceptively deep commentary on Paul's letter.

NOTES

1. Friedrich Nietzsche, "The Antichrist: An Attempted Criticism of Christianity," sec 42, in *The Complete Works of Friedrich Nietzsche*, vol. 16, ed. Oscar Levy (New York: Russell and Russell, 1964), 184.

2. Rosemary Radford Ruether, *Faith and Fratricide: The Theological Roots of Anti-Semitism* (New York: Seabury, 1974).

3. Lloyd Gaston, *Paul and the Torah* (Vancouver: University of British Columbia Press, 1987), 15.

4. For a discussion of this issue, see Caroline Johnson Hodge, *If Sons, Then Heirs: A Study of Kinship and Ethnicity in the Letters of Paul* (Oxford, New York: Oxford University Press, 2007), 19-58.

5. Shaye D. Cohen, *From the Maccabees to the Mishnah*, 2nd ed. (Louisville: Westminster John Knox, 2006), 40–46.

6. As argued by John M. G. Barclay, *Jews in the Mediterranean Diaspora: From Alexander to Trajan (323* BCE—*117* CE*)* (Edinburgh: T&T Clark, 1996), 381–95. Barclay actually calls him an "anomalous diaspora Jew."

7. Bultmann, *Primitive Christianity in Its Contemporary Setting* (New York, 1956), 66, cited in Gager, *Reinventing Paul* (Oxford: Oxford University Press, 2000), 32. The chapter where the quote is found is entitled "Jewish Legalism."

8. Pamela Eisenbaum, *Paul Was Not a Christian* (San Francisco: HarperOne, 2009), 67–132.

9. Two scholars who have made a thorough-going argument for a Gentile audience are Stanley K. Stowers, *A Rereading of Romans: Justice, Jews, and Gentiles* (New Haven: Yale University Press, 1994), amd John G. Gager, *Reinventing Paul* (New York: Oxford University Press, 2000).

10. Paula Fredriksen, "Judaism, the Circumcision of Gentiles, and Apocalyptic Hope: Another Look at Galatians 1 and 2," *Journal of Theological Studies* New Series 42:2 (1991), 532–64.

11. The idea that Jews have been atoning for their sins all along and therefore are in good standing in the covenant, even when their have been serious acts of disobedience, while Gentiles' sins have been accumulating, is found in 2 Maccabees 6:12-16. See also the discussion in Stowers, *A Rereading of Romans: Justice, Jews, and Gentiles*, 104–7.

12. The one major exception to this is Mark Nanos, who argues that the rival teachers are not followers of Jesus; see *The Irony of Galatians: Paul's Letter in First-Century Context* (Minneapolis: Fortress Press, 2002).

13. A reconstruction of the views of Paul's opponents can be found in J. Louis Martyn, *Galatians: A New Translation with Introduction and Commentary* (Anchor Bible; New York: Doubleday, 1997).

14. By translating the text as "Abraham believed . . . " the NRSV translators are assuming a dichotomy between faith and works in which faith is taken to be belief, and "works" is taken to be doing things, ritual in particular; the former implicitly meaning belief in God and that one is loved by God (=Christianity), and the latter meaning that one does things not as a matter of faith, but to earn God's favor in a kind of exchange, work for reward (=Judaism).

15. See Pamela Eisenbaum, "Paul as the New Abraham," in *Paul and Poltics: Ekklesia, Israel, Imperium, Interpretation*, ed. Richard A. Horsley (Harrisburg: Trinity Press International, 2000), 130–45; ibid., *Paul Was Not a Christian*, 205–7.

16. The word *ex* is the word *ek* spelled differently.

17. Fredriksen, "Judaism, Gentiles, and Apocalyptic Hope." Fredriksen argues that the other teachers in Galatia became concerned because of the delayed parousia. They began to doubt that it was in fact time for the ingathering of the nations, so they changed their views regarding the status of Gentiles: Gentiles needed to be circumcised for full inclusion into the community.

18. As Sam K. Williams says, "This curse that persons are 'under' is not the Law itself but rather the disasters that the Law forewarns will befall those who break the commandments." See Sam K. Williams, *Galatians*, Abingdon New Testament Commentaries (Nashville: Abingdon, 1997), 89.

19. Williams, *Galatians*, 90.

20. One still finds this view frequently in commentaries. See, for example, Hans Dieter Betz, *Galatians*, Hermeneia (Minneapolis: Fortress Press, 1979), 145–46: Frank Matera, *Galatians*, Sacra Pagina, vol. 9 (Collegeville: Michael Glazier, 1992), 123–24.

21. This was the primary argument of E. P. Sanders, *Paul and Palestinian Judaism: A Comparison of Patterns of Religion* (Philadelphia: Fortress Press, 1977).

22. For more on Paul's theology of grace, see Eisenbaum, *Paul Was Not a Christian*, 247.

23. A more literal translation of the Greek would be "But the law is not from faith," the last two words being *ek pisteōs*, which appear in the quotation from Habakkuk and are translated by the words "by faith."

24. Paul obviously does not mean that Jesus is a curse upon others, but rather that Jesus bore the curse, so as to prevent others being afflicted.

25. See Genesis 17:7-9; Micah 7:18-20 and the discussion in Eisenbaum, *Paul Was Not a Christian*, 91-2.

26. Williams, *Galatians*, 87.

8

AFRICAN AMERICAN APPROACHES

Rehumanizing the Reader against Racism and Reading through Experience

DEMETRIUS K. WILLIAMS

INTRODUCTION: AFRICAN AMERICAN BIBLICAL INTERPRETATION—"ABSOLUTE RUBBISH!"

I would like to introduce my formative thoughts on introducing the Pauline let-ters through the lens of African American biblical interpretation by sharing an encounter I had at the Society of Biblical Literature (SBL) annual meeting a few years ago in San Diego, California. On the Saturday evening of the conference that year, two of my former classmates—one African American and the other Anglo-American, both of them Hebrew Bible scholars—were standing outside of the main doors of our hotel, catching up on our lives and our careers since we last met at the SBL the year before (this is a part of our annual ritual after various receptions). As we conversed with one another, a young man who was also an SBL participant, perhaps in his early thirties, approached us and asked if anyone had a lighter, so that he might light his cigarette. I noticed right off that he had an Irish accent. As my Anglo-American friend pulled out a lighter to assist him, I noticed him glance at my SBL nametag, which had a ribbon attached that read, "Fortress Press Author." As he leaned back from the lighter, another conference attendee, a young man about the same age or so, and certainly British by his accent, approached us too and asked if anyone had a cigarette. My same friend with the lighter reached into his pocket and gave him a cigarette and offered him a light. No sooner than this was done, our first visitor asked me: "So you're an author.

What did you write?" I told him that I was a contributor to a newly published African American New Testament commentary, *True to Our Native Land*. What happened next no one standing there expected. He leaned back, looking rather aghast, and declared, "That's absolute rubbish! You're being racist! Christianity [or Christ] is universal." I smiled, taking no offense, thinking he was not really serious; nor perhaps did my African American friend, who laughed and excused himself to answer a cell phone call. I simply assumed that he was attempting to be provocative, offering an intellectual challenge. In this vein I was preparing to engage his intellectual duel, but the details of what ensued next would take too much time to narrate sequentially or sufficiently here, so allow me to summarize briefly the particulars as best as memory can serve.

First, the young Brit asked the Irishman, "Where do you get off insulting this chap, who are you, what have you done? You're the one being racist." The young Irishman replied with venom, "You don't say anything to me, I didn't know racism until I was taught it by the British. In my country I am a black man because I'm the minority" (meaning, I presumed, Irish Catholic). After this my Anglo-American friend chimed in, getting "into his face," much too close for comfort: "You're in America, my friend, and if you don't tone it down, we might have to go at it right now! I'm not going to let you insult my friend like that." I immediately stood between the two before they came to fisticuffs. After I had calmed everyone down and assured them that I was not insulted, apologies were eventually given between my Anglo-American friend and the Irishman. But there were no apologies made between the Brit and the Irishman: they exchanged expletives as the Brit and everyone else departed, leaving the young Irishman and me alone to talk.

In our private conversation my interlocutor assured me that while he was really trying not to be insulting or racist, he really did feel that to address differences effectively (that is, ethnic, social, national, and so on), one should not intensify differences through emphasizing particularity but seek unity, be universal. From his perspective, then, the goal of biblical studies is to provide a *universal* interpretation that is free of racial, gender, ethnic, national or any other *particular* concerns. I listened thoughtfully, seeking now not to offer a defense of my position, but to learn why he held his.

One may wonder why I have begun my assessment of introducing Paul with this personal narrative. On the one hand, as a result of our encounter and conversation, I plunged deeper into a reconsideration and assessment of why I held to my own interpretive perspective and approach to biblical interpretation and Paul. On the other hand, this real life narrative is indicative of the long and arduous struggle of African American biblical interpretation (and that of other marginalized persons, groups, and perspectives) against the normative interpretation of scripture, and also the struggle to enter the academic and scholarly discourse of biblical studies and interpretation (see also, for instance, the "Feminist Approaches," "Asian

American Perspectives," or the "Queer Approaches" chapters). In this way, the narrative can serve as an instructive model for introducing Paul and his letters in the African American interpretive tradition.

AFRICAN AMERICAN BIBLICAL INTERPRETATION: "HUMANIZING" THE READER

It has become clear to me that, like myself, my interlocutor had been well trained in traditional biblical criticism. Given its proposed scientific basis and approach, the discipline called for a very specific kind of reader—the reader as *a universal and informed critic*. Fernando Segovia critically notes that this proposed reader is supposed to assume a position of *neutrality* and *impartiality* with regard to the text through a careful application of the proper methodological tools of the discipline that would, in turn, apparently produce a *universal* interpretation of the text, applicable to all people at all times.[1] As a result, the proposed critic in this paradigm brought nothing of him/herself to the text in the process of interpretation—no issues related to his/her own gender, racial, ethnic, political, social, or national concerns. Such "issues," if brought to bear on the interpretation of the text, would "taint" or "corrupt" the *scientific examination* of the text. Segovia sees the clear problem with this paradigm or model of interpretation, as it calls for a "dehumanized" reader.

What I have come to realize in this regard, is that "humanizing" the reader has been one of the most significant challenges and contributions of African American biblical interpretation. To be sure, a contextual, "humanized" reading of the Bible—a reading perspective that did not seek to mask or hide the issues and concerns of the interpreter—was a vital necessity in the African American experience with the Bible. In this world, they were already "dehumanized"—through the slave system causing "social death," through the ideology of white supremacy (wherein they were initially considered three fifths of a human being), and through the U.S. empire-building enterprise in which they were used as chattel. Yet, African Americans found opportunities for "rehumanization" within the same Bible that was used also to support the ideology of their oppressors. What I mean is that they found within the Bible opportunities to intervene and to challenge the ideologies supporting their oppression and also to navigate and articulate strategies for freedom, humanity, survival, and liberation. In short, using the Bible to address their "real-life" contextual issues related to gender, racial, ethnic, political, social or national concerns "re-humanized" them and demonstrated also the power of the Bible to address real human concerns, general and particular. Given the opportunity this is some of what I might have shared with my interlocutor in San Diego. Here, I will share my more detailed insights with readers of this chapter.

In light of ever-present time and space constraints, allow me to share a brief assessment of African American biblical interpretation in general before moving on to the politics of introducing Paul and interpreting Paul's letters from the African American interpretive tradition and perspective.

A Brief Assessment of African American Biblical Interpretation

African American biblical interpretation did not begin with the significant publications of *Troubling Biblical Waters* (by Cain Hope Felder, 1989) or *Stony the Road We Trod* (edited by Felder, 1991). It did not begin with other significant contributions like *African Americans and the Bible: Sacred Texts and Social Textures* (Vincent Wimbush, 2000), *Yet with a Steady Beat* (edited by Randall Bailey, 2003), *True to Our Native Land* (edited by Brian Blount and others, 2007), or *The Africana Bible* (edited by Hugh Page Jr. and others, 2009). These are all important contributions to the academic development of African American biblical interpretation. However, the African American interpretive tradition began within the free and enslaved populations of African Americans and their oftentimes skewed introduction to the Bible. In some of their early encounters with the Bible, one could argue for a kind of *survivalist* reading of the text. But increasingly the tradition developed a more critical liberationist stance, which sought to oppose racism and oppression in American society—religion, politics, life, and culture. This long tradition has culminated in a budding, self-conscious, and intentional reading strategy. According to Randall Bailey, contemporary African American interpretation of the Bible seeks to accomplish several goals:[2]

1. To demonstrate African presence and Africans in the biblical text, and analyze what Africans are "doing in the text"

2. To expose racism in the history of biblical interpretation: for example, examining how the "household codes/duties" (in Colossians and Ephesians, for example) have been used to enjoin slaves to submission, or how Paul's epistle to Philemon has been used to support the U.S. slave regime (the Fugitive Slave Law of 1850)

3. To examine and explore the tradition and history of biblical interpretation in the African American Christian (and non-Christian) community; and

4. To examine, explore, and apply the African American story and experience as a "strategy for reading" biblical texts.

I would add a fifth aspect of recent development:

5. To reflect critically upon the "scriptures" as traditionally understood and develop a radical reorientation toward or even rejection of them.

This fifth and more recent aspect proposes that, instead of interpreting ("excavating") the "scriptures," the "master's" master text, in the conventional academic orientation, a different type of critical interpretive practice is envisioned. It calls for "excavating the work . . . that we make 'scriptures' do for us." This means focusing upon the socio-religious-political orientations associated with "scriptures," not the content-meaning of "scriptures."[3]

In considering these goals and developments, another aspect of African American biblical interpretation cannot be overlooked: the rise and development of womanist theology and interpretation. In the mid 1970s and early '80s, African American women began to challenge, on the one hand, black churches and black liberation theologians and their interpretation of the African American religious tradition and of the Christian faith with its sole focus on racism to the exclusion of sexism. On the other hand, they also critiqued white feminist scholars for not including a consistent and viable race component in their analyses of sexism. While white feminist and black male liberation theologians focused on sexism and racism, respectively, womanist theologians/interpreters highlight the interrelatedness of race, sex, and class as multidimensional factors in the reality of black women's oppression. "Womanist" is the name many African American women (clergywomen and scholars from a broad range of disciplines—theology, biblical studies, ethics, social science, education, and so on) have chosen to identify this interrelated focus. The term gained initial inspiration from a dictionary-styled definition of womanism that Alice Walker provided in her book *In Search of Our Mothers' Gardens: Womanist Prose.*[4]

Finally, African American biblical interpretation does not represent a particular method but a *reading strategy* that seeks to ask certain questions (as presented above). In this regard it can be seen as sharing similar concerns and also as participating in an overall *ideological* approach of reading biblical texts that is shared by several other, if you will, "marginal" readings of the Bible (see the "Feminist Approaches," "Postcolonial Approaches," "Asian American Perspectives," and "Queer Approaches" chapters, among others). In the following exposition on Paul, the uses of the second, third, and fourth African American reading strategies or interpretive goals will become even more apparent (particularly since the first interpretive goal is less common and more difficult to follow in reading Paul's letters).

PAUL THE APOSTLE IN THE AFRICAN AMERICAN INTERPRETIVE TRADITION

Assessment of Paul in the Pre-Scholarly African American Religious Tradition

Assessing Paul's legacy was a necessity for both free and enslaved African Americans. Proslavery advocates constructed an image of Paul that made him the cornerstone of antebellum Southern values. The Pastoral Epistles and especially Philemon supplied the backbone for the construction of the "proslavery Paul" who was "created in the likeness and image" of the slave-holding class to support their economic exploitation of slaves and to enjoin them to "obey your masters in everything" (Col. 3:22; cf. Eph. 6:5). According to Clarice Martin, the "Paul" of proslavery hermeneutics neither questioned the social condition of the slave nor threatened the privileged status of the master.[5] For this reason, "The usefulness of the Pauline letters to systems of domination and oppression is . . . clear and palpable."[6] Accordingly, African American slaves "found themes so supportive of the slave status quo that many vowed never to listen to Paul preached or, when and if they were so able, never to read Paul for themselves."[7] They believed that Paul religiously took away the freedom God and Jesus had so graciously offered. To be sure, "they held the apostle in righteous contempt. . . . because of the prohibitions placed upon them by the white oppressor."[8] Although they discovered liberative themes in the Hebrew Bible and New Testament, they did not find these themes in Paul's writings. Hence slaves and ex-slaves refused to accept biblical passages that justified their exploitation and humiliation. This means that they both interpreted and critiqued the biblical texts out of their experience.

Despite the proslavery portrayal of Paul, several blacks developed a more nuanced understanding of Paul. Instead of outright rejection, they sought instead to "put Paul back together again."[9] Although the letters and legacy of Paul were used to support slavery and oppression, black abolitionists believed that a different image of "Paul" could be reconstructed to support slavery's abolition and win Paul over for the cause of freedom. Black abolitionists, then, reconstructed "Paul" by using several strategies: (1) utilizing positive statements of Paul against those that were negative to critique slavery's mythological structures; (2) assuming a typological correspondence between Paul and the said abolitionist; and (3) seeking the general "spirit" of Paul. These strategies were used to sustain a hermeneutic of liberation using a reconstructed "Paul" as a cornerstone. The African Americans' "Paul" of liberation could be seen most clearly through the egalitarian vision of Galatians 3:28, which provided them with a "new principle" for understanding God, humanity and their social situation.

A New Principle: "All Persons are Equal before God"

Enslaved African Americans' encounter with the Christian religion confirmed within them an idea of "the equality of all people before God." Vincent Wimbush has noted that during the late eighteenth and early nineteenth centuries—during the period of the American Revolution and the rise of independent black churches—African Americans developed an ethical and moral principle that stressed the ideal of Christian unity.

> African Americans sought to institutionalize as an ethical and moral principle one of the rare New Testament passages they found attractive and even identified as a *locus classicus* for Christian social teaching—"There is neither Jew nor Greek, there is neither slave nor free, there is neither male nor female; for you are all one in Christ Jesus" (Gal. 3:28)... This and other passages were used to level prophetic judgment against a society that thought of itself as biblical in its foundation and ethic.[10]

Wimbush elaborates further in another study:

> [T]here was a certain cluster of passages from the New Testament, especially Galatians 3:26-28 and Acts 2; 10:34-36, that provided the evocative rhetorical and visionary prophetic critique and the hermeneutical foundation for this dominant "mainstream" African American "reading" of the Bible and American culture . . . They were often quoted and paraphrased in efforts to relate them to the racial situation in the U.S. by generations of African Americans . . . [11]

These select passages were also important because they confirmed within African Americans the idea of the equality of all people before God (see also the "Feminist Approaches" chapter). The majority of enslaved blacks, lacking literary skills, were nevertheless exposed initially to the idea of this equality before God by evangelical Christianity, in the form of prayers, sermons, and exhortations at camp and revival meetings. Through these means, evangelical Christianity impressed upon both master and slave that they were sinners equally in need of salvation. So impressive was the idea of "the equality of all people before God" that it became African Americans' basic source of authority and they have remained unreservedly committed to this biblical anthropology. The black Christian tradition came to be governed by the principle of non-racism. Thus, the tradition's most useful function was to give African Americans a fundamental principle with which to critique American oppression and society and to justify their endeavors for survival and social transformation. The discovery of this principle revealed to African Americans the contradictions implicit in the religion of white Americans, whose practice of racism and oppression contradicted this biblical understanding of humanity. This principle of equality served as a balance in which America was weighed and found wanting. Thus African Americans used this tradition to press America to live up to its rhetoric of "freedom, liberty and justice for all." Peter J. Paris states that the principle of "the equality of all people before God" was so important that "apart from [this] tradition it is doubtful that blacks would have been able to survive the dehumanizing force of chattel slavery and its legacy of racial oppression."[12]

Moreover, African Americans seized this understanding of God and humanity as a revolutionary hermeneutic for understanding scripture, starting with the slaves and continuing into subsequent generations. Based upon this understanding of God, enslaved African Americans were able to practice a nascent "hermeneutics of suspicion" long before this idea was articulated as a modern hermeneutical method.[13] This means that they were suspicious of whites' interpretation of the Bible and their practice of Christianity, both of which were used to support slavery and racism. They felt so strongly about this notion that they set out to form religious organizations where they could actualize this idea of equality and freedom, even if only within the confines of independent black churches. In this way, this important principle became institutionalized within the emergent independent black churches.[14]

Assessments of Paul in Contemporary African American Scholarly Interpretations

Like their forebears, contemporary African American interpreters have also been compelled to appraise Paul's legacy. Some contemporary black biblical scholars and theologians perceive liberating potential in Paul's thought,[15] while some have taken a *via media* ("middle road") in this regard, recognizing his ambivalence and ambiguity in the matters of class and sex.[16] Others have viewed Paul's thought as patently conservative and useless to the cause of human freedom.[17] This modern assessment of Paul is similar to that in the earlier African American interpretive tradition. In both cases, one has to confront Paul's ambivalence on the important matters of human freedom and oppression.

On this point Delores Williams wonders how biblically derived messages of liberation, especially from the Exodus and Paul, "can be taken seriously by today's masses of poor, homeless African Americans, female and male, who consider themselves to be experiencing a form of slavery—economic enslavement by the capitalistic American economy."[18] For Williams, Paul's ambiguity is insurmountable for those in oppressive situations today who need to hear a clear and unequivocal voice for liberation. Cain Felder proposes, however, that even if the position of Paul on various issues is unascertainable or unacceptable, his position alone does not determine a particular reading, hearing, or appropriation. The liberating message of the entire New Testament must be gleaned.[19] To be sure, Paul had an apparently ambiguous stance with respect to issues of human freedom. But his position alone does not limit the *liberating potential* of the gospel. Contemporary African American interpreters of Paul who anguish about Paul's ambiguity may well take note of Allen Callahan's reflections: "In the modulation of activism and accommodation African Americans appreciated with ambivalence, and, rarely, with hostility, Paul's canonical ambiguity. . . . It is this profound ambiguity that black folks have not only appreciated in Paul, but, perhaps, have shared with him."[20] Callahan's statement reminds us that the African American interpretive tradition is not monolithic (perhaps we should even say, interpretive "traditions"). There can be, at times, competing views on significant matters of interpretation, just as we have sketched above with respect to Paul. This is no less the case with regard to the interpretation of Paul's letters.

APPLYING AFRICAN AMERICAN BIBLICAL HERMENEUTICS: INTERPRETATION OF PAUL'S LETTER TO PHILEMON

In the following exposition on the interpretation of Philemon, which serves as a primary example of African American interpretation of Paul's letters, I will more fully elaborate upon the second, third, and fourth of the African American reading strategies/interpretive goals (described above) and will subdivide the analysis under each heading for clarity. In order to gain a clearer understanding of African American interpretation of Philemon, it will be set against the traditional interpretation, which claims that the *plain sense* of the *original context* along with *authorial intent* are the only determinants for a *valid* interpretation of the text.

Exposing Racism in the History of Biblical Interpretation

The traditional hypothesis surmises that the letter reflects the relationship between Paul; Philemon, a well-to-do householder; and the householder's slave, Onesimus, who ran away from his master, taking several of the master's items with him in his flight (vv. 15, 18-19). Under unknown circumstances this slave came under the influence of Paul's teaching and preaching and was converted while Paul was "a prisoner of [or "for the sake of"] Jesus Christ," under house arrest at some unknown locale (vv. 10-11). Once Onesimus was converted, Paul persuaded him to return to his master (v. 12), who had also become a Christian earlier under Paul in Asia Minor (v. 19) and in whose house a Christian congregation met (v. 2). Paul wanted the slave to return to his master because there were severe laws that punished those who interfered with the rights of the slave owner. It was Paul's duty by law to return him to his master (v. 14). Thus Paul goes to great pains, using every means possible to ensure that Onesimus's return to his master does not incur the harsh treatment of the Roman law usually received by runaways.

This use of Philemon to support oppression and racism can be most adequately depicted in a now commonly related incident in which Charles Colcock Jones, a white Presbyterian plantation missionary, recalled in his memoirs a sermon he gave before a slave congregation in 1833:

> I was preaching to a large congregation on the Epistle of Philemon: and when I insisted upon fidelity and obedience as Christian virtues in servants and upon the authority of Paul, condemned the practice of running away, one half of my audience deliberately rose up and walked off with themselves, and those that remained looked anything but satisfied, either with the preacher or his doctrine. After dismission, there was no small stir among them; some solemnly declared "that there was no such an Epistle in the Bible"; others, "that they did not care if they ever heard me preach again." . . . There were some too, who had strong objections against me as a Preacher, because I was a master, and said, "his people have to work as well as we."[21]

Several salient points can be observed from Colcock's reflections of 1833: 1) long before the Fugitive Slave Law (1850) was enacted as law, Paul's letter to Philemon was used to address and to discourage African American flight from slavery; 2) it was used to support human slavery and oppression (that is, the slave regime); and 3) enslaved African Americans showed marked discontent with the conventional interpretation and application of Philemon (and scripture as a whole). They were aware that ready support for slavery could be found in the normative reading of Philemon.

Exploring the Tradition and History of Biblical Interpretation in the African American Christian Community

Enslaved African Americans provided a "reading/hearing-response" to Paul's epistle to Philemon that was initially aural and oral. Their forceful rejection of the epistle and palatable discontent with its use expressed emphatically their refusal to apply its views to their own social-political situation. African American slaves responded to such use and application of Philemon with openly expressed dissatisfaction ("one half of my audience deliberately rose up and walked off with themselves, and those that remained looked anything but satisfied, *either with the preacher or his doctrine*" [emphasis mine]). Those slaves innately recognized the complicity of the text and its interpretation with the slaveholding system. Accordingly, the epistle was rejected ("some solemnly declared 'that there was no such an Epistle in the Bible'") and so also was the preacher and his explication of Philemon ("There were some too, who had strong objections against me as a Preacher"). The preacher's complicity with slavery was clear ("because I was a master, and [they] said, 'his people have to work as well as we'"). The African American interpretive tradition thus found Philemon and its interpretation incompatible with their experience of God and their quests for human dignity and social-political liberation.

This incident, moreover, reveals that enslaved African Americans did not and could not accept as "word of God" any scripture or interpretation thereof that could be used to uphold their oppression. Enslaved African Americans *were not* convinced that it was God's will for them to be slaves, no matter what the Bible, their "masters," or pro-slavery preachers and exegesis told them. To be sure, "Slaves distinguished the hypocritical religion of their masters from true Christianity and rejected the slaveholder's gospel of obedience to master and mistress."[22] Yet, the tradition of "rejection," or at least a "very cold reception," of this epistle continued in the ecclesiastical traditions of African American churches. My own experience since childhood in the black Baptist tradition resembles Allen Callahan's in the African Methodist Episcopal (AME) tradition: Paul's letter to Philemon was not a part of the "canon" for many African American churches by virtue of its absence and exclusion from sermons, Sunday school curricula, and Bible Class teaching.[23] In short, it played no essential role in their religious tradition and ecclesiastical life, most certainly because of the role it had played in supporting Fugitive Slave Law and, perhaps even more emphatically, the potential role it could play in endorsing slavery in general.

Lloyd A. Lewis, however, has attempted to employ a liberative African American hermeneutic to the interpretation of Philemon, although he accepts a fugitive/run-away slave hypothesis as the background for the letter's occasion.[24] Nevertheless, Lewis draws a link between Paul's appeal in Philemon and Galatians 3:1–4:7 (especially 3:28). He suggests that Paul uses familial language to reconfigure extensively the relationship between Philemon and Onesimus (for example, *brother* is used 4 times, vv. 1, 7, 16, 20; *sister*, v. 2; *child*, v. 10; *father*, v. 10). Lewis views Galatians 3:28 (a statement of Christian equality) as the basis of a liberative hermeneutic for reading Philemon anew for the African American Christian tradition. Important in this respect is Lewis's statement, "What African American readers look for is some vision of how as a church leader Paul understood the gospel's power in the face of this very present social situation [slavery]."[25] Lewis holds the opinion that the letter to Philemon broadly provides an answer to this question. What he and other readers in the African American interpretive tradition are attempting to do is provide a reading of Philemon that can positively recoup the letter for African American churches, readers and liturgical traditions.

In this regard Kirk D. Lyons seeks to address this very issue of providing a case for the homiletic usefulness of Philemon, which undoubtedly would be significant for the African American religious tradition. He recommends, then, a reading of Philemon that redirects the primary focus *from the request of* Paul to Philemon, toward *Paul's very act of requesting*. Rereading Philemon from this nuanced perspective reveals Paul's strategic use of language, which indicates his unwillingness to consecrate the social roles in his cultural environment. This move posits greater emphasis on Paul's action of requesting rather than the rhetoric of his request, for it is "through an analysis of Paul's action *through* rhetoric that we discover a public theology."[26] Lyons argues that the case of Onesimus provided Paul with an opportunity to test his theology against the empirical reality of a concrete situation and apply his theological evaluation consistently. Rather than consecrate certain social roles (master-slave), Paul determined instead to give priority to sanctifying the familial structure of the assembled community.

Perhaps the most radical departure from supposing any background of slavery for the interpretation of Philemon is the proposal of Allen Callahan. He proposes that the fifth-century CE church leader John Chrysostom theorized a background of slavery to address a mounting issue with Christian slaves in his own time. Callahan proffers, then, not only that slavery is an inappropriate background for reading Philemon but also that Onesimus is not a slave: he is the blood brother of Philemon! The letter to Philemon is not Paul's plea to a master on behalf of a runaway slave but an apostolic intervention between two estranged brothers. Philemon 16 is a critical verse for many readings and interpretations of Philemon as well as for the theological question of Paul's view of slavery, and Callahan builds his case for a rereading of Philemon based on this verse. His alternative *argumentum* builds also upon abolitionists' exegeses of v. 16, but Callahan elaborates the full exegetical and possible historical implications of such a proposal, recognizing that in traditional exegesis of this verse there is a certain unquestioned assumption: Onesimus is identified *literally as a slave* and *figuratively as a brother*. He has in turn reversed this assumption: for him Onesimus is *literally* Philemon's *blood brother* and *figuratively* identified as a slave.

Cain H. Felder, however, rejects Callahan's literal interpretation of "a beloved brother . . . " because it "moves the letter too far from the more common and ancient understanding of Onesimus as a runaway slave."[27] Both interpreters are attempting to sort out Paul's rhetoric in this passage because v. 16 is the only place where the term slave (*doulos*) is used. However, Callahan notes that Onesimus's servile identity rests solely on the exegesis of this word in traditional exegesis of

Philemon. But since Paul can use the term "slave" for himself and his coworkers in a figurative sense (cf. Phil. 1:1), might not the possibility obtain here also?

The possibility of Callahan's proposal is tested in his translation of *hōs* ("as"), which he argues can have the meaning "as though," indicating that "Onesimus's servile status is a thought or assertion on Philemon's part and not a point of fact."[28] Hence, he translates the first phrase of v. 16, "no longer *as though he were* a slave." The second part of the phrase, "but more than a slave, as a beloved brother," suggests that the figure of a slave (bereft of family ties) serves as the antitype of a blood relative. So Paul exhorts Philemon to cease his treatment of Onesimus *as if he were a slave,* and to treat him instead as a beloved brother, which he really and truly is. The final phrase of v. 16 bears the weight of Callahan's reading: "very much so to me, but how much more to you, both in the flesh and in the Lord." The driving force of Paul's language here indicates that Philemon and Onesimus are brothers, but now even more so, both literally (*in the flesh*) and spiritually (*in the Lord*). If they are now at odds with each other, this must be resolved because they are both *brothers* "in Christ." Onesimus has become a "child" of and a "brother in the Lord" to Paul, but Paul emphasizes the dual ties between Onesimus and Philemon when he stresses, "but *how much more to you* both in the flesh and in the Lord."[29] According to Callahan, then, "The problem that Paul engaged in the letter was not that Onesimus was a real slave (for he was not), nor that Onesimus was not a real brother to Philemon (for he was), but that Onesimus was not a *beloved* brother to Philemon."[30]

Thus, for Callahan, these observations warrant the proposition of an alternative hypothesis that would account for the epistle's truly main elements: (1) Paul's familial vocabulary used to describe the relationship between the principals,[31] (2) Paul's deferential (yet paternalistic) approach when addressing Philemon,[32] and (3) Paul's determined concern for the reconciliation of Philemon and Onesimus. He notes that, in the Greco-Roman culture of the day, one could find similar elements of paternal engagement, and a manifest concern to reconcile estranged friends, spouses, and brothers, in the biographies of contemporary philosophers. In this way Callahan offers a plausible historical reading and exegesis of Philemon that does not posit a framework of slavery for understanding the letter.

Using the African American Story and Experience as a Strategy for "Reading" Biblical Texts

The normative interpretive paradigm disavows the use of the interpreter's experience as a source for biblical interpretation. The only valid experience for interpretation is that of the original biblical audience. But this reading paradigm has muted the voices and alternative readings of scripture. So, for example, an erudite scholar within the normative paradigm makes the following statement in this regard with respect to the kinds of newer reading discussed above:

> All of these interpretations fail to take history seriously as the proper first context for interpretation . . . the first step toward valid interpretation of scripture . . . , which means the determination of the originally intended meaning of a text. "History as context for interpretation" does not refer to our own history, but to the original setting(s) of the biblical texts themselves.

He states, furthermore, "we insist that the universally applicable meaning of the text is related primarily to its originally intended meaning."[33]

But it is not that the newer readings "fail to take history seriously," but that history is not the only determinant for interpreting scripture: *experience* is important also—of "the original setting(s) of the biblical texts themselves" and of the flesh-and-blood readers who interpret them! In this way the normative paradigm seeks to mute the voices of other interpretive perspectives. For example, another recent commentary on Philemon clearly presents the normative paradigm in this regard:

> [W]e cannot adapt (distort) the teaching of St. Paul on slavery to suit the demands of certain voices of today, each stridently insisting on being "heard" at the dawn of the third millennium A.D. No, faith submits to what the Word of God has always said through the passing of the ages and does not gladly suffer the plain meaning of scripture to be twisted to suit constantly changing societal norms—a particular American "mentality" for example.[34]

From this perspective, scripture's meaning does not change through the centuries. But take serious note of the notion of the "plain meaning of scripture" because in the explosive debate over slavery in the U.S., proslavery interpreters also sought to proffer a "plain sense hermeneutic" when reading scripture. On this note Albert Harrell avers, "the proslavery spokesmen were holding the more defensible position from the perspective of historical criticism."[35] Unfortunately, this paradigm has consecrated the status quo.

Thus, the African American reading strategies seek to open the interpretive possibilities of the letter to Philemon by using the collective experience of African Americans as a starting point for interpreting scripture. It is clear that, in the African American interpretive tradition, black men and women read the Bible dialectically: that is, *they read the Bible through their experience* and *their experience through the Bible*. This is also how they read Paul and his letters. Moreover, in the more recent theological and exegetical investigations of African Americans trained in theological and biblical studies, liberative readings of Philemon have been offered that work both within the traditional framework of slavery and without positing slavery. Yet, interestingly enough, the African American experience and its interpretive history can converge to eliminate an "either/or" or binary approach to understanding Philemon. Such a convergence can be seen in the life and experiences of Francis J. Grimké.

Francis James Grimké (November 4, 1852–October 11, 1937) was a Presbyterian minister who was prominent in working for equal rights for African Americans. He was born in Cane Acres, a rice plantation near Charleston, South Carolina, the son of a wealthy white man and Nancy Weston, a black slave. After his father died and property rights over the slaves were exercised by his father's half-brother Montague, who had no intentions of manumitting them, Grimké ran away from home and joined the Confederate Army as an officer's valet, where he served until Emancipation (1865). After the Civil War, his white aunts, Angela and Sarah Moore Grimke, the aunts also of his white half-brother, acknowledged their kinship and helped him gain his education at Lincoln University in Pennsylvania. Grimké graduated at the head of his class in 1870 and began to study law, attending Howard University in 1874. At this time, he felt a call to the ministry and enrolled at Princeton Theological Seminary, where he graduated in 1878. He married and began his ministry at the 15th Street Presbyterian Church in Washington, D.C., where he remained until 1928. From his pulpit he preached and exhorted a national audience to agitate for civil rights "until justice is done." Grimké campaigned against racism in American churches and requested assistance from the Afro-Presbyterian Council to encourage black moral uplift and self-help. He joined with W. E. B. Du Bois at the Carnegie Hall Conference in 1906, which led to the Niagara Movement and the NAACP. He was a spiritual leader with a conviction for justice and passion for his people. Francis J. Grimké lived in Washington, D.C., until his death in 1937.[36]

What is it about Grimké's life and experiences that recommends him to a rereading of Philemon? His experience can inform us of the interpretive possibilities not only of rereading Philemon but also of abandoning binary interpretative perspectives. Grimké can be seen as an example both of one who could be a *literal slave* and a *literal brother* at the same time (Phlm. 16). He can also be seen within the traditional slavery framework as one who fled his brother's household to seek his freedom because of impending inequities on the horizon. Although he and his half-brother never reconciled, he did reconcile with his half-brother's aunts, who received and supported him, "no longer as a slave" but as a beloved nephew, assisting him in his education and the fulfillment of his ministry: a ministry in which he served faithfully.

CONCLUSION

Each of the reading strategies presented above emerged within various African American communities and are most likely to continue to develop in the coming years. These African American interpretive traditions offer opportunities to critically rethink and engage not only the traditional issues of race, class, and sex but also those of gender and identity. In such opportunities lies the possibility of reassessing and even reclaiming problematic texts; but one can expect that future challenges and developments will push these reading perspectives even further. As I reflect back on my experience at the SBL in San Diego with my Irish colleague and interlocutor, his challenge did just that: it caused me to critically reassess my training and scholarship in order to determine whether I was engaging in a hermeneutics that dehumanized or humanized the reader. I certainly hope I have been and will continue to operate within the latter category, as all African American approaches aim to do.

FURTHER READING

Bailey, Randall, ed. *Yet with a Steady Beat: Contemporary U.S. Afrocenric Biblical Interpretation*. Semeia. Atlanta: Society of Biblical Literature, 2003. Bailey edits several articles presented by a second generation of African American scholars who use new literary, historical, and other critical tools to broaden the issues and concerns of the discipline of biblical interpretation.

Blount, Brian, et al., eds. *True to Our Native Land: An African American New Testament Commentary*. Minneapolis: Fortress Press, 2007. Blount and the other contributors offer a signal achievement in African American biblical interpretation. The contributions call into question many of the canons of traditional biblical research, while at the same time highlighting the role of the Bible in African American history, accenting themes of ethnicity, class, and slavery.

Brown, Michael. *Blackening the Bible: The Aims of African American Biblical Scholarship*. Harrisburg: Trinity Press International, 2004. Brown offers an insightful overview of the emerging discipline of African American biblical interpretation through an examination of some exemplary voices from the late 1980s up to 2004.

Callahan, Allen D. *The Embassy of Onesimus: The Letter of Paul to Philemon*. Trinity Press International, 1997. Callahan proposes his radical interpretation of Philemon, which he gleaned through Anti-Slavery hermeneutics of the nineteenth century; namely, that Philemon and Onesimus are blood brothers.

———. *The Talking Book: African Americans and the Bible*. Yale University Press, 2006. Callahan utilizes biblical images of exile, exodus, and prophets as expressed in the lives of African Americans through history, spirituals, literature, politics, and culture.

Felder, Cain H. *Troubling Biblical Waters: Race, Class and Family*. Maryknoll: Orbis, 1989. Felder brings the African American experience and the Bible to bear on the issues of race, class and family.

————, ed. *Stony the Road We Trod: African American Biblical Interpretation*. Minneapolis: Fortress Press, 1991. A signal and significant collection of articles from the first generation of academically trained biblical scholars that ignited and initiated the field of African American biblical interpretation.

Martin, Clarice J. "The *Haustafeln* in African American Biblical Interpretation: 'Free Slaves' and 'Submissive Wives.'" In *Stony the Road We Trod: African American Biblical Interpretation*, edited by Cain H. Felder, 206–31. Minneapolis: Fortress Press, 1991. Martin offers an insightful examination of the blinders within the African American interpretive tradition's discussion and assessment of the place and equality of black women in the black church and society.

Smith, Abraham, Allen Callahan, and Richard Horsley, eds. *Slavery in Text and Interpretation*. Semeia. Atlanta: Society of Biblical Literature, 1998. Smith, Callahan and Horsley provide the reader with a collection of articles that critically reevaluate slavery across history. Important also for African American biblical interpretation are seminal articles by Smith, Callahan, and Clarice Martin.

Williams, Demetrius K. *"An End to This Strife": The Politics of Gender in African American Churches*. Minneapolis: Fortress Press, 2004. Williams utilizes African American biblical interpretation, history and theology to explore Galatians 3:28 as a liberative paradigm that can effectively address sexism in black churches.

Wimbush, Vincent L. *African Americans and the Bible: Sacred Texts and Social Textures*. New York: Continuum, 2000. Wimbush assembles in this work a broad collection of articles exploring the African American engagement with the Bible through a number of interpretive sources and disciplinary perspectives (such as semiotics, cultural anthropology and sociology).

NOTES

1. Fernando F. Segovia, *Decolonizing Biblical Studies: A View From the Margins* (Maryknoll: Orbis, 2004).

2. Randall C. Bailey, "The Danger of Ignoring One's Own Cultural Bias in Interpreting the Text," in *The Postcolonial Bible*, ed. R. S. Sugirtharajah (Sheffield: Sheffield Academic Press, 1998), 66–90, 81–84.

3. Vincent Wimbush, ed., *Theorizing Scriptures: New Critical Orientations to a Cultural Phenomenon* (New Brunswick: Rutgers University Press, 2008).

4. "Womanist. 1. From womanish. (Opp. of "girlish," i.e., frivolous, irresponsible, not serious.) A black feminist or feminist of color . . . 2. Also: A woman who loves other women, sexually and/or nonsexually. Appreciates and prefers women's culture, women's emotional flexibility (values tears as natural counterbalance of laughter), and women's strength. Sometimes loves individual men, sexually and/or nonsexually. Committed to the survival and wholeness of entire people, male and female. Not a separatist, except periodically, for health. Traditionally universalist . . . 3. Loves music. Loves the moon. Loves the Spirit. Loves love and food and roundness. Loves struggle. Loves the Folk. Loves herself. Regardless. 4. Womanist is to feminist as purple is to lavender." Alice Walker, *In Search of Our Mother's Gardens: Womanist Prose* (New York: Harcourt Brace Jovanovich, 1983), xi–xii.

5. Clarice J. Martin, "'Somebody Done Hoodoo'd the Hoodoo Man': Language, Power, Resistance, and The Effective History of Pauline Texts in American Slavery." *Semeia* 83/84 (1998): 203–33; 213.

6. Neil Elliott, *Liberating Paul: The Justice of God and the Politics of the Apostle* (Maryknoll: Orbis, 1994), 9.

7. Brian K. Blount, *Then the Whisper Put on Flesh: New Testament Ethics in an African American Context* (Nashville: Abingdon, 2001), 119.

8. Amos Jones Jr., *Paul's Message of Freedom: What Does It Mean to the Black Church?* (Valley Forge: Judson, 1984), 37.

9. Abraham Smith, "Putting 'Paul' Back Together Again: William Wells Brown's *Clotel* and Black Abolitionist Approaches to Paul," *Semeia* 83/84 (1998): 251–62.

10. Wimbush, "The Bible and African Americans: An Outline of an Interpretative History," in *Stony the Road We Trod: African American Biblical Interpretation*, ed. Cain Hope Felder (Minneapolis: Fortress Press, 1991), 81–97, 90.

11. Wimbush, "Reading Texts through Worlds, Worlds through Texts," *Semeia* 59 (1993): 129–39, 132.

12. Peter J. Paris, *The Social Teaching of the Black Churches* (Philadelphia: Fortress Press, 1985), 10–13. Paris states further: "Their raison d'être is inextricably tied to the function of opposing the beliefs and practices of racism by proclaiming the biblical view of humanity as they have appropriated it, that is, the equality of all persons under God. Thus their moral aim is theologically grounded. The doctrine of human equality under God is, for them, the final authority for all matters pertaining to faith, thought, and practice. In short, its function in the black experience is categorical, that is, it is unconditional, absolute, and universally applicable" (14).

13. Cf. Elisabeth Schüssler Fiorenza, *Bread Not Stone* (Boston: Beacon, 1985), 15–18. Schüssler Fiorenza herself has been influenced by and engages with the history of African American hermeneutics. This is expressed clearly in her edited volume, *Searching the Scriptures: A Feminist Critical Introduction*, vol. 1 (New York: Crossroad/Herder & Herder, 1993), which is dedicated to the memory of Anna Julia Cooper, the nineteenth-century black feminist/womanist of great learning and of committed advocacy for women's rights and equality.

14. Gayraud S. Wilmore, *Black Religion and Black Radicalism: An Interpretation of the Religious History of African Americans*, 3rd ed. (Maryknoll: Orbis, 1998), 78; Paris, *Social Teachings*, 10.

15. Jones, *Paul's Message of Freedom*.

16. Allen Dwight Callahan, "'Brother Saul': An Ambivalent Witness to Freedom," *Semeia* 83/84 (1998): 235–50; Smith, "Putting 'Paul' Back Together Again;" Clarice Martin, "The *Haustafeln* in African American Biblical Interpretation: 'Free Slaves' and 'Submissive Wives'" in *Stony the Road We Trod*, 206–31; Felder, *Troubling Biblical Waters: Race, Class and Family* (Maryknoll: Orbis, 1989).

17. Albert B. Cleage, *The Black Messiah* (New York: Sheed and Ward, 1968); James Cone, *God of the Oppressed* (New York: Seabury, 1975); Howard Thurman, *Jesus and the Disinherited* (Richmond: Friends United, 1981); Delores S. Williams, *Sisters in the Wilderness: The Challenge of Womanist God-Talk* (Maryknoll: Orbis, 1993).

18. Williams, *Sisters*, 146–47.

19. Felder, *Troubling*, 147.

20. Callahan, "'Brother Saul,'" 249.

21. Albert J. Raboteau, *Slave Religion: The "Invisible Institution" in the Antebellum South*, (Oxford: Oxford University Press, 1978), 294.

22. Raboteau, *Slave Religion*, 294.

23. Callahan, *The Embassy of Onesimus: The Letter of Paul to Philemon* (Harrisburg: Trinity Press International, 1997), 1–4.

24. "An African American Appraisal of the Philemon-Paul-Onesimus Triangle," in *Stony the Road We Trod*, 232–46. Later, Lewis still assumes slavery as the background for interpreting Philemon, but departs from viewing Philemon from the fugitive slave hypothesis. He states in that, Onesimus "either ran away from his master or was lent out by his master to serve an incarcerated Paul during one of his several times of arrest." See Lloyd A. Lewis, "Philemon," in *True to Our Native Land: An African American New Testament Commentary*, ed. Brian Blount, et al., (Minneapolis: Fortress Press, 2007), 437.

25. Lewis, "Philemon," 438; Orlando Patterson's reflections are pertinent here also ("Paul, Slavery and Freedom: Personal and Socio-Historical Reflections," in *Semeia* 83/84 (1998): 263–279): "It is preposterous then, to criticize Paul for not calling for the abolition of slavery, or for taking the Roman imperial slave system for granted. However, one can morally evaluate Paul in regard to the first level of confrontation with slavery: that of his face-to-face dealings with slaves of his time, because here there was a wide moral space within which he and his contemporaries ranged. And here the evidence points overwhelmingly to the fact that Paul was a humane, caring soul in regard to slaves and their plight. . . . The letter to Philemon makes this all quite clear and it is hard to imagine how it could be read in any other terms. . . . " (269).

26. Kirk D. Lyons, "Paul's Confrontation with Class: The Letter to Philemon as Counter-Hegemonic Discourse," *Cross Currents* 56, no.1 (2006): 116–32; 117–18.

27. Felder, "Philemon," in *The New Interpreter's Bible*, Volume XI (Nashville: Abingdon, 2000), 881–905; 886.

28. As the Latin side of the diglot codex Claromontanus tells us, Onesimus is to be no longer a "quasi-slave" (*iam non quasi servum*). Callahan's argument can be found in his *Embassy*, 44–50.

29. Chris Frilingos ("For My Child Onesimus": Paul and Domestic Power in Philemon," *JBL* 119.1 (2000): 91–104) notes that, "how much more to you (v. 16)—both Philemon and Onesimus are Paul's children, because Paul fulfills the paternal role (he is the paterfamilias)" (103).

30. Callahan, "Paul's Letter to Philemon," 368, 372 (my emphasis).

31. "Kinship imagery which Pliny's letter lacks, imbues Paul's letter with familial intimacy" (Frilingos, 92). Frilingos investigates the way the letter simultaneously expresses and counters claims to authority. Paul constructs a rhetorical household that counters Philemon's actual household (93).

32. See Andrew Wilson, "The Pragmatics of Politeness and Pauline Epistolography: A Case Study of the Letter to Philemon," *JSNT* 48 (1992): 107–19.

33. Gordon D. Fee, "History as Context for Interpretation," in *The Act of Bible Reading: A Multidisciplinary Approach to Biblical Interpretation*, ed. Elmer Dyck (Downers Grove: Intervarsity, 1996), 10–32, 11 and 14.

34. John G. Nordling, *Philemon* (Saint Louis: Concordia, 2004), 68–69.

35. J. Albert Harrill, *Slaves in the New Testament: Literary, Social, and Moral Dimensions* (Minneapolis: Fortress Press, 2006), 192; see also *The Manumission of Slaves in Early Christianity*, 2nd ed. (Tübingen: Mohr Siebeck, 1995; 1998).

36. *The Encyclopedia of African-American Heritage*, by Susan Altman. Copyright 1997, Facts on File, Inc. New York ISBN 0-8160-3289-0: http://www.aaregistry.com/detail.php?id=1210; accessed, 6/19/09. I would like to thank Rev. Dr. Charles Tindsley for the reference to Grimké as an example of how his experiences could be seen as a modern analogue to Callahan's reading of Philemon.

9

ASIAN AMERICAN PERSPECTIVES

Ambivalence of the Model Minority and Perpetual Foreigner

SZE-KAR WAN

After two weeks of trying with enticement, coaxing, and even threat to discourage my beginning students from translating Greek participles literally, I gave them an ultimatum: "Pay attention to how the participle is used in a sentence and find its equivalent in English. Don't translate it word for word. The Greek participle is much more complex than the English participle." Little did I know this throwaway linguistic commonplace would force me to countenance the viciousness of white supremacy, as well as its subtlety. A middle-aged woman, white and self-proclaimed "conservative," stormed past me after class, half-screaming into my ear: "I am sick and tired of you dumping on *my* language all the time. How dare you? How would you like it if I said something like that about Chinese!"

After I recovered, I sought the advice of my academic dean, herself also a middle-aged woman, white, but avowedly "liberal," a feminist scholar and a well-known gay-rights advocate. "I don't think it's racism," she volunteered, "I don't know why the student would say something like that about Chinese, because in fact I think your English is excellent." I was distressed a second time.

Two racial myths about Asian Americans can be seen in operation in these two episodes. The first is the myth of Asian Americans as the "perpetual foreigner," the other the myth of the "model minority."[1] Both produce in Asian Americans a sense of ambivalence, of both attraction and repulsion toward the dominant culture, because both come as a result of power differentials in society. An understanding of these myths and the resulting ambivalence on the part of Asian Americans will help us understand Paul's own ambivalence as a member of a model minority and a perpetual foreigner, first in the diaspora then as a member of the Jesus movement.

175

Paul in turn can help Asian American readers come to terms with the ambivalence of their own social location.[2]

THE ASIAN AMERICAN EXPERIENCE:
PERPETUAL FOREIGNER AND MODEL MINORITY

To the student in my Greek class, I was a foreigner, a guest-worker, whose technical knowledge could be exploited but who should not be allowed to own the master's and the mistress's language, and most certainly not to the extent of subordinating it to another language. I had no right to take what was not mine because, in the words of legal scholar Cheryl Harris, whiteness is a property, a status property, ratified, legitimated, and safeguarded by law, a condition that still obtains today.[3] As property, whiteness could be defended like any other property, and it is within the whites' right to do so. Whiteness as property also implies a hierarchy of race, a social construction according to which "whites" have privileges that those labeled "nonwhites" do not—including the privilege of "owning" the English language. The legal system further gives whites the absolute right to deny those legally established as nonwhites the use of that property:

> The right to exclude was the central principle . . . of *whiteness as identity,* for mainly whiteness has been characterized, not by an inherent unifying characteristic, but by *the exclusion of others deemed to be "not white."* The possessors of whiteness were granted the legal right to exclude others from the privileges inhering in whiteness; *whiteness became an exclusive club whose membership was closely and grudgingly guarded.* The courts played an active role in enforcing this right to exclude—determining who was or was not white enough to enjoy the privileges accompanying whiteness. In that sense, the courts protected whiteness as any other form of property.[4]

In other words, whiteness is a social and legal construct that depends not on any racial or ethnic category, or on any "inhering unifying characteristic"—not accent, not social class, not origins, and most definitely not phenotypes like skin color—but on what "whites" are not. Exclusion of "nonwhites" is as much a part of affirming who "whites" are as discovering what "whites" have in common. Stripped to its core, it is a naked power play by which those in this "exclusive club" use legal instruments to keep others from entering.

To the extent that I was excluded as a nonwhite by the student in my Greek class, I was treated no differently from how African Americans and Native Americans had historically been treated. My dean's comment to me reveals a far subtler form of white supremacy, however. By complimenting me on my English, she foregrounded my nonwhite status by reminding me English was not my mother tongue. Even though she granted that I had learned it well, it was nevertheless a *learned* skill and therefore an acquisition or borrowing extrinsic to the nonwhite status with and into which I was constructed. That it was *discovered* as a learned skill further allowed her to appeal to and to reaffirm the race hierarchy, according to which the native speaker who possessed English as a racial marker of whiteness now was entitled to judge whether I had acquired the skill properly. If whiteness was a property, it was her duty to arbitrate whether I had amassed sufficient capital to entitle me to the rights to that property. With her "liberal" leaning, she did not exclude me from whiteness as had my student, but she interpreted my request for consultation as a bid for property claim to whiteness, a bid she actually would have supported. But implicit in that very interpretation and her support for entrance into an exclusive club was her unexamined and therefore unquestioned assumption about the normativity of race hierarchy. She, the insider, taking for granted her whiteness as property, adjudicated who could or could not be admitted into the club. Even though I had been in this country for nearly my whole life, I was racialized as a "foreigner"; and even though her liberalism would normally sensitize her to the faintest hint of racism against historical victims of discrimination such as African Americans and Native Americans and new victims such as women and gays, action toward a "foreigner" was filed under a different ideological category. Her implied racism was no different from the student's overt racism in the final analysis: both found racism against Asian Americans tolerable, even acceptable. But because it was unknown to her, it was more insidious.

My dean's awkward compliment on my English casts light on a second racial myth about Asian Americans, the myth of the "model minority." This myth was historically spawned by liberal anxieties to whitewash racial differences in the U.S. According to the racial reasoning of this myth, I had earned my right to whiteness, and my student was wrong in questioning it. Put differently, I was an "honorary white," as a liberal white acquaintance once called me, intending it to be flattery. (My open annoyance brought a premature end to a dinner party to which I have not been invited back.) In "honorary white" we run up against the more subtly racial construct of the "model minority." This myth trades on the whites' perception of theirs being a fair and meritocratic society that provides all comers open and equal access to resources and opportunities.[5] It absolves them of the inequity endemic in a white society constructed to protect the power of the elite. And it places the onus on the minoritized groups and the "foreigners" to assimilate into the host society. The lowly Asian immigrants, so goes this narrative, through hard work and education succeeded in lifting themselves out of poverty and have now "ascended" to the cusp of "whiteness."

In this mythography, the two stereotypes of perpetual foreigner and model minority are mutually inclusive and in fact require each other to wreak their desired racial havoc. The more foreign Asian Americans are, the more remarkable are their supposed success and implied abilities to adapt to the host society; the greater the affirmation of the existing structure and value; and the less necessary it is for the dominant culture to examine the logic of its racial hierarchy. On the other hand, the more successful Asian Americans are perceived to be, the more pronounced is the difference between them and the power holders. As Harris highlights: "In a society structured on racial subordination, white privilege became an expectation and . . . whiteness became the quintessential property for personhood."[6] The allure and the discursive power of a title like "honorary white," after all, derive from a normalized expectation of white privilege. That is why Asian Americans must be perpetually foreign; the construction of whiteness requires them to be so. Asian Americans are forever "whites-to-be," poised at the cusp but never admitted into full whiteness.[7]

Deferred Whiteness

But for whom are Asian Americans a "model"? Frank Chin answers, "Whites love us because we're not black."[8] Since the end of World War II, the attempt to replace the increasingly politically costly category of race with ethnicity prompted liberal social scientists to develop a model of assimilation. According to the chief architect of this model, Robert Park, full integration of blacks into the American ethnicity should happen in four stages: "initial contact between the outsider and the host society, economic and political competition, economic and cultural accommodation of the ethnic to the host society, and finally, assimilation into the host society."[9] This model was drawn mainly from the experience of European immigrants who were thought to be able to "achieve whiteness" in a generation following the prescribed course of assimilation.

This assimilation model is today discredited for its one-sided emphasis on personal initiative to the exclusion of systemic change. It fails to dismantle institutional racism and its legal infrastructure by dangling the promise of a "colorblind" society. Two results from this ethnicity theory continue to influence U.S. race relations today, however. The better known is the use of Asian Americans to reinforce the dominant ideology that the U.S. is a just society that provides a level playing field to all who acquiesce to the social demands of industry and good citizenship. As Gale A. Yee observes, "The supposed accomplishments of Asian Americans divert attention away from the fact that racial discrimination is a structural feature of U.S. society, produced by centuries of systematic exclusion, exploitation, and disregard of racially defined minorities."[10] The "success story" of Asian Americans is used to show how a minoritized group could follow the path of assimilation and become successful in American society—provided they work hard and keep their mouths shut.

A "model" for whom? For African Americans, Native Americans, Latinos and Latinas, and any other minoritized groups who "whine" about racism. Not only does the model-minority myth leave intact the racist structure, it incites minority groups to compete for privilege to be doled out by the power holders.[11] "Race," writes Ian Haney López, "remains a social system in which persons from different positions in the racial hierarchy seek, or contest their exclusion from, social and material status."[12] It keeps us from raising questions about the unequal power relation between whites and nonwhites, and shifts our attention to how nonwhites must compete among themselves before they could be accorded "white privilege." The myth of model minority pits Asian Americans against other racially minoritized groups and resulted in racial skirmishes in Queens, New York, in the late 1980s and in the 1992 burning of Los Angeles.

A second result of the assimilation model is the categorical denial of whiteness to Asian Americans. The term "ethnic" was originally used to describe European immigrants such as the Irish, Italians, Greeks, and Jews who were not yet "white."[13] Historically, it was the presence of Asian immigrants that forced a collapse of these European ethnics into "whiteness," belatedly and reluctantly. In that process, Americanness was equated with whiteness and race became the criterion for national identity. As Susan Koshy observes, "Both blacks and Asians *helped make* the liminal European groups white, an identity that would have been less tenable in their absence."[14] An ethnic reasoning was thus set up. It stipulated that the Irish, the Greeks, the Jews, and the Italians were white because they were *not* Asian or black or Native American. The implication was that Asian Americans could not be white if the Irish, the Italians, the Greeks, and the Jews were.

Today the myth of the model minority is maintained for much the same purpose: to buttress the dominant ideology and to forestall dismantling structural racism. Asian Americans remain minoritized, racialized as non-white, but also as perpetual "whites-to-be." Deferred whiteness is held out at once as enticement to and as prevention from full American membership. Meanwhile, systemic racism operates now as before.

Ambivalence as a Reading Strategy

Asian Americans respond to the model-minority myth with a discomforting sense of ambivalence. A term borrowed from psychoanalysis, ambivalence describes the feeling of wanting one thing and, simultaneously, its opposite. The postcolonial theorist Homi Bhabha first used the concept to characterize the colonial subjects' complex mixture of attraction and repulsion toward the colonizers (see also the "Postcolonial Approaches" chapter). But the resulting relation between the colonizers and subjects is neither purely oppressive nor purely resistant but both. The colonizers demand that the colonized acknowledge and accept the superiority of the colonizers' culture, especially by attempting to adapt aspects of it in acquiescence. When the colonial subjects try to imitate their masters, the result is imperfect and their mimicry turns into mockery because the clash and mutual interpenetration between the worlds of the subjects and of the colonizers is by nature adaptive, creative, and finally transgressive. The subjects' ability to "be like" their colonizers becomes a menace, as it undermines the colonizers' claim to "cultural superiority."

In the Asian American relation to the dominant culture, ambivalence fittingly describes their experience of the twin myths of model minority and perpetual foreigner. The earlier generations of Asian immigrants sought the U.S. shores to flee from economic hardship or political persecution. The initial relief and hope soon gave way to bitter despair as they encountered the reality of institutionalized and popular racism. For example, in the shadow of the Chinese Exclusion Act of 1882, Asian American immigrants, mainly Chinese Americans, were detained on Angel Island off the coast of San Francisco, even when they had legitimate entrance documents. Detention often lasted months, even years. Poems composed by these early twentieth-century Chinese immigrants and etched on wooden walls while they languished on Angel Island give voice to this ambivalence.[15] Even before they officially set foot on American soil, the harsh treatment they received colored their perception of the U.S. as a hostile land, a place they would stay only for sake of survival.

> Myriads and myriads of verses on the walls,
> All grievances and plaintive galls.
> If I shed this prison and prevail,
> I will remember this bygone tale.
> Daily needs I will myself curtail,
> Lest extravagance my youth to fail.
> My kinsfolk, you must never omit:
> Small gains then straightway homeward commit.[16]

Protest against injustice is given voice in another poem:

> America has might but no justice,
> Imprisoning us the innocent they practice.
> How cruel they are to heed no reason!
> I bow my head: what hopeless despondence I notice![17]

Yet, in spite of their anger, and even after they had been driven out from town to town up and down the west coast, Asian Americans stayed.[18] This willingness to endure unspeakable pain and isolation imposed by a racist society gives us a glimpse of the profound ambivalence of being in two places at once, being simultaneously repulsed by legally protected violence and attracted by the opportunities afforded them in the new land. Such a hybrid identification meant they were somehow both Asian and American but at the same time neither Asian nor American.

This ambivalence is today crystallized most clearly in the model-minority myth. The myth engenders tremendous pride among Asian Americans, especially during the 1970s and '80s when images of the Asian whiz kids were on the covers of *Time Magazine* and the *New York Times*. This "we have arrived" euphoria, however, was and still is always accompanied by alienation, for the model-minority myth trades on exoticizing the very subject it extols. It embodies a statement that such success, while celebrated, is the exception rather than the rule. It normalizes the foreignness of Asian Americans, all the while giving them an appearance of acceptance. The flip side of the model-minority myth is that of the perpetual foreigner.

Asian Americans therefore exist in the tension between locations and loyalties. They occupy the empty interstitial space between ancestral homelands that no longer welcome them and America where the hulking structure of white supremacy dominates the landscape.[19] It is a permanent diaspora of endless sojourn with no Promised Land, a perpetual exodus with no Jordan River.

This is the essence of the ambivalence that colors how Asian Americans read the biblical text. We read our very ambivalence into the text, to perform a hermeneutics of immersion, as it were. We do so by discovering how the web of power relations encoded in the biblical text has created the same ambivalence in biblical characters that defines the Asian American experience. Gale A. Yee uses this method successfully to read Ruth.[20]

An Asian American reading of Paul's letter to the Galatians might proceed in the same way. By examining how the twin myths of perpetual foreigner and model minority function in the text, Asian Americans might find in Paul a prototype of their experience. In so doing they also inscribe the Asian American experience in the biblical text. I hasten to add this is not a "method" as such. If anything, it is an anti-method. It is a self-understanding or perhaps a "pre-understanding" that enables us to approach the biblical text with boldness and humility. Besides, any attempt to formulate an Asian American "method" would run up against the impossible and inadvisable task of defining who is "Asian American" and what an "Asian American biblical hermeneutics" is.[21]

READING GALATIANS THROUGH ASIAN AMERICAN AMBIVALENCE

Ambivalence is produced by power differentials, and this expresses itself in two dimensions. Vertically, the state of powerlessness produces in the colonial subjects both attraction to the empire and a repulsion. Horizontally, it also produces in one minoritized group ambivalence toward other minoritized groups or members within the same group. Both of these can be richly documented in the Asian American experience. Conflicts and contradictions engendered by the empire at the state level are transformed at the social level as competition between groups for inclusion in the dominant culture. The empire, which controls all membership to the dominant culture, is therefore always relevant by its insistent presence.

Like Asian Americans, Paul was a member of a model minority and a perpetual foreigner in the Roman Empire. He was a high achiever living in the diaspora. Chances are he was not a Roman citizen, which makes him a resident alien from the land of Judea, subject to taxes by the local authorities for being a foreigner. His ambivalence toward his colonizers is difficult to access and assess, since he makes few direct statements about the Roman Empire as such. But we can approach the problem via his ambivalence toward the Jerusalem leadership of the Jesus movement, since it is common, often necessary, to transpose opposition against the Empire to opposition against symbolic representation or a mere reminder of the Empire. In the Jesus movement, Paul found a temporary home where his talents were put to good use and his ethnicity did not make him a foreigner. But this movement also replicates the imperial structure, with its capital centered in Jerusalem and its leaders installed as heads of state. Subsequently, Paul reacted to the Jerusalem hierarchy in the same way he would have reacted to the Empire. If so, his ambivalence toward the empire would have mirrored his ambivalence toward the Jerusalem leaders (see also the "Postcolonial Approaches" chapter).

Inviting comparison to the Jerusalem leadership, Paul recounts his accomplishments and portrays himself as a "model minority." Paul tells his readers: "I advanced in the study of Judaism far beyond those of the same age among my people, being far much more zealous for my ancestral traditions" (1:14). Since "ancestral traditions" form the content of a young Jew's education, the statement is tantamount to saying he was a child prodigy in the rabbinic school, a star student who graduated summa cum laude, at the top of his class.[22] This model minority might not be a racial or ethnic minority in relation to a dominant group in a metropolis, but he presents himself as a minoritized member in terms of power *vis-à-vis* the Jerusalem leaders who are themselves minoritized by the Empire. If we take the Gospel accounts seriously, the Pillars, James, Peter, and John, were of peasant stock from the north countries, while Paul facilely boasted of his finely honed rabbinic education. They likely were Aramaic speakers with a Galilean accent, while Paul was fluent in Greek, the prestige language of the Empire. Just how his education and language are indispensable tools in his work among Greek-speaking Gentiles is amply corroborated by his success among them. His personal qualifications and success, he feels, should earn him a place at the table. This is the genesis of the Jerusalem meeting of 2:1-10.

Power Struggles in Jerusalem

One scholarly consensus on Galatians is that it reflects a debate between Paul and traditionally minded missionaries over the necessity of circumcision for Gentile followers of Jesus. Emissaries show up in Galatia advocating that the Gentiles undergo circumcision (5:2-3, 6; 6:12-13; cf. 5:6; 6:15). That they would valorize circumcision is indicative of their Jerusalem-Antioch pedigree. Some time ago, in Antioch, Paul had split from the powers that be over the observance of the Jewish Law (Gal. 2:11-14). To understand the debate, we need to examine the power dynamics behind Galatians, in particular Paul's tortuous relationship with Jerusalem chronicled in Galatians 1:13–2:10.

The narrative leads to a climax in the Jerusalem meeting of 2:1-10. Three groups play central roles in the story: the reputed "Pillars" of Jerusalem, James, Peter, and John (2:9); the Antioch delegation of Barnabas, Titus, and Paul; and the opposition whom Paul derisively calls "false brothers" (2:4). Why the last named group opposed the Antioch delegation Paul does not make explicit, except to say that "[they] came in through the side door to spy on our freedom which we have in Christ Jesus, in order that they might enslave us." Since later in Galatians Paul ties freedom and slavery to observing the Jewish Law (see the Sarah-Hagar story in 4:21–5:1; also 5:4, 18), it is likely that the opposition insisted that Gentiles follow the "works of the law." The phrase most likely refers to ritual aspects of the Torah such as dietary requirements and circumcision. Paul resists their effort, "in order that the truth of the gospel might remain with you" (2:5). If the debate is over observing the ritual Torah, "truth of the gospel" must refer to a ritual-free gospel that does not require Gentiles to circumcise or to keep the food law.

Who has the authority to convene the meeting? The Pillars in Jerusalem, no doubt. They have the authority to overrule the opposition: Paul tells his Galatian readers that the Gentile convert Titus is not "forced" to be circumcised (2:3). The Jerusalem leaders refuse to side with the opposition, to impose the Torah across the board to Gentile followers of Jesus. At least not yet. The Pillars have jurisdiction over Paul as well. Paul has "[to lay] (*anatithēnai*) before them the gospel that [he] preached among the Gentiles"—for approval—"lest somehow [he] was running and had run in vain" (2:2). This is an extraordinary admission in view of the snide remarks he makes about the Jerusalem leadership elsewhere (see below). The word *anatithēnai* means laying something before someone for consideration or communicating something to someone with a request for opinion. If so, Paul presents himself to the Jerusalem Pillars as a model minority hoping that his success among Gentiles can bring him recognition, status, and power. For their part, the Pillars also treat Paul as a model minority, commending him for his ability and success ("recognizing the grace that had been given me," 2:9), promising him partnership ("gave me . . . the right hand of fellowship," 2:9), but as events unfolding later in Antioch (2:11-14) tell us, ultimately conceding to him no real power.

In spite of Paul's best effort to cover up the unequal relationship between himself and the leadership, therefore, his account betrays a palpable power differential between them. The Antioch delegation has to travel to Jerusalem for the meeting, Paul's appeal to revelation notwithstanding (2:2a). Paul has to explain to the Jerusalem leaders the nature and content of his preaching, even though he again tries to save face by adding that he met the leadership "in private" (2:2c). They alone, in other words, not the opposition, are in a position of power.

While Paul has to submit to the Pillars, he acknowledges their authority grudgingly. He uses the phrase *hoi dokountes* ("those who appear or are reputed [to be something]") four times (2:2, 6 [2x], 9), a phrase dripping with irony and ambiguity. He uses it in a general exhortation to warn against empty self-deception: "If anyone is reputed to be something but is not, he is deceiving himself" (6:3). In 2:6, he calls the Jerusalem Pillars *hoi dokountes einai ti* ("those who are reputed to be something"), and immediately qualifies it with a Hebrew proverb, "God shows no partiality." The Pillars' appearance is contrasted to their substance, which does not impress him: "*Of what sort of men* they presumably were makes no difference to me" (2:6). He calls James, Peter, and John not "Pillars," only "*reputed* Pillars" (*hoi dokountes styloi*, 2:9). If there is any doubt about his antipathy toward the Pillars in Jerusalem, his equation of the heavenly Jerusalem with the free woman Sarah and *earthly Jerusalem* with the slavery of Hagar (4:21–5:1) removes it.

In the last analysis, Paul has no choice but to submit to the Pillars, even though he makes a valiant effort to elevate his own status *vis-à-vis* the leaders. He suggests that the reputed leaders have to acknowledge the divine authority with which he is vested. They realize that he is entrusted with the gospel as much as Peter is (2:7), he is empowered (literally, "energized") for the apostolate just as Peter is (2:8), and he is endowed with the same grace as the Pillars are (2:9a). Paul presents himself as the sole leader responsible for defending the welfare of Gentiles through his liberal use of the first person singular. Paul alone goes to Jerusalem (*anebēn*, "I went up," 2:1), and he does so "according to a revelation" (2:2), lest one thinks he is summoned. He says nothing of Barnabas's attendance; he claims he is the sole leader of the delegation, and he alone submits his gospel to the scrutiny of the Pillars (2:2). Paul makes it clear that it is he, not Barnabas, who takes Titus to the meeting (2:1), leaving the impression that he is also responsible for the well-being of Titus and his not being compelled to circumcise (2:3). He claims active agency only for himself. At the end there is no camouflaging the stark reality that it is the Pillars who "gave" the Antioch delegation their stamp of approval or "right hand of fellowship" (2:9), not the other way around. It is the Pillars who exact a financial promise from the Antioch congregation to collect money from Paul's Gentile congregations for Jerusalem (2:10), not the other way around.

The Ambivalent Paul

Judging from the reaction of the power clique at the Jerusalem meeting and from their subsequent imposition on Antioch (2:12-13), they never intend to grant Paul the power he is seeking. Their actions are consistent with how the dominant culture treats the model minority. They offer a glass ceiling to entice the eager status-seekers and simultaneously to block them from promotion. Their purpose is to cultivate a coterie of hardworking, subservient workers without upsetting the current structure of inequality. At first blush, the Jerusalem leaders seem willing to concede Paul and the Gentile mission a measure of autonomy, giving the Antioch delegation "the right hand of fellowship, in order that [Paul] should go among the Gentiles and they among the circumcised" (2:9). Paul takes this to mean a power-sharing agreement has been reached. The mission field would be divided into the circumcised and uncircumcised, with the Gentile mission gaining independence and him installed as its leader. Paul's self-confidence leads him to over-interpreting the Pillars' action. James' imposition of a stricter ritual-centered gospel on Antioch (2:12), and indirectly on the Gentile mission, indicates that Jerusalem never intends to relinquish or even to share control of the worldwide mission. Moreover, the imposition of a financial obligation on the Gentile congregations (2:10), probably modeled on the temple tax, is a reminder to Paul and company that they must submit to the power center. The power differential vested in the status quo is thereby upheld and reaffirmed. By the time of the writing of Galatians, Paul has finally recognized the Pillars' true intention for what it is. Outsiders arrive in Galatia, which Paul takes to be his, preaching the ritual-centered gospel of Jerusalem-Antioch. Paul interprets this as Jerusalem's reneging on a supposed power-sharing arrangement.

If the Jerusalem leaders hold all the cards, one wonders if Paul's confidence might not be an over-compensation for a position of weakness. His repeated claim of divine appointment is designed to distance himself from the Jerusalem leadership. His self-introduction stresses the divine appointment of his apostolate: "Paul an apostle not from human beings, nor through a human being, but through Jesus Christ and God the father who raised him from the dead . . . " (1:1). The content of the gospel he preaches to Gentiles is said to come not from any human source but from God directly (1:11-12).

In speaking of his revelation, Paul is interested less in the experience itself than in the independent locus of authority—that is, independent from Jerusalem—the experience supposedly gave him: "When God who set me apart from my mother's womb and called me through his grace was pleased to reveal his son in me, that I might preach him among the Gentiles, straightway I did not consult flesh and blood, nor did I go up to Jerusalem to the apostles who came before me. Instead, I went away into Arabia and returned again to Damascus" (1:15-17). The revelation itself is mired in a subordinate clause, while the main clause is a self-defense of his independence from Jerusalem: "straightway I did not consult flesh and blood, *nor did I go up to Jerusalem*" (1:16b-17a). He goes instead into Arabia before returning to Damascus. He recounts his earlier persecution of the Jesus-followers (1:13) and his reception by the Judean followers of Jesus. The latter are surprised by his radical transformation (1:22-24) for the same reason: his former violent opposition could not have given him a chance to learn "the gospel of Jesus Christ" from anyone, least of all the Jerusalem congregation he sought to destroy.

In this narrative Paul cannot resist jabs at the Jerusalem leaders, and in this we catch a glimpse of his ambivalence towards them. He calls Peter and others "the before-me apostles" (1:17), thus thrusting himself into the ranks of apostles. The Opposition, named or unnamed, are just like me but they are also different. The leaders in Jerusalem are apostles just like me if not for the minor fact that they were appointed before me. He calls his opponents in Jerusalem "false brothers" (2:4). While Paul stresses his differences from them, he is willing to call them "brothers." Even when he warns the Galatians of a perverse gospel from the ritual-centered missionaries (1:6-9), a gospel "different" from (1:6) that which Paul preached (1:8) and the Galatians received (1:9), Paul still calls it a "gospel." Perverted it might be, it is a "gospel."

It is only through the lens of this same-yet-different ambivalence toward Jerusalem that we can fully appreciate Paul's account of his visit with Peter and James in Jerusalem: "Then after three years I went up to Jerusalem *to visit and receive information from* [*historein*] Cephas and remained with him for fifteen days; any other of the apostles I did not see, except James, the Brother of the Lord" (1:18-19). The word *historein* means both "to visit" and "to visit for the purpose of getting information." While scholars debated endlessly on which of this Paul meant, the answer is both. The ambiguity of the word gives verbal expression to Paul's ambivalence.

Meanwhile, the Opposition does not stand idly by. The Pillars did not initially rule in their favor, but they soon gain an upper hand. Not long after the Jerusalem meeting, James sends his lieutenants to impose the ritual gospel on Antioch (2:12). Peter, Barnabas, and the other Jewish members comply (2:13), while Paul refuses (2:11, 14). That refusal earns him an expulsion from the Antioch-Jerusalem axis. The Opposition now decisively has the upper hand, and Paul is once again reduced to a wanderer, a perpetual foreigner in his own movement, consigned by the Jerusalem-Antioch metropolis to its periphery. Paul is excluded a second time, this time by members of his own group.

CONCLUSION

Paul's ambivalence toward the Jerusalem hierarchy led to a contentious relationship with its leaders. Having been brought up in the diaspora and having endured the twin stereotypes of model minority and perpetual foreigner, he thought he had found a home in the Jesus movement. His early success in Greek-speaking cities led him to believe he might play a more central role in the large movement. Leaders ensconced in Jerusalem, however, had other ideas. Their direct and personal contact with Jesus had given them a privileged status, one which they were not ready to share with an upstart returnee from the diaspora. They treated Paul in much the same way the dominant culture treated him. They used the same stereotypes to keep him at arm's length from the center of power. Ultimately, Paul was forced out altogether. We witness, therefore, in Paul the same double exclusion experienced by modern Asian Americans, who are marginalized by the white culture in the U.S. and also by their ancestral cultures in Asia. They, like Paul, are perpetual foreigners no matter where they go.

What is impossible to ignore in both Paul's and our times, however, is the hulking presence of empire. Its presence is more than mere background to what appears on the surface to be an intramural squabble. In both cases empire provides the hierarchical model that is founded on power struggle and exclusion. The Jerusalem hierarchy replicated the Empire and ended up treating Paul the same way the Empire had done. Similarly, the struggles of Asian Americans for acceptance might be institutional (for example, corporation, university, government, and so on), but that is because the organizational rationale used in these institutions is modeled after the dominant white culture.

Even more impinging than modeling conflicts, empire is also the material cause for internal conflicts. In Paul's case James's imposition of rituals on the early Jesus followers was likely a necessary response to the political and ethnic unrest experienced in Jerusalem. The unrest would explode into full-scale revolt fifteen years later, but evidence suggests the unrest had been a constant feature of life in Jerusalem ever since Rome installed Herod the Great as a puppet king to rule Judea. Today, the American Empire has assiduously cultivated a geopolitical world of power blocs and competitive divisions that operates on the principles of enmity and power differentials between the U.S. and other countries, in particular "emerging" Asian countries. The Asian Americans' experience of double exclusion is the result of an intentional American policy. Reading Paul as model minority and perpetual foreigner, then, Asian Americans find in Paul a mirror to understand their own experience of ambivalence.

FURTHER READING

Harris, Cheryl. "Whiteness as Property," *Harvard Law Review* 106 (1993): 1707–91. A discussion of the legal protection of whiteness.

Koshy, Susan. "Morphing Race into Ethnicity: Asian Americans and Critical Transformations of Whiteness," *Boundary 2* 28 (2001): 153–94. Discusses the inter-connected history of constructing race and ethnicity for Asian Americans and whiteness.

Lee, Robert G. *Orientals: Asian Americans in Popular Culture*. Philadelphia: Temple University Press, 1999. A social analysis of how Asian Americans are portrayed in popular culture.

Liew, Tat-Siong Benny. *What Is Asian American Biblical Hermeneutics?* Honolulu: University of Hawaii Press, 2008. An attempt at defining Asian American identity and hermeneutics inductively.

López, Ian Haney. *White by Law: The Legal Construction of Race*. Rev. and updated 10th anniversary ed. New York and London: New York University Press, 2006. A historical account of race construction in the U.S. and the legal infrastructure erected in support.

Osajima, Keith. "Asian Americans as the Model Minority: An Analysis of the Popular Press Image in the 1960s and 1980s," in *Contemporary Asian America: A Multidisciplinary Reader*, edited by Min Zhou and James V. Gatewood, 449–58. New York & London: New York University Press, 2000. A historical analysis of the "model minority" myth in the popular media.

Wan, Sze-kar. "Betwixt and Between: Towards a Hermeneutics of Hyphenation," in *Ways of Being, Ways of Reading: Asian-American Biblical Interpretation*, edited by Mary F. Foskett and Jeffrey Kah-Jin Kuan, 137–51. St. Louis: Chalice, 2006. A hermeneutical discussion of the social and geopolitical location of Asian Americans.

———. "Does Diaspora Identity Imply Some Sort of Universality? An Asian-American Reading of Galatians," in *Interpreting Beyond the Border*, edited by Fernando F. Segovia, 107–31. The Bible and Postcolonialism, 2. Sheffield: Sheffield Academic Press, 2000. An Asian American reading of Galatians as ethnic construction.

Yee, Gale. "'She Stood in Tears Amid the Alien Corn': Ruth, the Perpetual Foreigner and Model Minority," in *They Were All Together in One Place? Toward Minority Biblical Criticism*, edited by Randall C. Bailey; Tat-siong Benny Liew, and Fernando F. Segovia, 119–140, in Semeia Studies 57. Atlanta: Society of Biblical Literature, 2009. Reading of the book of Ruth as an Asian American biblical scholar, along the line of the two myths of model minority and perpetual foreigner.

———. "Yin/Yang Is Not Me: An Exploration into an Asian American Biblical Hermeneutics," in *Ways of Being, Ways of Reading: Asian-American Biblical Interpretation*, edited by Mary F. Foskett and Jeffrey Kah-Jin Kuan, 152–63. St. Louis: Chalice, 2006. An excursion into the difficult place of not being fully accepted either in the U.S. or in Asia.

NOTES

1. Gale Yee has enumerated "perpetual foreigner" and "model minority" as the two defining characteristics of the Asian American experience. See her "'She Stood in Tears Amid the Alien Corn': Ruth, the Perpetual Foreigner and Model Minority," in *They Were All Together in One Place? Toward Minority Biblical Criticism*, ed. Randall C. Bailey, Tat-siong Benny Liew,

and Fernando F. Segovia; *Semeia* Studies 57 (Atlanta: Society of Biblical Literature, 2009), 119–40, especially 120–26.

2. I want to thank Drs. Gale Yee and Patrick Cheng for their careful reading of an earlier draft and their helpful suggestions. This chapter is infinitely better because of their contributions.

3. Cheryl Harris, "Whiteness as Property," *Harvard Law Review* 106 (1993): 1707–91; see 1734–36 for her notion of "status property." Appealing to James Madison's view of property as "[embracing] every thing to which a man may attach a value and have a right," Harris takes this to mean the totality of a person's legal right: "Whiteness defined the legal status of a person as slave or free. White identity conferred tangible and economically valuable benefits and was jealously guarded as a valued possession, allowed only to those who met a strict standard of proof" (p. 1726).

4. Harris, "Whiteness as Property," 1736; emphasis supplied.

5. Articles in the popular press in the 1960s and 80s all reinforce these same American values. See Keith Osajima, "Asian Americans as the Model Minority: An Analysis of the Popular Press Image in the 1960s and 1980s," in *Contemporary Asian America: A Multidisciplinary Reader*, ed. Min Zhou and James V. Gatewood (New York & London: New York University Press, 2000), 449–58, 451, 453.

6. Harris, "Whiteness as Property," 1730.

7. The phrase "whites-to-be" is Susan Koshy's: "Morphing Race into Ethnicity: Asian Americans and Critical Transformations of Whiteness," *Boundary 2* 28 (2001): 153–94; see 187.

8. Frank Chin et al., eds., *Aiiieeee! An Anthology of Asian-American Writers* (Washington, DC: Howard University Press, 1974); cited in Robert G. Lee, *Orientals: Asian Americans in Popular Culture* (Philadelphia: Temple University Press, 1999), 145. See also, Osajima, "Asian Americans as the Model Minority," 450–51.

9. Summary provided by Lee, *Orientals*, 158.

10. Yee, "'She Stood in Tears amid the Alien Corn,'" 125.

11. Data show that not all Asian American groups progress at the same rate and that, while Asian American professionals might do well overall, they invariably run up against the glass ceiling. All this shows that race-based discrimination still persists in the American workplace today. See Lucie Cheng and Philip Q. Yang, "The 'Model Minority' Deconstructed," in *Contemporary Asian America*, 459–82.

12. Ian Haney López, *White by Law: The Legal Construction of Race*, rev. and updated 10th anniv. ed. (New York and London: New York University Press, 2006), Preface. Haney López goes on to say, "Justice lies, then, not in embracing Whiteness (that is, advantage), but in seeking to dismantle race as a system that correlates to power and privilege."

13. See Richard Alba, *Ethnic Identity: The Transformation of White America* (New Haven: Yale University Press, 1990); and Koshy, "Morphing Race into Ethnicity," 188–90.

14. Koshy, "Morphing Race into Ethnicity," 165–66; emphasis supplied.

15. These poems that are now collected in Him Mak Lai, Genny Lim, and Judy Yung, eds., *Island: Poetry and History of Chinese Immigrants on Angel Island 1910-1940* (San Francisco: History of Chinese Detained on Island, 1986). For a history of the Angel Island project, see introduction on 8–29.

16. My translation; Chinese original in Lai et al., *Island*, 67.

17. My translation; Chinese original in Lai et al., *Island*, 59.

18. For a history of the systematic expulsion of Chinese Americans from the west coast, see Jean Pfaelzer, *Driven Out: The Forgotten War against Chinese Americans* (Berkeley: University of California Press, 2008).

19. For this double exclusion of Asian Americans, see Sze-kar Wan, "Betwixt and Between: Towards a Hermeneutics of Hyphenation," in *Ways of Being, Ways of Reading: Asian-American Biblical Interpretation*, ed. Mary F. Foskett and Jeffrey Kah-Jin Kuan (St. Louis: Chalice, 2006), 137–51, especially 147–49.

20. Yee, "'She Stood in Tears amid the Alien Corn.'"

21. Yee lends a personal voice to this dead-end question in "Yin/Yang Is Not Me: An Exploration into an Asian American Biblical Hermeneutics," in *Ways of Being, Ways of Reading*, 152–63. Liew's proposal of skirting the what-question by "inventing a tradition" of *all* self-avowed Asian and Asian American biblical writers in a move he calls "referencing without referentiality" (*What Is Asian American Biblical Hermeneutics?* [Honolulu: University of Hawaii Press, 2008], 2–9) is a wise one, even if I question its cogency and practicality.

22. The educational context of the statement is what motivated me to translate *ioudaismos* ("Judaism") as "*study of* Judaism." Paul here is not speaking of a "former Judaism" as opposed to a "present Christianity," a construct possible only if the later split between Judaism and Christianity is read back into Galatians. At this time, Paul had no notion of "Christianity" or a supposed obsolescence of Judaism (see the "Historical Approaches" and "Jewish Perspectives" chapters).

10

POSTCOLONIAL APPROACHES

Negotiating Empires, Then and Now

JEREMY PUNT

INTRODUCTION

Our world today is marked by a range of factors and influences—globalization, diverse forms of neocolonialism, the devaluing and commercialization of human life, and on-going violent and armed conflicts—so many of which have religious subtexts. Many postcolonial thinkers have assessed the enduring political, cultural, and economic impact of these factors, yet a postcolonial optic is not only valuable in accounting for our modern-day, contemporary contexts, and their impact on biblical interpretation. In the first-century CE Mediterranean context, the very existence of life in its various forms was determined by the seemingly omnipresent and omnipotent Roman Empire in its various guises. True to imperial ideology, the empire was ubiquitous in tangible and visible ways. The reigning emperor and the current and past imperial families made their presence felt through the "mass media" of the time: statues, coins, monuments, and temples (see also the "Spatial Perspectives" and "Visual Perspectives" chapters). These made it clear, though, what their presence stood for: power and control.[1] The material reality of imperial imposition largely determined the social fabric, the reality of life for first-century people. This imperially informed context was constantly reinforced by visual images and verbal and written decrees, through military presence and social systems such as patronage.

Empires, then, have had an impact on the history and culture of both ancient and more contemporary contexts. A postcolonial approach to any of these contexts is not simply to perform an anti-imperial reading of this impact, though. Because empires have their own attractions as well as dangers, a postcolonial approach needs to extend its reach to investigate and consider the imperial context in broader scope, incorporating but then also going beyond the perceptions and workings of a dominating political order or state apparatus. The political systems and mechanisms of empire were ably assisted by various social constructs that promoted social buy-in, tacit support, and even overt promotion. These functioned in subtle and sublime, public and confrontational ways to sustain uneven power relationships across the spectrum of first-century life. Since everybody was affected in one way or another, all first-century people were negotiating empire.

Paul's letters were created, circulated, and read within this socio-historical setting, amidst and as part of the Roman Empire. Paul lived under the reign of this empire, as did those communities who received and then distributed his letters. As will be explained below, it was a reign that expanded beyond military domination and included a whole range of socio-political notions, systems, and structures. Further, in more recent history, biblical literature and interpretation, or biblical texts and ideas, have also been used to justify, reinforce, and support imperial regimes and movements. Such regimes use every available social, cultural, political, and economic factor to support themselves, including politics, gender, sexuality, economics, religion, family structures and various others.

As a result, postcolonial thinking tends to go beyond simply describing the binaries of oppressor and oppressed, in order to expose and rewrite these relations. Postcolonial approaches inquire into *both* the structural and relational nature of life for those living on the down side of power *and* the sustaining power of the imperial venture and its operations. The basic scope and value of a postcolonial approach for reading and studying Paul's letters are addressed here, then, in three broad sections, dealing first with the development of and terminology in postcolonial thinking, followed by a consideration of its value for New Testament studies, and finally a brief postcolonial exploration of 1 Thessalonians.

WHAT IS POSTCOLONIAL BIBLICAL CRITICISM?

Postcolonial biblical criticism is a critical theory of interpretation, particularly interested in investigating the uneven and complex power relations that result from imperialism, colonialism, and other forms of marginalization. It draws upon the work of postcolonial thinkers and theorists, like Edward Said, Gayatri Chakravorty Spivak and Homi Bhabha, among others. Before considering aspects of their work, and their usefulness for the analysis of biblical texts, though, it is important to define the terms used in such forms of analysis. Broadly speaking, postcolonial studies engage the geopolitical and dialectical relationship between center and margins, metropolis and periphery. As a result, biblical scholar Fernando Segovia distinguishes between imperialism as that which concerns the center or metropolis and colonialism as that which is related to the margins or periphery. This corresponds to Said's way of defining the two concepts, where imperialism is "the practice, the theory, and the attitudes of a dominating metropolitan city ruling a distant territory," while colonialism is a consequence of imperialism and is specifically about "the implanting of settlements on distant territory."[2]

For the purposes of our discussion, then, the primary use of postcolonial will be as a conceptual, philosophical, or even political marker of resistance to the practices and effects of colonialism and similar geo-political forms of hegemony, both historically and discursively. As the brief reference to the first-century example (above) already suggests, empires work not only by imposing political force but also by generating ways of thinking and being. Thus, postcolonial is not mainly a historical marker (some time "after" colonialism), it refers to the full extent of the continuing practical effects and conditions of colonialism, even after its "official" end. A postcolonial approach involves creating awareness, or "conscientizing" about "the problematic of domination and subordination in the geopolitical realm."[3] Since to be colonized is to be removed from history, postcolonial writing involves the arduous task of reentering a history from which the colonized were excluded.[4] But a colonized mind-set involves more than consciousness about exclusion, as it also entails the awareness of rivalries between colonized groups competing for scarce resources and for the favor of the colonizers. Thus, one must become more attuned to how the colonized consent to colonialism.[5] In this sense, then, colonialism's power is maintained by colonial forms of knowledge.

Unlike many other approaches, a postcolonial approach to biblical interpretation is keen to acknowledge and reflect upon its social location, and have it interact with other similar but also different and even oppositional approaches. Postcolonial scholars in biblical, religious, and theological studies frequently acknowledge their connections to or commonalities with liberation theology, black theology, or feminist approaches, particularly since interdisciplinary interactions with postmodernism and poststructuralism, feminism and gender studies, race and ethnicity studies, and Marxism can often be important but difficult (see the "Economic Approaches," "Feminist Approaches," "African American Approaches," and "Asian American Perspectives" chapters).[6] This might explain why there is not just one method or strategy for postcolonial approaches. As the postcolonial biblical critic R. S. Sugirtharajah notes: "It must be stressed that it [postcolonialism] is not a homogenous project, but a hermeneutical salmagundi, consisting of extremely varied methods, materials, historical entanglements, geographical locations, political affiliations, cultural identities, and economic predicaments."[7]

At first, postcolonial studies developed in part out of various anti-colonial independence movements, particularly in Africa and Asia in the twentieth century.

These movements were in resistance to a number of dominant European colonial powers which, like the Romans centuries earlier, ruled not only by force but also by creating or reinforcing certain social constructs that all the colonized subjects had to negotiate. Resisting these Eurocentric empires will thus require more than establishing formal independence. This problematic is why Edward Said's *Orientalism* (1978) should be understood as an important marker for the development of postcolonial studies. Said adapted ideas and frameworks of thinkers like Michel Foucault and Jacques Derrida to articulate and analyze those social constructs developed by European colonial powers. The analysis of colonial discourse, then, would prove to be important for understanding the continuing, even lingering effects of colonialism. *Orientalism*, in particular, showed how knowledge formations justify imperial and colonial arrangements, and how the West constructed an "Other" in their colonizing discourse—the "Oriental." In Said's words: "the Orient has helped to define Europe (or the West) as its contrasting image, idea, personality, experience."[8]

As a result, attention must be paid to the multiple, overlapping discourses that both define and support imperial and colonial powers, including especially various racisms. One important mechanism for the maintenance of imperial-colonial regimes was in terms of racialized thinking (like Orientalism), often with devastating lingering effects. But, when racism is demystified and put into political perspective, it emerges as a strategy of scapegoating, devised to enable the West to cling to power despite the violent reaction it evoked from the colonized. The colonized is construed "as a population of degenerate types on the basis of racial origin, in order to justify conquest and to establish systems of administration and instruction."[9] Such claims about degeneracy reflect not only racialized but also sexualized ways of arguing. For example, another complementary, and particularly favored, strategy of the colonizers was to claim colonized people engaged in "strange" or even "savage" gender and sexual roles and practices as further justification for colonial rule and "civilization."[10] The study of colonialism, then, can hardly be simply only about colonial center and periphery.

This engagement with other peoples, and the imperial urge to portray them as different from the (imperial) norm, resulted from imperial travels, conquering journeys of "discovery" and "conquest." Apart from the evident economic and other material gains entailed in the conquest of other people's land and resources, such acquisitions also required a colonizing perspective about the conquest, discovery, and salvation of the people themselves. In biblical studies, Musa Dube has particularly stressed the importance of considering these imperial journeys to distant territories as part of postcolonial and postcolonial feminist analysis.[11] The mission narratives of many biblical texts (and the cultures that carried the texts with them on their journeys) can be read as imperialist, sanctioning authoritative travelers and reducing all nations to obedient student disciples of Jesus or the apostles (and, thus, their new representatives among the colonizers). These biblical views of travel involved not only cultural imposition but also support for political and economic submission to an empire, elements which at the time were thoroughly interlinked with the religious.

As Said's work revealed, and this previous example makes clear, what counts as true in Eurocentric settings was far from objective, value-free, or scientific. Postcolonialism, then, shares in the critiques made in postmodernism, in allowing and inviting other, different readings. However, unlike postmodernism, postcolonialism has both a dismantling and constructive energy, implying a theory of agency and social change, and a concern "to speak truth to power" given the suffering of the majority of the world's population.[12] Postcolonial studies' interrogation of ruling regimes and of the constructions of exploitative economic relationships and structures also indicate some of its affinities with Marxist ideas and practices.

Postcolonial approaches can therefore be presented as both identifying how justifications work (in a Said sort of way), as well as in decentering such discourses by reentering, by writing the excluded back into the dominant narratives on the colonized's own terms. A postcolonial approach interprets with suspicion but also toward retrieval or restoration. Interacting with colonial history and its aftermath, a postcolonial optic focuses on histories of repression and repudiation, but through exposé engages also in restoration and transformation. Given this enduring legacy, discursive colonialism probably deserves more attention than simply a recitation of the history of colonialism. Systems of meaning are always linked to the exercise of power in the perpetuation of dominant social systems.[13]

Postcolonial studies accommodates two archives, then, in addressing this discursive impact of colonialism. First, it seeks out and examines writing from the underside, writing by the marginalized in places previously (and currently) colonized. Second, it traces the hegemonic ideologies to which the colonized responded and analyzes how they developed their particular practices of resistance to colonial discourse. Even as such strategies depend upon an ethical commitment to those affected by colonizing discourse, Sugirtharajah commends postcolonial interpretations as "alternative and counter-readings of biblical texts which, like other resistance readings, complicate and fracture the received interpretation and refuse to adopt a simple and single reflection on reality."[14] Accordingly, postcolonial reading allows one to search for "alternative hermeneutics while thus overturning and dismantling colonial perspectives. What postcolonialism does is to enable us to question the totalizing tendencies of European reading practices and interpret the texts on our own terms and read them from our own specific locations."[15] This means that postcolonial criticism involves both a hermeneutic of suspicion and a hermeneutic of retrieval or restoration. It studies not only colonial history, where it sees imperialism and hegemony operating in different forms and at different levels, but also the complex aftermath of colonialism, which is shaped by a history of repression and repudiation. In short, it involves exposé as well as restoration and transformation. It represents a shift in emphasis, a strategy of reading that attempts to point out what was missing in previous analyses, as well as to rewrite and correct.

This does bring us, however, to problems of representing colonial/colonized subjects, how to rewrite such subjects into history. As mentioned earlier, those subaltern groups that find themselves in contexts with unbalanced power relations often try to negotiate both the powerful and other subaltern groups in their attempts to secure power. This could lead to a wide variety of political maneuvers and overtures to the imperial powers. The act of taking up the terminology of the powerful and adjusting it for the subalterns' own purposes can be understood as a *catachresis*. In her discussion of the subaltern, Gayatri Spivak introduced catachresis as a concept for use in postcolonial thought, suggesting that it can describe how the colonized can recycle or redeploy parts of colonial and imperial culture and propaganda for their own purposes (and in conflict with their first, or more "proper" uses). Catachresis, then, is at once an act of creative appropriation that turns the rhetorical instruments of their colonial owners against them. As a device of subversive adaptation, it redirects the incursions of imperialist discourse and creates a parody of the empire through strategic misrepresentation. If interested in tracing how the subalterns register their resistance against empire, though, one might also need to account for some of the strategic, even subtle ways this might have been done. Here is where one can use another helpful notion, from political scientist James C. Scott. Scott recognizes that subtle opposition to imperial claims is necessary, as explicit opposition can be quite dangerous to express publicly. Therefore, one must look for the "hidden transcripts" of the oppressed in a "social space in which offstage dissent to the official transcript of power relations may be voiced."[16] Thus, appropriations might not take the most obvious forms in colonized cultures, making their history more difficult to trace.

Postcolonial analysis also involves a critique of the ideology of the colonizing discourse, since texts always have vested interests. Such analysis can expose the overt self-interest and more covert forms of justification for the dominant in these texts. But, postcolonial approaches do not just focus on domination and resistance, especially because the effects of colonialism on culture are wider and far more variable, leading to ambivalences and ambiguities. In fact, the creative appropriation described above can develop in such ambiguous contexts through practices like colonial mimicry (a concept considered by Homi Bhabha, but see also the "Asian American Perspectives" chapter). Since colonization also works through culture, the colonizers often try to impose their culture on the colonized, compelling the latter to (try to) imitate or mimic the supposedly superior culture. Internalization, then, would mark their acceptance and subservience to this culture. This replication of the colonizers' culture, however, is never perfect, but it can become subversive. The supposedly inferior colonized people's ability to become more "like" the colonizer undercuts their rationale for empire: their superior culture. Mimicry can become a form of mockery, showing how the apparent distinction can be repeated and in ways the colonizers do not intend. In the case of Paul, his mimicry of empire may create the impression that he had *both* internalized and replicated the colonizer's culture *and* employed the ambivalence of colonial or hegemonic discourse to his own advantage.

From the discussion it is evident that a single, all-inclusive description or summary of postcolonial approaches is impossible. Nevertheless, postcolonial work on the New Testament would include attention to the relationships between texts and power at the geopolitical level in different ways. Postcolonial work links up with various other critical theories to consider the complex and ambiguous constellations of power communicated in the texts, and their enduring legacies. In the following section a number of strategies for accomplishing such work in the Pauline letters are discussed.

POSTCOLONIAL KINDS OF APPROACHES TO PAUL

As noted above, the context for the creation and circulation of Pauline literature was determined by the Roman Empire. While on face value some of these texts appear to be "pro-imperial" (like Rom. 13:1-7), a wide range of them can be understood as reflecting power concerns in society broadly and the Jesus movement-communities in particular. Texts such as Romans 1:16-17 may echo and even parody concerns about imperial ideology and the emerging imperial cult.[17] The reversals presented in 1 Corinthians 1:18-31 probably suggest that the current powers and their accompanying conventions, the normalized and domesticated imperial world, are overturned.[18] The hymn to Christ in Philippians 2:6-11 seems to make claims about the power of another lord (besides the emperor) for a community that has now become a "colony of heaven" (3:20), an advance guard of the project to bring the whole world under the sovereign rule of Israel's God. Even Paul's use of Jewish scriptures, as in Romans 15:12, can insist on confirming Jesus Christ as a Davidic Messiah, the hope of all nations.

An increasing number of scholars are convinced that these and other texts in the New Testament exhibit an anti-imperial stance or notions. Some have suggested that terms found in Paul would have resonated with the recipients of his letters given the imperial context, evoking analogies between Roman and divine empires. In fact, many have gone so far to suggest that Paul's use of these terms would not only have invoked but also challenged imperial claims as well as the prevailing social order, which of course often went hand in hand in the first century. A term like *dikaiosynē* looks differently when one emphasizes its potential meaning as "justice" (instead of "righteousness"). In the context of this empire, the "good news" (*euangelion*, or "gospel") would have been more commonly used to describe Caesar Augustus' ascension to power. In fact, the herald announcing the approach of an emperor like Augustus would be an *apostolos* ("messenger" rather than apostle) with a message of the *parousia* ("arrival" rather than Christ's return) of the *kyrios* ("lord," one of many titles given to the emperor). In this light, then, it becomes compelling to recall that the term commonly translated as "church," *ekklēsia*, was used to describe a political gathering, and *ta ethnē* functioned as a reference to all those "nations" or "peoples" under Rome's dominion (rather than just the Gentiles).[19] In such a light, scholars like Richard Horsley have declared that: "the most significant way in which a postcolonial reading of Paul disrupts the standard essentialist, individualist and depoliticized Augustinian-Lutheran Paul, consists in the rediscovery of the anti-imperial stance and program evident in his letters."[20]

The position of Paul's letters with regard to the Empire is nevertheless complex, even ambivalent. On the one hand, Pauline texts indeed appear to issue an anti-imperial challenge and critique of centralized, autocratic power. On the other hand, they also show signs of condoning an imperial point of view, absorbed in the language and structure of this power—a phenomenon not uncommon in contexts of unequal power relationships. Given such ambiguity in the Pauline letters, a postcolonial reading is valuable. It allows one to recognize and account for such tensions and strains in dealing with texts from the underside of empire, without absolving the tension or ambiguity. Furthermore, this seems particularly relevant, since each of Paul's letters was directed to different assembly communities, variously situated in particular imperial-colonial settings: formal colonies (Philippi), utterly destroyed and resettled colonies (Corinth), colonized provinces still negotiating the empire (Galatia in Asia Minor), and even the very heart of the empire (Rome).

Paul's social location in this empire may also explain the apocalyptic tenor of his letters. A postcolonial reading could show how the "seductive realism" of empire and imperial theology is confronted[21] and its true character exposed by unmasking reality. For Paul this meant of course first and foremost the Roman Empire, who through idealization of the Roman government ironically propagated the idea of the *Pax Romana*, or peace brought about by the Romans. This so-called peace was authoritarian and oppressive and led to the growing misery of the masses, which contributed to political and economic instabilities and gave rise to widespread materialism and opportunism. It was not only at the macro-political level where the impact of Roman imperialism was felt, but the Jews with their long and revered tradition relating to sacral law and custom found "a thousand irritants in the day-to-day encounters with the Roman provincial administrators."[22] Apocalyptic literature can enable endurance amidst oppression, but it serves also as a medium to respond, for example through resistance, indicating that Pauline letters could also be viewed as protest literature. Apart from everything else it is and does, apocalyptic literature poses a challenge to the existing order, securities and powers. However, its involvement in the discourse of power, as will be argued below, can also see it implicated in similar structures it condemns; so, it too harbors a darker side.

Paul's written or textual strategy reveals his ambivalent position. Paul's writings engaged the powers of the day while also exercising and increasingly formulating his own discourse of power. Paul, like other early followers of Christ, found himself in a marginalized position. Christ-followers were members of a *religio illicita* (an unpermitted religion) and thus outsiders to the broader political scenario and established forms of religion. Yet, Paul's rhetoric of power, although dictated in part by his marginal position, at times comes close to the rhetoric of empire that he engaged and deflected in his letters. The basic ambivalence, whereby the apostle along with the majority of others suffered marginalization but also vied for power, is extended through participation in a colonial/imperial context. In the context of an authoritarian, imperialist society, subalterns typically challenge each other for the favor of the powerful as they vie with one another to establish their power and influence.

These dynamics will be important to consider when engaging in a postcolonial approach to any of Paul's letters. While texts like 1 Thessalonians 4-5 may include explicit rebukes of the Roman imperial claim to provide "peace and security" (5:3), taking a postcolonial angle to such a text raises at least five concerns to investigate: anti-imperial strands within the letter; the ambivalence of imperial engagement given a colonized mind-set; the negotiation (of Empire) among subalterns; overlapping aspects of embodiment including race and gender; and, conquering travels as triumph over local peoples.

AMBIVALENCE OF AN ANTI-IMPERIAL TEXT: 1 THESSALONIANS 4–5

Thessalonica was made the capital of Macedonia in 146 BCE, and enjoyed special commercial and civic privileges, including the right to mint coins. Local industries and proximity to the Via Egnatia, an important trade route, ensured commercial prosperity and facilitated security. Despite the city's checkered history in terms of local governors' actions, and its support for Antony in the Roman civil wars (in the first century BCE), the city eventually bestowed various honors upon Octavian, who became Augustus (after defeating his rival Antony). Shortly before the end of the first century BCE, a series of coins was minted containing the laureate head of Julius Caesar and the word *theos*. Fragments of imperial statuary of the first century CE were recovered in Thessalonica, attesting to the visual presence of the empire. Apart from other sanctuaries, archeological studies suggest the most important cults in Thessalonica during the early Roman period were those of the gods of the city, of the emperor and of Roma and Roman patrons.[23] It was from within this empire-saturated context that the first letter to the Thessalonians was heard and interpreted.

In the *first* place, Paul used some of the terms that empire-critical scholars have claimed are better read as anti-imperial, including *kyrios* throughout (4:1, 2, 6, 15, 16, 17; 5:2, 9) and the coming (*parousia*) of the *kyrios* (4:15), who brings *sōtēria* (often "salvation," but also "security," 5:9). Paul's reference to the well know slogan of what the Romans claimed to have achieved in the *Pax Romana*, "peace and security" (5:3), can be read as a further, direct challenge to the normalization of the empire. Paul's insistence on the falsity of the *Pax Romana* threatens to expose it for what it was, an ideological smokescreen for imperial violence. It was neither *peace* for the majority of people living from hand to mouth nor a *world* peace since it was limited to the boundaries of the empire, existing only in as far as violence continued within it.[24] Its violent underside was particularly disconcerting for subjugated nations, as imperial peace was not the counterforce of violence but was established and maintained only through (the threat of) violence.[25] The *Pax Romana* slotted in with the imperial cult that spread its religious sentiments throughout the empire, ensuring that imperial peace was religiously inscribed. Augustus' Peace Altar of 14 BCE on the fields of Mars in Rome and Vespasian's Peace Temple of 75 CE emphasized the *Pax Romana* as means of dominating other nations.[26] Further, if this passage is also making an intertextual reference to the false peace described in Jeremiah 6:14 ("saying 'Peace, Peace,' when there is no peace"), the phrase becomes a possible parody of empire.[27]

When read in light of this parody of peace and security, the letter's contrast between light and darkness (5:5-6) could refer to the in-group and imperial authorities respectively (5:5-6). In this way empire is mimicked and mocked, amidst the polarization of the situation of oppression. Indeed, constant references are made to a context of suffering, involving both the Thessalonians (for example 1:6; 2:14; 3:3) and Paul (2:2; 2:9; 3:4; 3:7). Even if these probably did not describe state-authorized persecution, they belie the imperial utopian claims of peace for all in the empire. Rather, the pervasive military enforcement of the imperial context explains why Paul described ethical alertness with references to military gear: the breastplate of faith and love, and the helmet as hope of salvation, or "security" (5:8).

But probably more than mimicry, such claims already start to show how a colonial mind-set impacted Paul in an ambivalent way (including in his claims to power, a topic we will return to below). In 1 Thessalonians 4–5 we are, *secondly* then, not just in the presence of resistance to empire. The quietism of 4:11-12 (especially *hēsychazein*, "live quietly," 4:11) suggests more than an anti-imperial thrust to this letter, demonstrating that still other aspects require consideration, particularly in terms of the ambiguities in these chapters. Contrary to some traditional idealist and other one-sided notions about peace in the New Testament, certain voices are not heard in 1 Thessalonians, from inside and outside the community. Such concerns are important in an oppressive context, where the subalterns negotiate (with) empire, competing with others for power in order to achieve superior positions. At a time when religious activities and affiliation were constituent elements of identity and community, informing reality and life, the Thessalonians' association with Paul and the Jesus-follower community would have been tenuous. The silence of the unheard voices takes on a particular ominous ring in light of Paul's troubling advocacy of what must now be seen as a disconcerting quietism (although in 5:14 "the idle" are criticized). Both the silence of the text and the ambivalent promotion of quietism are strange if trying to state simply that Paul is anti-imperial (or proimperial). Further, the letter stops just short of addressing the recipients as soldiers, evoking the militarized imagery like the apocalyptic battle of 5:8, or the trumpet (supporting royal calls or orders) and the battle-command in 4:16. Does this mean that the community is militarized against the empire, or like the empire, or both?

The ambivalence of Paul's sentiments in 1 Thessalonians 4–5 can be partly explained if his letters were largely "hidden transcripts," with an apocalyptic tenor. Paul's apocalyptic framework, without being "otherworldly," required a retooling of the universe by setting up an anti-structure,[28] but it is a scenario in which one can also get caught. The violently dualistic nature typical of apocalyptic discourse is at work in the discussion of the children of light and of the dark (5:4-5, noted above). An eschatological scenario where the sky is the place for apocalyptic battles further helps to explain the militarized and often violent perspectives found in Paul and in 1 Thessalonians 4–5 in particular. The day of the Lord is eagerly awaited, while Paul and the audience look forward to the judgment and destruction of others (4:15; 5:3), much like other empires have. For Paul the scope and nature of Messianic peace differed from the Roman version but without severing the link between peace and violence. The tension is palpable in Paul's alignment of God with peace (5:23), while already earlier invoking God's wrath for the destruction of *tōn idiōn symphyletōn* ("your [the Thessalonians'] own countrymen" 2:14). Since the letter depicts the audience as suffering things from their "countrymen," just as some "Jews/Judeans" (apparently) killed Jesus and the prophets (2:14-16), it also develops a contrast between an in-group whom "God has not destined for wrath" (5:9) and those implicitly destined for such a fate. Such an opposition stands in shrill contrast to the apostle's own appeal not to repay evil with evil (5:15). In short, fighting empire is no guarantee against the attraction to empire; resisting empire does not preclude availing oneself of its apparatus.

Third, in attending to how empire is negotiated among its subalterns, one must also consider the ambivalent impact of empire-related discourses. On one level the strained relationships typical among subalterns in a context of uneven power relationships emerge among the Thessalonians, together with resulting tensions and rivalries. The early insistence that Paul brought the message while under pressure (2:2), as did the Thessalonians receive it in much affliction (*en thlipsei pollē*, 1:6), may be about more than sharing in the rhetoric of overcoming adverse circumstances; it may voice some of the lingering tensions in the community. Although no explicit opponents of Paul are mentioned in the letter, subtle hints in 5:5-6, 12-13 (cf. 3:5, 10) suggest the presence of opposition to Paul in the community. In an imperialist context rivalries were often brought on by the need for colonized groups to compete for scarce resources and seek the favor of their colonizers to secure (even a little) more resources for their group. The presence of such rivalries may explain the notoriously tricky passage to interpret in 4:6 (*to mē hyperbainein kai pleonektein en tō pragmati ton adelphon autou*; "that no man transgress, and wrong his brother in this matter" RSV). Not only was there considerable tension between Paul and the Thessalonians but apparently among Jesus-followers as well. Could one of Paul's final remarks, that the letter should be read to *all* the brethren (*pasin tois adelphois*, 5:27), be an indication that the recipients may have been one faction only in the community and may have been tempted to monopolize the letter?

Since, on another level, Paul himself can be included among the subalterns vying for power, the letter gives many indications that Paul felt pressure in negotiating power in an imperial context. Paul seems to have felt compelled to look after his own interests too. Early claims about divine sanction for Paul and his work extended to his claim that also the Thessalonians fall within the ambit of God's sanction (1:4; 1:6; 2:12). Paul insinuates and asserts God's approval for his work (1:5b; 2:4-6; 2:10), and applies this approval to his activities in the community. Paul's statement about proclaiming his message *en pollō agōni* (amidst much struggle [or opposition], 2:2) can refer to the opposition from his rivals, but it can also be a reference to the generally antagonistic context typical of an imperial setting. Whether Paul included himself among those "set/presiding over you" in 5:12 (*proistamenous hymōn*) is not immediately clear, there are other indications that Paul was concerned about his status. The letter's emphasis on the importance of following both Paul and the Lord (1:6) implies Paul's link with Christ and Paul's own exemplary status, which is why disobedience to him (in 4:8) can take on a divine flavor. Furthermore, Paul's calls to imitate him ("you became imitators of us and of the Lord,"1:6; cf. 1:7; 2:16) were an important mechanism for him to stabilize his own discourse of power.[29] Through mimesis and other devices, Paul not only claimed divine sanction for his person and authority, he also extended such claims to his message and actions. In negotiating empire Paul and the community members in Thessalonica were engaging each other as subalterns competing for power and control.

Fourth, a postcolonial reading should also explore the hegemonic space of empires and colonies as deploying a range of social relations, particularly through dynamics of embodiment. Imperial designs of domination use overlapping and interlinking forms of race and gender vital to maintaining domination and hegemony. Since such ways of thinking are common in colonized settings, they can help to explain the ethnic stereotypes and the lateral violence of rivalries reflected in the letter. For instance, Paul not only claims to present the will of God, but formulates it through strong sexualized and gendered claims in 4:3-7, where fornication, impurity, and lust is what makes one like the "Gentiles" (or "nations"). Beyond his use of such gender and ethnic stereotypes, the male point of view of the letter is reflected in how the community and Paul himself are described. Both groups' patriarchal position is reinforced by the way Paul addresses the community continuously as "brothers" (1:4; 2:1, 9, 14, 17; 3:7; 4:13; 5:1, 4, 12, 14, 25), and describes himself as the "father" of the community (2:11). Yet, when Paul speaks of his engagement with and longing for them, he refers to himself in the role of a *trophos* (nurse-nanny, or even mother, 2:7). But Paul could do this without losing his (masculine) authority, since the members of the community were simultaneously cast in their subordinate role as of *ta heautēs tekna* ("her [own] children," 2:7).

Racial implications were of course already explicit in Paul's characterization of the Thessalonians' own countrymen (2:14) in a context loaded with confrontation (*epathete*, "you suffered," 2:14). A brutally negative description of *tōn Ioudaiōn*, the Jews or Judeans in 2:14-16, portrays them as the people who killed Christ and the prophets, persecuted Paul, displeased God, opposed all people and prevented Paul's work among the nations. Regardless of its dubious historical worth (see the "Historical Approaches" chapter), such portrayals reflect the lateral violence of empires, where subject peoples are divided and played against each other. This can account for why Paul would repeat further explicit ethnic stereotyping in places like 4:3-7. The stereotype of the "nations" and their inability to control their desires (4:5) is a well-worn colonial mechanism that connects ethnicity with sexuality, here functioning in service to Paul's own claims of dominion over these people(s). Paul used this ethnic, sexualized, and gendered image both as a deterrent and as an endorsement: if they do not want to run the risk of becoming like these terrible others, the community should follow him (4:1-2)!

Fifth, as is common in colonial discourse where travels to distant lands and the triumph over the indigenous people are common themes, this letter explicitly repeats these themes in describing Paul's conquering travels. Travel is a key element in Paul's work and his letters in general, not only in 1 Thessalonians. In this letter Paul refers to his experiences in Philippi (2:2) and encounters with assemblies in Judea (2:14). He also indicated the role played by the Thessalonian community in Achaia and Macedonia (1:7-8). In 2:18, Paul expressed his frustration in not having been able to visit the Thessalonians but referred to Timothy who travelled as Paul's substitute. Earlier the Thessalonians themselves apparently also travelled (1:8). Even the very letter is part of Paul's broader program of missionary travels, acting as substitute for Paul's conquering presence and maintaining the dominance of his voice as expressed in the letter.

The apocalyptic nature of Paul's letters helps to clarify how Paul was using conquering travel. On the one hand, apocalyptic with its ultimate, final, radical scenarios presents divine conquering travels (4:14-17), sudden and unexpected (5:2). On the other hand, Paul presents himself as the eminent emissary, as the ultimate traveler within an apocalyptic context collecting and leading the others toward the final journey (4:16-17). Even as he offers praise for and appeals to communal love and support (4:9-12) in their own land, it is in anticipation of "conquering" other communities that Paul travels and invited others to follow suit (as 1:8 seems to suggest already happened). While these and other images (pointed out in the other sections above), could be viewed as anti-imperial in one sense, Paul still tends to speak on the same terms as the empire, repeating or perhaps perpetuating an imperial discourse—and in the process he does not so much destabilize empire as he replaces it with another.

To conclude, it is most likely correct to argue that Paul was opposed to Caesar's empire not because it was an empire but because it was *Caesar's* (and because Caesar claimed divine status and honors that Paul believed belong only to God).[30] As a result, we should also be alert to the possibility that Paul is engaging in a construction of empire through his own discourse of power. One has to be careful not to try so hard to rehabilitate Paul that one becomes oblivious to Paul's own tendency to assert a subtle form of hegemony. Paul's position was always ambiguous. It is understandable that some can claim that "[t]he successors of Paul today are the theologian-activists, Christian thinkers-and-doers who call the affluent church to live truly in the service of the crucified, who is present in the persons of the struggling poor, the marginalized and oppressed, the sinned against and erased from history, nonpersons (1 Cor. 1:28-29)."[31]

However, did not Paul's anti-imperial challenge contain the very sentiments that would allow these letters to establish and sustain hierarchy and imperialism, domination and entrenched power, and the ideological manipulation of others in the history of the Christian church and Western world? Paul's broad concern with the well-being of others did not preclude his preoccupation with achieving his own goals socio-politically, culturally, and theologically. It is therefore not strange to find that those early Christianities that developed shortly after also followed in the footsteps of the Roman Empire in developing their own all-encompassing rhetorical strategy, a rhetoric of empire.[32]

On the one hand, Paul was the apostle to the "others" in the eyes of the Jewish tradition, that is, a marginal Jew in his own way challenging the hegemonic power of discursive Roman imperialism and engaging some of its agents along the way. On the other hand, he was keen to impose his authority and to ensure that he kept the upper hand in the discourse of power that he established and maintained throughout his letters. 1 Thessalonians 4–5 was Paul's public transcript to a Mediterranean community that served also as a hidden transcript in relation to the empire whose propaganda was built upon a top-heavy ideology of the beneficence of their rule. Paul interacted with imperial sentiments and seemed set on counteracting the impact and consequences of imperial claims on his proclamation of Christ. Then again, he bought into imperial rhetoric and constructed an ideology, which likely reflects his own implication in this imperial discourse. In dissenting deference Paul's mimicking challenge to the empire creates the impression that he was intent on subtly subverting imperialist propaganda. However, Paul also internalized and replicated imperial culture, in his employment and deployment of the ambivalence of hegemonic discourse, to his own advantage.

CONCLUSION

A postcolonial reading is not a new "tool" to apply in a mechanical way to the business of Pauline studies—postcolonial is concerned about coming to terms, theoretically and otherwise, with the politics and practice, the setting and contents, of New Testament studies. Postcolonial work incorporates a range of critical perspectives and positions, investigating the interrelationship between texts and power, amidst all the ambiguities and ambivalences involved. In Pauline studies a postcolonial approach, assisted by insights from other critical theories, is particularly well situated to identify the interactive but complex relationships that form both the colonizer and colonized while also providing conceptual, analytical tools for their investigation. A postcolonial reading enables both an examination of Paul's challenge to the powers of the day as well as how the powers impacted him, shaping his response to the powerful, influencing his stance to his addressees, and framing his perspective generally. Given the global context today, it is just as important to consider the ambivalent impact of these imperial and colonial dynamics, in and outside of Paul's letters.

FURTHER READING

Postcolonial Approaches

Bhabha, Homi K. *The Location of Culture*. London: Routledge, 1994. One of the most important contributions to postcolonial thinking, introducing various important concepts often used in postcolonial work.

Gandhi, Leela. *Postcolonial Theory: A Critical Introduction*. New York: Columbia University Press, 1998. Valuable general introduction to the development of postcolonial thinking and theory outside of religious/biblical studies.

Said, Edward. *Culture and Imperialism*. New York: Knopf, 1993. Key analysis of literature in postcolonial studies that plots and discusses the relationship between Western imperialism and the culture that reflected and sustained it.

Spivak, Gayatri Chakravorty. "Can the Subaltern Speak?" *The Post-Colonial Studies Reader*, edited by Bill Ashcroft, Gareth Griffiths, and Helen Tiffin, 24–28. London: Routledge, 1995. Landmark article on the problems of representing subalterns in the discourse and texts of the powerful.

Paul, Empire, and Postcolonial Approaches

Dube, Musa W. *Postcolonial Feminist Interpretation of the Bible*. St. Louis: Chalice, 2000. Exploring the intersections between postcolonial and feminist thinking from a decidedly African perspective.

Elliott, Neil. *Liberating Paul: The Justice of God and the Politics of the Apostle*. The Bible and Liberation, 6. Maryknoll: Orbis, 1994. Advocating a rereading of the Pauline letters beyond the traditional as well new perspective on Paul, focusing rather on Paul's anti-imperial thrust.

Horsley, Richard A., ed. *Paul and Politics: Ekklesia, Israel, Imperium, Interpretation—Essays in Honor of Krister Stendahl*. Harrisville: Trinity Press International, 2000. Edited work with excellent contributions that critically and diversely interact with the intersections between Pauline letters and Roman Empire.

Marchal, Joseph A. *The Politics of Heaven: Women, Gender, and Empire in the Study of Paul*. Paul in Critical Contexts. Minneapolis: Fortress Press, 2008. Interacting with postcolonial, feminist and imperial studies, this book renders a fresh, critical reading of Paul's letter to the Philippians.

Punt, Jeremy. "Paul and Postcolonial Hermeneutics: Marginality and/in Early Biblical Interpretation," in *As It Is Written: Studying Paul's Use of Scripture*, edited by Stanley Porter and Christopher D. Stanley, 261–90. Symposium, 50. Atlanta: SBL, 2008. Article that explains and shows how postcolonial approaches affect the interpretation of Paul, in ways that impact traditional investigations as well.

Segovia, Fernando F. "Mapping the Postcolonial Optic in Biblical Criticism: Meaning and Scope," in *Postcolonial Biblical Criticism: Interdisciplinary Intersections*, edited by Stephen D. Moore and Fernando F. Segovia, 23–78. The Bible and Postcolonialism. London: T&T Clark, 2005. Excellent overview article, providing both a historical grid and conceptual clarity regarding postcolonial work in biblical studies.

——— and R. S. Sugirtharajah, eds. *A Postcolonial Commentary on the New Testament Writings*. The Bible and Postcolonialism. New York: T&T Clark, 2007. One-volume commentary on the New Testament documents, showing the breadth and scope of postcolonial work.

Sugirtharajah, R. S. *Postcolonial Criticism and Biblical Interpretation*. Oxford: Oxford University Press, 2002. Broad yet detailed investigation of the how postcolonial work can provide for new dimensions of interpretation as well as social locations.

NOTES

1. See John Dominic Crossan, "Roman Imperial Theology," in *In the Shadow of Empire: Reclaiming the Bible as a History of Faithful Resistance*, ed. Richard A. Horsley (Louisville: Westminster John Knox, 2008), 59–73.

2. Edward W. Said, *Culture and Imperialism* (New York: Knopf, 1993), 9–10.

3. Fernando F. Segovia, "Mapping the Postcolonial Optic in Biblical Criticism: Meaning and Scope," in *Postcolonial Biblical Criticism: Interdisciplinary Intersections*, ed. Stephen D. Moore and Fernando F. Segovia, *The Bible and Postcolonialism* (London, New York: T&T Clark, 2005), 23–78, 65.

4. Georg M. Gugelberger, "Postcolonial Cultural Studies," in *The Johns Hopkins Guide to Literary Theory and Criticism*, ed. Michael Groden and Martin Kreiswirth (Baltimore and London: Johns Hopkins University Press, 1994), 581–84, 582.

5. Leela Gandhi, *Postcolonial Theory: A Critical Introduction* (New York: Columbia University Press, 1998), 173.

6. See the various contributions in Stephen D. Moore and Fernando F. Segovia, eds, *Postcolonial Biblical Criticism: Interdisciplinary Intersections*, The Bible and Postcolonialism (London, New York: T&T Clark, 2005).

7. R. S. Sugirtharajah, "Biblical Studies after the Empire: From a Colonial to a Postcolonial Mode of Interpretation," in *The Postcolonial Bible*, ed. R. S. Sugirtharajah, The Bible and Postcolonialism 1 (Sheffield: Sheffield Academic Press, 1998), 15.

8. Edward W. Said, "Orientalism," in *The Post-Colonial Studies Reader*, ed. Bill Ashcroft, Gareth Griffiths, and Helen Tiffin (London and New York: Routledge, 1995), 87–91, 87.

9. Homi K. Bhabha, *The Location of Culture* (London & New York: Routledge, 1994), 70.

10. See Anne McClintock, *Imperial Leather: Race, Gender and Sexuality in the Colonial Contest* (New York and London: Routledge, 1995); Sara Mills, *Gender and Colonial Space* (Manchester: Manchester University Press, 2005); and for biblical studies, see Musa W. Dube, *Postcolonial Feminist Interpretation of the Bible* (St. Louis: Chalice, 2000); Kwok Pui-lan, *Postcolonial Imagination and Feminist Theology* (Louisville: Westminster John Knox, 2005); and recently Joseph A. Marchal, *The Politics of Heaven: Women, Gender, and Empire in the Study of Paul*, Paul in Critical Contexts (Minneapolis: Fortress Press, 2008).

11. Dube, *Postcolonial Feminist Interpretation*, 140–41.

12. See Linda Hutcheon, "Circling the downspout of Empire," in *Past the Last Post: Theorizing Post-Colonialism and Post-Modernism*, ed. Ian Adam and Helen Tiffin (New York: Harvester Wheatsheaf, 1991), 167–93, 183; and Robert Allen Warrior, "Response," *Semeia* 75 (1996): 207–09, 209.

13. Gandhi, *Postcolonial Theory*, 77.

14. R. S. Sugirtharajah, ed. *The Postcolonial Biblical Reader* (London: Blackwell, 2006), 131.

15. Sugirtharajah, "Biblical Studies," 16.

16. James C. Scott, *Domination and the Art of Resistance: Hidden Transcripts* (New Haven and London: Yale University Press, 1990), xii.

17. See the discussion in Neil Elliott, *Liberating Paul: The Justice of God and the Politics of the Apostle*, The Bible and Liberation, vol. 6 (Maryknoll: Orbis, 1994).

18. See Jeremy Punt, "Paul and Postcolonial Hermeneutics: Marginality and/in Early Biblical Interpretation," in *As It Is Written: Studying Paul's Use of Scripture*, ed. Stanley Porter and Christopher D. Stanley, Symposium Series 50 (Atlanta: SBL, 2008), 261–90.

19. Elliott, "The Apostle Paul and Empire," in *In the Shadow of Empire*, 98.

20. Richard A. Horsley, "Submerged Biblical Histories and Imperial Biblical Studies," in *The Postcolonial Bible*, ed. R. S. Sugirtharajah, The Bible and Postcolonialism (Sheffield: Sheffield Academic Press, 1998), 152–73, 167–68.

21. Elliott, *Liberating Paul*, 180.

22. Wayne A. Meeks, *The Moral World of the First Christians* (Library of Early Christianity. Philadelphia: Westminster, 1986), 31.

23. Holland Hendrix, "Thessalonica," in *Anchor Bible Dictionary*, vol. 5, ed. David Noel Freedman (New York: Doubleday, 1992), 523–27, 525.

24. See Klaus Wengst, *Pax Romana and the Peace of Jesus Christ*, trans. John Bowden (London: SCM, 1987), 17.

25. See Philip L. Tite, *Conceiving Peace and Violence: A New Testament Legacy* (Lanham: University Press of America, 2004), 39–40; Luise Schottroff, "The Dual Concept of Peace," in *The Meaning of Peace: Biblical Studies*, ed. Perry B. Yoder and Willard M. Swartley, trans. Walter W. Sawatsky, Studies in Peace and Scripture, vol. 2 (Louisville: Westminster John Knox, 1992), 156–63.

26. See John Dominic Crossan and Jeffrey L. Reed, *In Search of Paul: How Jesus's Apostle Opposed Rome's Empire with God's Kingdom—A New Vision of Paul's Words and World* (New York: HarperSanFrancisco, 2004).

27. Schottroff, "The Dual Concept of Peace," 157.

28. See Elliott, *Liberating Paul*, 140–80.

29. Elizabeth Castelli, *Imitating Paul: A Discourse of Power*, Literary Currents in Biblical Interpretation (Louisville: Westminster John Knox, 1991).

30. See N. T. Wright, "Paul's Gospel and Caesar's Empire," in *Paul and Politics: Ekklesia, Israel, Imperium, Interpretation—Essays in Honor of Krister Stendahl*, ed. Richard A. Horsley (Harrisburg: Trinity Press International, 2000), 160–83, 164.

31. Richard B. Cook, "Paul the Organizer," *Missiology* 9 (1981): 485–98.

32. See Averil Cameron, *Christianity and the Rhetoric of Empire: The Development of Christian Discourse*, Sather Classical Lectures, vol. 57 (Berkeley: University of California Press, 1991), esp 20.

11

QUEER APPROACHES

Improper Relations with Pauline Letters

JOSEPH A. MARCHAL

"Well, doesn't the Bible say . . . ?" "Didn't Saint Paul tell us . . . ?" Questions like these often aren't really questions, coming as they frequently do at key points in conversations where interlocking issues of religion, history, sexuality, and authority are raised. Whether such questions mark the start of a proclamation or a mid-conversation intervention to settle a matter (supposedly once and for all), the users of such arguments treat these biblical texts and figures as stable, clear, and uncontroversial. There is hardly anything queer about reading and interpreting the Bible, and certainly not Paul. Or so most users of biblical (and biblical-sounding) arguments presume.

The approach of this chapter indeed presumes and proceeds otherwise; it attempts to move queerly, that is, not typically. Contrary to the predominant perception and use of biblical materials, often to give us "the biblical stance on sexuality," I suggest that bringing biblical studies and queer studies into closer relations with each other provides a more dynamic and compelling vision socially, politically, and ethically than if they had never "known" each other at all. To illustrate this suggestion, I need first to introduce you to what queer theories are and then to elaborate upon queer approaches to biblical and especially Pauline interpretation. Given the way people have used Paul's letters to either endorse or vilify all manner of social and cultural practice (and not just about gender and sexuality), it will be vital to engage this historical and rhetorical heritage (see also the "Jewish Perspectives," "Feminist Approaches," "African American Approaches," "Asian American Perspectives," and "Postcolonial Approaches" chapters). Yet, queer approaches suggest other ways forward and out of these dynamics, a suggestion that can be briefly elaborated by an example of some potential queer uses of Paul's letter to the Galatians.

WHO OR WHAT IS QUEER? (AND NOT JUST IN THEORY)

In contemporary English (especially U.S. English) practice, the term *queer* is generally used in a couple of different ways. Often *queer* is used as an adjective, even as a term of identification or description. In such contexts one can meaningfully say: "I am queer," or "we're here, we're queer, get used to it." In practice, this use of *queer* has often functioned as a replacement for a series of cumbersome abbreviations like LG, LGB, LGBT, or even LGBTIQA, for lesbian, gay, bisexual, trans, intersex, queer or questioning, and ally (though *asexual* is also peeking through in some contexts and communities). *Queer* can be a convenient umbrella term, then.

Of course, the selection of this particular word is purposeful, given *queer's* previous (and often still current) pejorative or derogatory uses. As a term that aims to pathologize or marginalize its targets, *queer* means "odd," "abnormal," or "perverse." It has been used both as slang for homosexuals and as a homophobic term aimed at those who apparently do not fit adequately (enough) with dominant points of view. Therefore, its use for a different purpose indicates a spirit of reclamation and even defiance in the face of insult and injury. The force and often the excitement of this term comes from the resignifying, even the reversal in its evaluation. Those groups and scholars who have reclaimed this word will not dispute that it connotes abnormality or nonconformity; rather they will dispute that such a contrary relation to "the normal" and often "the natural" is a negative thing. Queer, then, can indicate a challenge to regimes of the normal, a desire to resist and contest such a worldview. In this second sense, then, queer is less an identity and more a disposition, a mode of examining the processes that cast certain people and practices into categories of normal and abnormal and then of interrogating the various effects of such processes. *Queer* can also work more like a verb or adverb: to "queer" an arrangement of power and privilege, or to interpret queerly by attending to certain dynamics. This is mostly how I use the term (as one might have noted by the description thus far).

Queer studies, then, could involve study about, or from the perspective of, LGBTIQ people and/or study about these processes called "normalization" (which have often been used against LGBTIQ people). One key thinker in the development of queer theories, Michel Foucault, is helpful for elaborating upon the meanings and functions of normalization. Foucault describes *normalization* as those exercises in power that perform and combine five particular operations by (1) comparing activities, (2) differentiating between them, (3) arranging them into a hierarchy of value, (4) imposing a homogenized category to which one should conform (within this hierarchy), and (5) excluding those who differ and are, thus, abnormal.[1] As Foucault's various works on power and sexuality became available in English translations (particularly his *History of Sexuality*, Volume One), such techniques for analysis found wider audiences and contributed to the rise of queer theories in the 1980s and '90s.

The theories and perspectives that would come to define queer theories coalesced in response to and out of a number of different movements and practices of this period. Various queer theories draw promiscuously from a range of partners and participants besides Foucault, including: historians of sexuality, feminists in and outside of the academy, scholars in lesbian and gay studies, theorists adapting poststructuralist and psychoanalytic concepts, and activists attending to a range of issues, including lesbian feminisms, rights for sexual minorities, and the AIDS crisis. Another founding figure for queer theories (and a key thinker for feminist theories), Judith Butler has insisted that there is no "proper object" for queer theories. Though it has historical and topical ties to lesbian and gay studies, queer studies are not confined to the study of sexual minorities or the topic of sexuality. In fact, the coining of the term *queer theory* is frequently attributed to a key essay by another feminist, Teresa de Lauretis, in which she calls for lesbian and gay studies to pay greater critical attention to differences within and between sexual minority communities in light of dynamics of gender, race, class, and geography.[2] Thus, queer studies aims not to divide its labors between the study of various categories and dynamics of normalization. To do so would inhibit any attempt to interrogate how certain norms are created and enforced, particularly given how people socially construct the meaning of something like "sexuality" differently with and through gender, race, ethnicity, class, religion, age, ability, and national or colonial factors. *Intersectional* forms of analysis are needed, then—modes that grapple with how multiple factors of power and identification intersect and reinforce each other.

The resistance that many queer theorists show toward defining their tasks to one set of limited questions and concerns indicates the mobility of a term like *queer*. Instead of being a source of frustration, this quality of queer theories makes it quite useful, given how it adapts to new contours and critically reflects on its own practices. Since the queer is arrayed in a contesting relation with and against the normal, there is an underlying suspicion about imposing only one meaning or insisting that there is only one task for a queer thinker and activist. Thus, it is important to keep in mind that no definition and description of queer theories can be exhaustive; in fact, any claim to be giving the final and definitive version of what queer theories are or do would itself be *un*-queer. Thus, my chapter can only briefly introduce *some* of the unique and useful directions queer interpretations can and do take.

Since queer theories direct us to interrogate basic assumptions and critique received narratives, you or I could even question why I have begun with thinkers like Foucault and Butler when there are other ways to organize and describe queer sorts of approaches and analyses. Other stories can be told about work that, for instance, precedes Foucault and exceeds his focus. One of the longest critical engagements of the operations of sexuality as it intersects with a wide range of social dynamics can be found in the work of "women of color feminists" like Audre Lorde, Barbara Smith, and Gloria Anzaldúa.[3] Queer theories meet their critical potential when they recognize how the subjects of gender and sexuality are not fixed but are enmeshed and moving in trajectories within and between intersecting differences and multiple dynamics of power. When queer modes fail to recognize this, and, in turn, reinforce certain normalizing trajectories, it is justifiable to ask "what's queer about queer studies now?" The charge to think and work in increasingly intersectional ways might just be recalling one of the impulses behind de Lauretis's first use of queer theory (precisely at a time when feminists had themselves been grappling with differences within and between women). Such multiple genealogies for queer theories suggest that readers and users of this text would be wise to attend to and mix insights from those chapters that engage critical approaches to gendered, sexual, racial, ethnic, economic, class, colonial and national dynamics, among others.

Queer theories, then, often begin by questioning the foundations through which arguments and claims to identity, authority, or power proceed—even their own. In this regard, a number of queer thinkers follow influential interrogations like the ones found in work(s) by Judith Butler. Butler's analysis of *performativity* challenges many of the commonly received notions about the sexed body, the seemingly stable basis for arguments about gender, desire, sexual practice, and sexual orientation.[4] Butler asserts: "Gender is the repeated stylization of the body, a set of repeated acts within a highly rigid regulatory frame that congeals over time to produce the appearance of substance, of a natural sort of being."[5] Gender is performative, because one's gender is recognizable only through certain actions. It is only when one "does" gender "properly" that others identify one as belonging to and "being" a gender. Thus, Butler maintains that it is not an innate sense of being that causes us to do gendered things, rather, it is the repeated doing that creates a sense of stably being a particular kind of gender, body, and sexuality. Butler's formulation demonstrates that what counts as "proper" gender is conditioned by the regulatory frame of *heteronormativity*, the system that presumes that heterosexual desire and behaviors are the only normal and natural options.

However, Butler's conceptualization subverts the basis of this regulatory frame by denaturalizing sex-gender. Gender only appears natural, only seems to be based on the substance of the body, and this appearance occurs only when one's gender is read as "normal" within a heterosexual matrix. Because it must always be repeated (to be recognized as normal/natural), gender is unstable. Yet, if gender is itself unstable, so too is heterosexuality, requiring as it does a desire for an "other" (*hetero-*) gender. Thus, what appears as only "natural" or "normal"—one's gender, body, sexuality—is not a straightforwardly innate part of one's identity: rather this sense of identity is only an effect of the incessant doing that must be done in order for one to be readable in the regulatory frame. Heterosexuality is revealed as inherently unstable, even panicked, needing constant explanation and reiteration to produce itself as the natural. It requires copies of copies of copies of what it is producing as the "natural." Such an operation leads Butler to observe that "*gender is a kind of imitation for which there is no original*, in fact, it is a kind of imitation that produces the very notion of the original as an *effect* and consequence of the imitation itself."[6] Butler thus turns on its head the heteronormative claim that homosexuality is a secondary, derivative, or imitative form of sexuality (after the "naturally" occurring heterosexuality). Performativity shows that any gender and any sexuality is an imitation, an attempt to copy the cultural process by which it is regulated.

While these cultural processes that produce (our ideas of) genders, sexualities, and bodies are never complete, one can't exactly get "outside" such processes of regulation. Yet, their instability and repeatability can make them sites in which to "trouble" norms; their "citationality" provides opportunities for subversion. If one must cite and repeat the norms of embodiment, one might find ways to develop subversive repetitions, to "fail to repeat loyally." The issue is not whether one repeats gendered scripts or cites erotic norms, but how one does so. This also reveals the potential instability of normativity (the conditions produced by normalization as described above); it is open to rearticulation precisely because it always only works if it is constantly being reinstalled as the norm, as the normal practice that must be cited and repeated. Since they are always requiring repetition, norms are never fully or completely realized. There is room within this process for subversive improvisation.

The work of Eve Kosofsky Sedgwick often stresses that spaces for subversion can be found within the orders of normalization.[7] Heteronormativity, for instance, requires the concept of homosexuality to constitute a differentiation between sexual orientations. Within this order, "abnormal" desires are simultaneously unspeakable and omnipresent in their silence. Thus, as she discusses in *Epistemology of the Closet*, the image of the "closet" and its relationship to ignorance and revelation structures not only homosexual life but also heterosexual life. Heteronormativity demands that one not "know" of other desires and practices, enforcing a silence that both conceals and reveals. The attempt to enforce silence or ignorance demonstrates the persistence and the continuing possibility of the queer: it is always just around the bend, or even all around, because it is (mostly) silently embedded within the very structures of gender and sexual identity. The queer is officially not there, even as this relation of revelation and ignorance pervades nearly every element of society, even and especially when it seems most absent or silent. This silence and ignorance is useful in continued marginalization, but since these operations require that which they disavow, the queer cannot help but crop up in (what only seems like) the unlikeliest of places.[8] In short, the queer inheres.

By attending to processes like closeting internalization, gendered performativity, flexibly mobile intersectionality, and normalization in general, these kinds of queer theoretical practices attempt to counter how sexuality is so often used to manage social anxieties. As Gayle Rubin has demonstrated, ideas about sexuality can be adapted to generate "moral panics," occasions when biblical argumentation might especially be deployed. Rubin highlights that these moralizing practices are possible because of sexual essentialism and negativity, the hierarchical evaluation of certain acts, the misplaced scale of alarm over sexuality, and the lack of a concept of benign sexual variation.[9] Queer approaches, then, can begin with different assumptions than these, but they must also attend to the social practices that evoke or stoke anxiety and even panic. Queer theories have generated resources for interrogating and contesting these dynamics and highlighted opportunities for taking matters to political and ethical elsewheres.

IN A QUEER AND PRESENT DANGER, WHAT ARE PROPER AND IMPROPER USES OF THE BIBLE?

As my opening indicated, biblical texts are often cited and treated as authoritative arguments when people want to settle various matters related to gender and sexuality. It is not surprising, then, that an intense amount of ink has been spilled in biblical studies to address what "the biblical stance" on sexuality (and gender) might be, particularly when the mostly heteronormative academic, ecclesial, and political communities want to "debate" homosexuality. Most biblically influenced conversations about queer desires and practices start with the interpretation of four particular biblical passages, often called the "clobber passages" (Gen. 19; Lev. 18:22 and 20:13; Rom. 1:18-32; and 1 Cor. 6:9-10), two of which are in Paul's letters. Similar to the development of queer theories, the responses to such interpretations draw upon a range of resources including feminist approaches, critical histories of sexuality, activists, leaders, and practitioners in religious communities, and eventually the queer theories discussed above. The responses to such rhetorical practices have generated three kinds of approaches, each of which I can briefly discuss below: a historical-contextual approach, an apologist-affirmative approach, and a queerly resistant approach more explicitly drawing upon queer theories.

The first of these approaches, the historical-contextual, takes argumentative practices about these four texts head-on and, thus, are most helpful for giving a crash course on these bashing passages before reflecting on how this approach operates in contemporary situations. This kind of response is most frequently practiced by professionalized academic biblical scholars who insist upon placing biblical texts and cultures properly in their ancient historical contexts.[10] Rather than showing how "the Bible condemns homosexuality," studies of these texts' socio-historical and linguistic contexts demonstrate that they focused on matters rather different from contemporary concepts of gender and sexuality.

All four of these texts reflect ancient attitudes about the body and gender that do not exactly correspond to our own contemporary (albeit fraught) views of these. For instance, they assume that receptivity and passivity are characteristic of females' secondary social status, and such practices depict femininity itself as problematic. This asymmetry in ancient gender roles also corresponds, then, with expressions of xenophobic stereotyping: all four of the clobber passages argue that these are the things that "other" people do.[11] These passages reflect how dynamics of gender, sexuality, status, and ethnicity intersect in what feminist biblical scholar Elisabeth Schüssler Fiorenza describes as *kyriarchy* (the dominating sociopolitical order that differentiates ruler and ruled in several, intertwined ways). All four passages operate with the assumption that sex acts can simply be forms of aggression, but they are always extensions of the social status of the participants. The one inserting (what some might call "the top" today) should be higher in a social hierarchy than the one receiving (perhaps "the bottom"); thus an act must correspond to interlocking gendered, social, ethnic, economic, and imperial differentiations. These texts reflect an ancient erotic ethos centered around penetration, not necessarily pleasure or reproduction.

Thus, when only one of these texts finally (if only briefly) touches upon the possibility of female-female contact in Rom 1:26, correspondence to this social and political order is what makes an act "natural." Bernadette Brooten has demonstrated that Paul's condemnation is based upon a set of assumptions about women's subordination that he shared with the wider Greco-Roman world (Paul does not just "get it" from Torah or a Jewish context). An erotic act is "unnatural" if it treats a social inferior, like women, slaves, or defeated foreign peoples (those lower in kyriarchal systems), as anything more than this role, or worse, if that inferior takes the supposedly superior role of penetration. (Such acts are forms of gender transgression but also run contrary to the predominant social order.) This explains why the ancient Greek word used in this passage and in many other expressions for erotic acts is *chrēsis*, that is, "use" (1:26), not just "intercourse" or "relations" as some more neutralizing translations suggest. An act "according to nature" requires that a superior makes *use* of another, inferior body as a receptacle of their penetration (see also the "Visual Perspectives" chapter). Paul's vision in Romans 1 is, indeed, a far cry from the idealized version of contemporary romantic relations in which one is often encouraged to find a match and an equal (and where affectionate contact might also be described in terms of reciprocal enjoyment and mutual benefit).

When Paul's vice list in 1 Corinthians 6:9-10 places the *arsenokoitai* and *malakoi* among the kinds of people that will not be a part of his divine kingdom, he is still situated within this kind of social order. As Dale Martin has demonstrated, while the Greek term *arsenokoitēs* is extraordinarily rare, poorly attested, and radically uncertain in its meaning, *malakos* (or "softness") is quite common and means a whole host of things associated with femininity or effeminacy.[12] While a male who

is penetrated by another male could be called *malakos*, it is associated more frequently with a male pursuing penetration of a female! As a term of mockery, *malakos* is rankly misogynist, as the problem it names is too great an association with
anything feminine. *Malakos* describes things like over-eating, wearing nice clothing
(or anything on the head), or just generally doing anything too much, including
what we might call heterosexual sex. This excess is part of what makes a person or
practice femininely "soft." It reflects a worldview strikingly different from many
contemporary points of view, even as many of our modern-day insults do similar,
if not exactly parallel work. (Our reasons for insulting a male for being effeminate
may differ, but this is still an effective way to insult someone; it reflects a very different kind of sexism.)

There are some who see taking this historical-contextual approach as the solu-
tion to the social, ethical, and political problems posed by the use of these texts.
Indeed, one can use this kind of research to argue that these texts have very different assumptions and worldviews than we do. In this light, Paul does not even have
our modern concept of sexual orientation; the Sodomites didn't even do sodomy;
and Leviticus also bans mixed fabrics like cotton-poly blends. These texts cannot
condemn or ban such a thing as homosexuality, because they do not imagine either
heterosexuality or homosexuality, only the right kinds of penetrative use and the
wrong kinds of acts that violate or challenge this order. Indeed, even Paul conceives
of the origins of these "unnatural" practices differently, claiming that they are the
by-product of the "idolatry" of Gentiles, their different worship practice (Rom.
1:21-25), not in the terms of some later Christian claims about "the Fall."[13] Such
arguments operate with ethically fraught forms of gender, ethnic, and ultimately
religious differentiation.

Highlighting such discontinuities between then and now is a kind of "historiographic trump," a defensive argument that counters the use of a clobber passage.
It tries to short-circuit homophobia and/or heteronormativity by insisting that the
first century and the twenty-first century are not the same, this past is not relevant to our present. In short, the defensive move at the heart of the historiographic
trump responds: "that's not what these texts *meant.*"

While this historical-contextual approach draws upon a wealth of compelling
historical work on the ancient world and the biblical texts, it is still centered around
these "bashing" passages. It can even insist on defending these texts as much as
defending those who have been targeted by their use. Proper understanding of the
texts ostensibly will lead to proper use of the texts, even if this means that such use
will be rather limited. Another kind of response to arguments about the "biblical
stance" on sexuality, though, does not begin with these texts. Rather, it begins with
an explicitly gay-affirmative strategy, where religious (typically Christian) readers look to passages where biblical figures act as queer stand-ins or parallels for
contemporary LGBTIQ folk. Mostly lesbian and gay religious interpreters point to

David's love for Jonathan (since it "surpassed the love of women," 2 Sam. 1:26), Ruth's bonds with Naomi ("Where you go, I will go," Ruth 1:16), Jesus' reclining next to his beloved disciple (John 13:23-25; cf. 19:26-27; 20:1-10), or even the Ethiopian eunuch (Acts 8:27-40) as signs that queer folks do positively belong in biblically based communities.[14] In response to those communities and interpretations that have condemned, excluded, or marginalized LGBTIQ people, such practices are compelling ways for LGBTIQ (mostly religious) people to claim a sense of belonging and their own authority to interpret biblical image and argument.

One could even call this strategy an apologist-affirmative approach since it not only affirms the place of LGBTIQ folk in religious life, but it also adopts an apologists' perspective toward the biblical text as a whole, affirming that it can have a positive impact on those who have been bashed by the use of other biblical passages. Thus, for example, Episcopal Bishop John Shelby Spong can maintain that the reason Paul argued against certain erotic practices was because he was himself a struggling and self-loathing gay male.[15] This suggestion has even taken root through such cheeky reclamations as a page for Paul on a "Gay Heroes" website (www.gayheroes.com/paul.htm). From such a vantage point, even Paul's letters, in Romans 16:1-23 and Philippians 4:2-3, could attest to an affirmative view of same-sex pairs committed to working together in these first-century communities.[16] This apologist-affirmative approach seems to hold that properly understanding what the relationships between these biblical figures *meant* provides explicit support and explanation for what biblical arguments *mean* today. This approach aims to recuperate biblical argumentation, albeit by turning to different kinds of biblical texts and biblical interpreters.

Rather than the dissociative turn of the historiographic trump, this second approach is associative or connective, seeking models in the texts with whom contemporary readers can identify. Yet, by recuperating biblical argumentation as a source, it also manages to reinscribe the authority of biblical image and argument. In doing so, it does not displace the authority by which normalizing and naturalizing interpretations operate in the past and present. Thus, both the historical-contextual and the apologist-affirmative approaches do not adequately grapple with how biblical argumentation functions in problematic ways. Whether one is discussing scripture in general, or "Saint Paul" for Christians, these conceptual figures all operate as norm-producing machines. When they claim that one just needs to find the "right" biblical text or hero, or the "appropriate" historical context, in order to have the "proper" understanding of the text, these approaches trace the path of this normalization without contesting or subverting this function of scripturalization. These approaches can also leave the intersecting dynamics of power and privilege uninterrogated in previous cultures when they focus only on certain kinds of connections (gay heroes) or in current cultures when they hold that there are no connections or continuities between then and now (historiographic trump).

The lingering quandaries of these approaches suggest that an additional queer approach is needed to grapple further with the normalizing and naturalizing functions of biblical argumentation. This kind of approach should involve a shift in focus from the text or from the history as "source" to a development of the process of interpretation as itself a critical "resource" for engaging the persistent rhetorical function of biblical argumentation (see also the "Rhetorical Approaches" and "Feminist Approaches" chapters). Some biblical scholars have already begun to engage the developments in queer theories outlined above in order to practice just such strategies. Just as the term *queer* can connote both an identification and a mode of critique, there are at least two different ways to describe queer approaches to biblical texts. One such approach can be called queer because it is the kind of approach taken by those who identify as queer. While certainly some of the apologist-affirmative and historical-contextual approaches have been taken by LGBTIQ people, this way of describing a queer approach entails not only an eccentric positionality but also a critical reflection on and from that social location to interrogate the function of normalization in people's lives.[17] Without such critical reflexivity, though, categories of power and identity can be naturalized rather than questioned. This leads to what queer biblical scholars like Ken Stone would describe as a second but better description of a queer approach: one whose starting point is to contest and interrogate normalization, in all of its configurations, including with and through the Bible.[18]

This kind of queerly resistant interrogation does not draw its ethical force from being a "proper" kind of scholarly move or having an "appropriate" biblical model. In fact, to the degree that biblical arguments and biblical interpretations (scholarly and otherwise) have played roles in generating and maintaining normalization, a queer strategy aims to be *inappropriate* to such trajectories and domains. As Stephen Moore has argued, this kind of queer reading will need to attend not only to regimes of the normal but also to their ancient antecedents, the regimes of the natural. Echoing perhaps both Foucault and Sedgwick, then, "'queer' is a supple cipher both for what *stands over against* the normal and the natural to oppose, and thereby, define, them, and what *inheres within* the normal and the natural to subvert, and indeed pervert, them."[19] It is through these modes of analysis, then, that queer approaches to biblical interpretation begin having "inappropriate relations" with queer studies from outside of religious studies.

WHAT'D YOU SAY ABOUT MY MOMMA?

To give the reader some historical background, the previous section spent much more time with the first, historical-contextual approach, than the third, more queerly resistant approach. In this section, though, all three of the approaches will be demonstrated, even as the third kind will be developed the most. Since matters of the "appropriate" approach are far from settled in understanding biblical texts (most especially about gender and sexuality), then, I suggest that it might be time to consider "inappropriate" approaches and conversation partners from queer studies, to allow for a greater range of creative, critical, constructive, and conscientious modes of interpretation and argument. One is not required to show what the texts *must* have meant (past tense), as if determining this will mean one must follow it—and, further, as if the historical project were that stable (see the "Historical Approaches" chapter). One also does not need a recuperated or rehabilitated biblical hero as a salvific model to follow. What does seem vital, though, is to deal with how biblical arguments are used (past and present), to challenge the ethically and politically troubling uses, and to suggest more subversive and possibly even enjoyable uses of biblical argument and interpretation.

Thus, there is a distinct need to develop different strategies of resistance to the processes of normalization and naturalization. In doing so, these interpretations can draw upon facets of the first two kinds of responses. While not recuperating them, this queer approach can shift attention to texts besides the four typical bashing passages, much like the apologist-affirmative strategy. Furthermore, while keeping a persistent eye out for their contemporary continuities, this approach can address multiple and interlocking power dynamics and historical specificities, much as the historical-contextual strategy can.

Interpreting some of the images and arguments in another of Paul's letters, particularly in Galatians 4, then, could provide other ways forward and out of these dynamics, as I will briefly show below. Indeed, this chapter comes fast on the heels of Paul's justly famous quoting of a baptismal formula: "there is neither Jew nor Greek, neither slave nor free, not male and female; for all of you are one in Christ Jesus" (3:28). Certain kinds of affirmative readings have certainly begun with this passage in order to present Paul as offering a radical message of inclusion. Here the image of Paul as the "apostle to the Gentiles" plays a key role in narrating Paul's boundary-breaking role in bringing his message to non-Jews. This argument for Paul's role in the inclusion of the nations can be applied by way of analogy to contemporary sexual politics in religious communities. Just as Paul extended his vision to include a surprising group of people, those members of the nations beyond Jews, so now one can follow Paul's lead and extend visions of community to another surprising group: LGBTIQ Christians.[20] Indeed, this kind of argument certainly would correspond to an apologist-affirmative strategy, given how it maintains and reinforces the authority of this Pauline letter and offers Paul as a model for behavior today.

Other kinds of queer approaches, though, might ask about the basis of the inclusion offered by this passage and/or this interpretation of it. Read in another light,

Paul's application of this baptismal formula functions to naturalize certain kinds of power, gender, and sexual arrangements in the community. The arguments developed immediately after this passage (3:29–4:7) describe communal belonging in terms of being sons, not slaves, and inheritors of a paternal legacy. If interested in placing such arguments in historical context, then the context of this passage requires reflection on the kyriarchal intersection of power dynamics within and across not only patriarchal family structures but also elitist social and economic structures: sons are contrasted with slaves and depicted primarily as inheritors. Rather than erasing or transcending gender (as some claim 3:28 does), the argument of this section reinforces a particular gender role in all of its connections to power through certain kinds of sexual, ethnic, economic, and (in its Roman context) imperial exchange. Paul's application of the baptismal formula operates in all five of the ways Foucault describes normalizations (above): it compares roles, differentiates them hierarchically, homogenizes those who will belong, and excludes those who do not conform to this role. In short, the argument functions as a kind of normalization.

Yet, one of the main reasons to queerly reconsider Paul's argument in the fourth chapter of Galatians is the striking image of Paul as a mother in labor, an image that has fascinated yet perplexed scholars. In addressing the Galatians, Paul specifically depicts them (and "himself") as "my children, with whom I am again in labor pains" (*ōdinein*, in 4:19). Given how carefully Paul has argued from a particularly male place, this image reflects not only a maternal Paul but also a transgendered maternal Paul, a Paul who has transformed from male to female.[21] If one also takes into account Paul's insistence upon his own singleness (in 1 Corinthians 7:7, for instance), the argument further reveals a single transgendered mother. Certainly, such an image of this saint stands in stark contrast to supposedly biblically-based claims about "family values" in a variety of contemporary contexts. In this instance, perhaps a closer contemporary analogue than the heterosexually married nuclear household would depict Paul more like RuPaul, or as the head of one of the shade-throwing vogue houses featured in the controversial queer documentary "Paris is Burning"—"Mother Paul" in the House of Paul. As Sedgwick's work would likely remind, the queer can inhere within the most normalizing of domains: though silenced, she can still surprise.

Of course, such an image of a transgendered and maternal Paul can also correspond with the trend of identifying with biblical figures in more apologist and affirmative approaches. Paul again is cast as a transgressive figure, breaking boundaries and standing in solidarity with those who are oppressed. Since this is a lot for a single image to bear, it requires that one also attend to earlier images in this section of the letter's argument. For instance, Paul describes himself as one who had a "weakness in the flesh" (4:13) when he first came to the Galatians. This image certainly corresponds to the Roman imperial perspective on conquered peoples: weak, submissive, defeated, and penetrated (see the "Visual Perspectives" and "Postcolonial Approaches" chapters). Briefly, there are at least two different ways to interpret this "effeminized" Paul, weak in the flesh and laboring to give birth. One way is to argue that Paul took on the position of the dominated and displaced in radical solidarity with all who would be seen as femininely "soft" and submissive in the Roman Empire.[22] Yet, another way could highlight that when Paul wants (briefly) to depict himself as vulnerable, weak and soft, like the Galatians, he chooses these feminine or effeminizing terms and images of embodiment.

Though these images are certainly surprising, it is not at all clear whether interpreting Paul in light of these images helps to counter normalizing and naturalizing uses of biblical argumentation. To clarify, one will need to weigh whether the association of certain qualities with particular kinds of bodies and genders is being resisted or reinforced by the arguments in this letter. Would it have been possible to resist or reinforce these gendered scripts if Paul had chosen to depict himself as weakened *without* immediately going to an image of femininity, without briefly transforming into a "her"? Indeed, the choice of gendered image is striking in this light, considering that Paul briefly casts himself as a mother. Such a role seems hyper(hetero)normative, focusing an audience's attention to one particular role for women and reinforcing what is still often seen as women's "natural" position. In keeping with the ancient ethos of penetration, women's bodies were receptacles of male seed (see also Galatians 3:16 twice, 19, and 29) and conveyors of those who will be sons to these fathers (as Paul has already identified the Galatians). The letter's argument reflects an instrumental view of bodies, particularly female bodies as conduits. By remaining within the gendered tropes of the ancient erotic ethos, Paul does not scramble the codes of his time, even if and as he briefly "descends" into the role of a mother.

This interpretation of the maternal imagery in the letter, though, must also grapple with the view of women's bodies in the extended allegory that follows the image of Paul in labor pains (4:22–5:1). Reflecting on such arguments gives the distinct impression that women's roles have been *reduced* to the maternal in this letter. Indeed, aside from the "not male and female" pair quoted in the baptismal formula, this is the only role women play in Galatians (in contrast to other Pauline letters). In this allegorical section the contrast between two (mostly unnamed) mothers is to highlight the difference between two different kinds of sons of Abraham. The argumentative focus is not upon the mothers, but upon the results of Abraham's penetrative use of them as receptacles for seed, then sons. In distinguishing between the free woman and son and the slave woman and son, the argument also reflects rather than resists the exploitative conditions of slavery, including especially the sexual uses of slaves.[23] The Hagar story was one of the more chilling examples of this instrumental use of slave bodies found in the Torah, and it is now repeated in Paul (but without the accompanying divine consolation at its conclusion). Paul's presentation presumes and flows out of this element of slavery, a system based upon social status and economic structures, as well as gendered assumptions and erotic practices. Attention to such intersecting kyriarchal forces and structures is crucial. Paul's argument reminds readers that the setting of these letters was not just an empire but an empire dependent upon slave labors of all sorts.

Ironically, so too is Paul's argument dependent upon the labor of a slave for his allegory to "work." The argument naturalizes slavery as a vector of difference since many slaves are simply slaves by nature of their birth (4:22, 24-25). Further, this slave child's birth out of a "slave girl" (*paidiskē*, 4:22, 23) makes him a product of the flesh (4:23, 29) and, thus, one with whom the audience should not identify (4:28-5:1). The two female figures and Abraham's offspring by them function as symbols for two different paths, two different covenants: slavery and the flesh versus freedom and the promise. As with Paul's previous allusion to flesh (the "weakness in the flesh" of 4:13), this form of embodiment is negatively evaluated and, thus, to be avoided. Paul's argument exhorts the audience as free males to choose not to become slaves and thus become eligible for the promise (and the inheritance) of Abraham. Such a viewpoint skirts the involuntary and coercive aspect of slavery (slaves do not get to choose), adopting elite philosophical notions of the "moral forms" of slavery that freeborn males must work to avoid.

Tracing this element of Paul's argument resituates claims about this letter's focus on "Christian freedom." When framed on the terms of degrading flesh and denigrated slave bodies, the normalizing and disciplinary trajectories of this call to embrace a certain kind of "freedom" become more apparent. The argument is meant to inculcate a particular disposition and response in the audience; they should internalize Paul's worldview. This freedom means they would only be "free" to act in conformity and obedience to this worldview.[24] To accept and internalize Paul's argument is to be disciplined to think that any other option is akin to slavery. In following (rather than resisting) this argument, one submits to a disciplinary regime of "normal" modes of inheritance, the "natural" means by which elite males reproduced themselves (and the accompanying power dynamics that support this position and privilege).

And yet, this is *Paul's* elaboration of the meaning of the baptismal formula he quoted in 3:28. Paul's own citation of the phrases "neither slave nor free, not male and female" presumes that the Galatians know them, raising the question if there are *other uses* to which such phrases can be put. How would a community that lived by different readings of these—not immediately flowing into sonship, inheritance, and freedom or fleeing flesh, slavery, and the feminine—appear and operate (then or now)?

One way to answer such a question is to think more creatively and critically about the kinds of argument Paul seems to prefer in his letters, especially those that call for imitation.[25] In Galatians, one such exhortation forwards Paul as a model figure: "become as I am, for I also have become as you are" (4:12). Though seemingly reciprocal in style, the argument is trying to get the audience to imitate Paul and follow the path he articulates in this chapter: the path of sonship and inheritance, not slavery (3:29–4:7), in continued contrast with both flesh and slavery (4:22–5:1). A Foucauldian kind of queer analysis might highlight the normalizing force of Paul's argument for obedience via imitation (as I have already done). Yet, further, as Butler reveals through performativity, all forms of imitation are unstable and insecure; they must be repeated. An order only comes to appear natural to the extent that it is faithfully cited and performed. So, another queer perspective insists that Paul needs them to cite his arguments to perform his vision; he is not a model without copies or "followers." So long as a group accepts a regulatory frame and acts, repeats, cites, and performs within it, in and through their bodies, the argument works and appears substantive, natural, true, and authoritative.

But this substantiation or naturalization of an argumentative vision is not a foregone conclusion, for those interacting with Paul in either the first or the twenty-first century. Butler's conceptualization provides opportunities to re-imagine both the historical scenarios of the ancient world and the contemporary contexts for biblical citation and use. Neither is bound by what is presented in the letter to the Galatians and its interpretation. Indeed, what is notable about the audience is the way Paul describes their reception of him even though he only came to them through his weakness in the flesh (4:13). Paul will soon exhort them to not imagine themselves in terms of the flesh and slavery but to act like free and inheriting sons. Yet, the Galatians apparently received the weakened Paul quite well, though they could have scorned him. They even "received me as a messenger of God, as Christ Jesus" (4:14). Their actions indicate that the Galatians could have been drawing upon a different model or performing a similar model according to a different script, one that frames their experiences and embodiments in ways different from the norms of "the natural." These could be communities where weakness, receptivity, and/or fleshiness are recognized as "feminine" but not necessarily inferior; or, alternately, where these matters matter less or materialize differently. Indeed, this might be why Paul cites the baptismal formula, since the Galatians already cite, repeat, and perform it but to different ends than Paul promotes in the letter.

In this light Paul's argument in the letter is a sweaty effort, even a panicked reaction. The Galatians are doing their own kind(s) of imitation, based on some of the same figures Paul uses (God and Christ) but proceeding differently than how Paul exhorts. While most interpreters of Paul too often presume and construct him in an authoritative and pre-eminent position for an audience, his letters bear clear signs that Paul's perspective and model were hardly the "original." If the Galatians receive someone weak in the flesh in ways akin to Christ, it is no wonder that Paul must work so hard to convince them to think otherwise about weakness, flesh, femininity, and slavery.

Thus, it is possible for contemporary users of these texts to also take them elsewhere; not because one might now have alternative models for embodiment and belonging in the Galatians but simply because the performative aspect of arguments for imitation are themselves already unstable and open to different kinds of repetitions. Since norms are always in the process of being realized, but never fully or completely so, Paul's attempt to argue for an obedient conformity and imitation can never be complete. The way that recent readings offer, for example, a transgendered Paul can be demonstrations of this provisional, even transitional possibility for interpretation, a failure to repeat Paul loyally or "faithfully." So long as such queer interpretations grapple with the naturalizing and normalizing impacts of these kinds of arguments, they represent illuminating and enlivening improvisations in the scenes of constraints constructed by such dynamics. Interpretation as a process itself becomes a site to trouble the obvious naturalness and normalcy of Paul's arguments (and those arguments that lay claim to Paul and his arguments).

BY WAY OF CONCLUSION

Images like a transgendered maternal Paul provide opportunities for such queer uses, destabilizing the obviousness of what people are supposed to do with texts (but not offering a transgendered saint as an all-purpose savior either). The exercise of queer reading can become an efficacious exercise, not solely for how it produces meaning but for how it generates effects, how it is involved in the production of new concepts of self and society. The Galatians might just have generated rather different concepts of body and belonging in the community. Regardless if they did or did not do so historically, reflecting upon them in and through the argumentation of this letter indicates how such counter-visions inhere and are internal to Paul's efforts to convince audiences not to proceed and persist with other views of Christ and community. If it operates as a continuing argument, then the letter bears other repetitions of itself as queer potentialities. In such approaches the authority moves from the text, the tradition, or the saint, to the ethical reflection upon interactions, citations, and repetitions between texts and interpreting communities. Thus, a queer process of critical interrogation becomes a resource for us to think about what attitudes toward embodiment, fleshiness, fellowship, and belonging are more politically and ethically generative than those that build on exclusionary imagery and kyriarchal structures or those that further efforts to normalize certain dispositions and naturalize problematic power dynamics. Reflecting upon and trying the three different kinds of queer approaches, particularly the more queerly resistant kind, is tremendously helpful in such efforts. Sometimes it's just that important to pursue "improper" subjects through "inappropriate" relations between biblical and queer studies.

FURTHER READING

Key Readings for Queer Studies

Butler, Judith. *Undoing Gender.* New York: Routledge, 2004. While her *Gender Trouble* is a signal contribution to what would become queer theory, this more recent work is often a more accessible discussion of performativity and the constraints of gender and sexuality (among other things).

Eng, David L. Judith Halberstam, and José Esteban Muñoz, eds. "What's Queer about Queer Studies Now?" *Social Text* 23:3-4 (2005). This special double edition presents a series of challenges to what have become the norms of queer studies, encouraging a more persistent and variegated set of analyses and interventions for the present and future.

Foucault, Michel. *The History of Sexuality: Volume 1: An Introduction,* translated by Robert Hurley. New York: Vintage, 1978 [1976]. Probably the most popular text for grappling with the construction of the regime we now call "sexuality," as his strategies have been adapted widely in queer studies.

Rubin, Gayle. "Thinking Sex: Toward a Radical Theory of the Politics of Sexuality," in *Pleasure and Danger: Exploring Female Sexuality,* edited by Carole S. Vance, 267–319; London: Pandora, 1989 [1984]. A challenging and path-breaking essay of what one might justifiably call proto-queer theory, particularly in its attention to the situatedness of social standards of approval for sexual behaviors and her distinctive response to this system.

Sedgwick, Eve Kosofsky. *Between Men: English Literature and Male Homosocial Desire.* New York: Columbia University Press, 1985. First of many works to trace the tensions, contradictions, and attractions of ostensibly normal literature and culture (see also her *Epistemology of the Closet*).

Key Readings for Queer Approaches in Biblical Studies

Brooten, Bernadette J. *Love between Women: Early Christian Responses to Female Homoeroticism.* Chicago: University of Chicago Press, 1996. Expansive and landmark resource for collecting and analyzing ancient views of female homoeroticism, before an extensive commentary on Romans 1:18-32.

Hornsby, Teresa J. and Ken Stone, eds. *Bible Trouble: Queer Reading at the Boundaries of Biblical Scholarship.* Atlanta: Society of Biblical Literature, 2011. Latest volume to attempt to trouble the ways biblical scholarship is done with the help of various queer theories and styles (and a few entries on Paul's letters).

Martin, Dale B. "*Arsenokoitēs* and *Malakos*: Meanings and Consequences," in *Biblical Ethics and Homosexuality: Listening to Scriptures,* edited by Robert L. Brawley. Pages 117–36; Louisville: Westminster John Knox, 1996. One of several key articles that debunk common heteronormative assumptions about what Paul's letters "say" about homosexuality (see also his book *Sex and the Single Savior*).

Moore, Stephen D. *God's Beauty Parlor: And Other Queer Spaces in and around the Bible.* Stanford: Stanford University Press, 2001. An audacious, incisive, and humorous introduction to queer approaches, including an extensive consideration of Paul's strange positioning and argumentation.

Stone, Ken. *Practicing Safer Texts: Food, Sex, and Bible in Queer Perspective.* London: T&T Clark, 2005. An insightful culmination of years of work in queer biblical hermeneutics (mostly in the Hebrew Bible), exemplifies how queer approaches can address much more than gender, sexuality, and desire, without ignoring them either (the introduction alone is adventurous, challenging, and helpful).

NOTES

1. Michel Foucault, *Discipline and Punish: The Birth of the Prison*, trans. Alan Sheridan (New York: Vintage, 1979), 182–84.

2. Teresa de Lauretis, "Queer Theory, Lesbian and Gay Studies: An Introduction," *differences* 3, no. 2 (1991): iii–xviii.

3. See the discussion in Roderick A. Ferguson, *Aberrations in Black: Toward a Queer of Color Critique* (Minneapolis: University of Minnesota Press, 2004).

4. See Judith Butler, *Gender Trouble: Feminism and the Subversion of Identity* (New York: Routledge, 1990); "Imitation and Gender Insubordination," in *Inside /Out: Lesbian Theories, Gay Theories*, ed. Diana Fuss (New York: Routledge, 1991), 13–31; *Bodies That Matter: On the Discursive Limits of "Sex"* (New York: Routledge, 1993); and *Undoing Gender* (New York: Routledge, 2004).

5. Butler, *Gender Trouble*, 33.

6. Butler, "Imitation," 21.

7. Eve Kosofsky Sedgwick, *Between Men: English Literature and Male Homosocial Desire* (New York: Columbia University Press, 1985); *Epistemology of the Closet* (Berkeley: University of California Press, 1990); and *Tendencies* (Durham: Duke University Press, 1993).

8. See, for example, Sedgwick, *Between Men*.

9. Gayle Rubin, "Thinking Sex: Toward a Radical Theory of the Politics of Sexuality," in *Pleasure and Danger: Exploring Female Sexuality*, ed. Carole S. Vance (London: Pandora, 1989 [1984]), 267–319, especially 275–83.

10. See, for instance, Bernadette J. Brooten, *Love between Women: Early Christian Responses to Female Homoeroticism* (Chicago: University of Chicago Press, 1996); Dale B. Martin, "*Arsenokoitēs* and *Malakos*: Meanings and Consequences," in *Biblical Ethics and Homosexuality: Listening to Scriptures*, ed. Robert L. Brawley (Louisville: Westminster John Knox, 1996), 117–36; and Martti Nissinen, *Homoeroticism in the Biblical World: A Historical Perspective*, trans. Kirsi Stjerna (Minneapolis: Fortress Press, 1998).

11. See, for example, Kwok Pui-lan, "A Postcolonial Reading: Sexual Morality and National Politics; Reading Biblical 'Loose Women,'" in *Engaging the Bible: Critical Readings from Contemporary Women*, ed. Choi Hee An and Katheryn Pfisterer Darr (Minneapolis: Fortress Press, 2006), 21–46.

12. Martin, "*Arsenokoitēs*."

13. Martin, "Heterosexism and the Interpretation of Romans 1:18-32," *Biblical Interpretation* 3 (1995): 332–55; and Brooten, *Love*.

14. See, for instance, Robert E. Goss, *Jesus ACTED Up: A Gay and Lesbian Manifesto* (San Francisco: Harper, 1993); Nancy L. Wilson, *Our Tribe: Queer Folks, God, Jesus, and the Bible* (San Francisco: Harper, 1995); and Theodore W. Jennings Jr., *The Man Jesus Loved: Homoerotic Narratives from the New Testament* (Cleveland: Pilgrim, 2003).

15. John Shelby Spong, *Rescuing the Bible from Fundamentalism: A Bishop Rethinks the Meaning of Scripture* (San Francisco: Harper, 1991), 116–25.

16. See, for instance, Mary Rose D'Angelo, "Women Partners in the New Testament," *Journal of Feminist Studies in Religion* 6 (1990): 65–86; and Thomas Hanks, "Romans," in *The Queer Bible Commentary*, ed. Deryn Guest, Robert E. Goss, Mona West, and Thomas Bohache (London: SCM, 2006), 582–605.

17. See Ken Stone, *Practicing Safer Texts: Food, Sex, and Bible in Queer Perspective* (London: T&T Clark, 2005), 15.

18. Ken Stone, "Queer Theory and Biblical Interpretation: An Introduction," in *Queer Commentary and the Hebrew Bible*, ed. Stone (Cleveland: Pilgrim, 2001), 11–34, 33.

19. Stephen D. Moore, *God's Beauty Parlor: And Other Queer Spaces in and around the Bible* (Stanford: Stanford University Press, 2001), 18.

20. See Jeffrey S. Siker, "Homosexual Christians, the Bible, and Gentile Inclusion: Confessions of a Repenting Heterosexist," in *Homosexuality in the Church: Both Sides of the Debate*, ed. Siker (Louisville: Westminster John Knox, 1994), 178–94; and Thomas Bohache, "'To Cut or Not to Cut': Is Compulsory Heterosexuality a Prerequisite for Christianity?" in *Take Back the Word: A Queer Reading of the Bible*, ed. Goss and West (Cleveland: Pilgrim, 2000), 227–39.

21. See Brigitte Kahl, "Gender Trouble in Galatia?: Paul and the Rethinking of Difference," in *Is There a Future for Feminist Theology?*, ed. Deborah F. Sawyer and Diane M. Collier (Sheffield: Sheffield Academic Press, 1999), 57–73; Kahl, "No Longer Male: Masculinity Struggles behind Galatians 3:28?" *Journal for the Study of the New Testament* 79 (2000): 37–49; and Davina C. Lopez, *Apostle to the Conquered: Reimagining Paul's Mission* (Minneapolis: Fortress Press, 2008).

22. See Lopez, *Apostle*; and Kahl, *Galatians Re-Imagined: Reading with the Eyes of the Vanquished* (Minneapolis: Fortress Press, 2010).

23. Sheila Briggs, "Galatians," in *Searching the Scriptures: A Feminist Commentary*, Vol. 2, ed. Elisabeth Schüssler Fiorenza with Ann Brock and Shelly Matthews (New York: Crossroad, 1994), 218–36.

24. See, for instance, the argument in Stephen D. Moore, *God's Gym: Divine Male Bodies of the Bible* (New York: Routledge, 1996), 17–30.

25. See, to start, Elizabeth A. Castelli, *Imitating Paul: A Discourse of Power* (Louisville: Westminster John Knox, 1991).

Glossary

PREPARED BY KELSI MORRISON-ATKINS

allegory: A form of extended metaphor in which the characters, setting, and/or plot of a text correspond to a symbolic meaning that lies outside of the narrative itself.

androcentric: "Male-centered," focused upon, or from the point of view of, males. Often, androcentric texts are those written by males for an implied or explicit male audience, and tend to ignore, exclude, or cast pejoratively the perspectives and/or activities of women.

apostle: From the Greek "one who is sent out," refers to a person sent to convey a message or to complete the instructions on behalf of another; a messenger.

BCE: "Before the Common Era," refers to ancient time periods before the year that Jesus is said to have been born (previously B.C.: "Before Christ"). This abbreviation is meant to replace the traditional BC/AD dating system that presupposes the dominance of Christianity and certain Christian themes.

CE: "Common Era," or the time period after the presumed birth of Jesus. Corresponds to and replaces the previous A.D. demarcation (*Anno Domini*, Latin for "Year of our Lord"), but does not presume the authority of Christianity or certain Christian themes or images (including a lordly or dominating divine).

colonization (adj., colonial; cf. colonialism): Originally derived from the Latin for farmstead or settlement (*colonia*), a system of domination in which a powerful minority of non-indigenous people (frequently from a distant territory) create settlements and either rule or eliminate most of the previous inhabitants. *See also* neocolonialism, below.

229

diaspora: From the Greek for "spread throughout" or "scatter," refers to those who identify as part of an ethnic and/or religious group but live outside of the group's established homeland. In the ancient world, it can refer to Jewish communities outside of Israel or Judea, but more recently, it has also been used for a range of groups (the African diaspora, Indian diaspora, and so on).

dikaiosynē: Greek term, commonly translated as "righteousness" or "justification" in the study of Paul's letters, but more broadly refers to justice.

ekklēsia: Greek term, commonly translated as "church" in the study of Paul's letters, but more broadly refers to an "assembly" of people gathering together, particularly to discuss critically political issues (an *ekklēsia* can be a deliberative body within the government of an ancient city, or *polis*).

eschatology (adj., eschatological): From the Greek "last," refers to the expectation of what will happen at the end of the world (or, at least, the "end" of the world as it was known).

exegesis: From the Greek "to lead out," the critical analysis of a text or texts.

feminism: A variety of movements based upon an ethically and politically driven advocacy stance that supports the political, economic, and social equality for all women (or wo/men, *see* below). Often requires a critique of or resistance to current structures of oppression and domination like sexism or androcentrism. *See also* womanism, below.

Hellenism (adj., Hellenistic or Hellenized): The process that asserted the preeminence of Greek (or Hellenic) culture (including rhetoric, education, language, and other conventions) over the eastern half of the Mediterranean world. This most notably and especially affects the study of ancient Judaism(s), so that one can describe Jews as Hellenized Jews, or mark out a time period of Hellenistic Judaism. This process accounts for the importance of Greek language and culture, even under the Roman empire.

hermeneutics: From the Greek for "interpretation," describes the process of interpreting texts, but can include more nuanced meanings and a range of tasks, including translation, exposition, or particular reading strategies (such as feminist or postcolonial hermeneutics). *See also* hermeneutics of suspicion, below.

hermeneutics of suspicion: A critical reading stance and strategy in which the positive authority and impact of a biblical text is not taken for granted but often challenged by critically evaluating the structures of domination inscribed within the texts.

humanization: A strategy of reading that is critical of the notion of an objective interpretation of any text that does not take into account the varied experiences of readers. Humanizing interpretive methods forefront experience as an unavoidable, and even integral, aspect of interpretation. *See also* postmodernism and standpoint epistemology, below.

hybridity: A combination of two seemingly quite different or incompatible notions of identity, or the complex interaction of two or more cultures in which differing languages, cultures, and ethnicities are blended or contested. In postcolonial studies, hybridity is often seen as creating spaces for subversion or resistance to colonial cultures or forces.

ideology (adj., ideological): The use of symbols in order to construct a representation of "reality" for people that helps them to navigate complex and otherwise unintelligible issues and to perceive their place in the world as legitimate, naturally occurring, and imperative.

imperialism (adj., imperial, cf. empire): Originally derived from the Latin for authority or command (*imperium*), a system of domination in which one people or nation exploits another less powerful people or nation, typically for economic gain. Colonization (*see above*) is a particular form of imperialism.

kyriarchy (adj., kyriarchal): A new term, coined by Elisabeth Schüssler Fiorenza, which refers to the "rule of the lord." As a substitute for the term *patriarchy*, kyriarchy takes into account the interlocking systems of domination in which elite men rule over women as well as most other males on the basis of more than sex or gender, but other factors including race or ethnicity, property and poverty, imperialism and colonialism (*see also* wo/men, below). The Greek word *kyrios* was used for emperors, slave-masters, husbands, and fathers, indicating how these roles can overlap.

mimesis: The rhetorical use of imitation of established authorities in order to reach a particular argumentative aim.

myth: Although colloquially understood as an impossible phenomenon or fictitious story, myth actually refers to stories about supernatural entities or the origins of a community that function to solidify communal identity or explain the nature of the material world. (Thus, referring to a narrative as "myth" is not the same as saying that it is "untrue.")

neocolonialism: The notion that, after the collapse of the major European empires that spanned the globe, a new form of exploitation is currently occurring in which powerful groups or nations are using economic and cultural institutions (like the World Bank or corporate mass media) to their advantage as a form of domination. *See also* colonization, above.

"New Perspective" (on Paul): An interpretive perspective that reacts to and attempts to correct the rampant anti-Semitism that accompanied the traditional "conversion" interpretation of Paul by locating Paul as a lifelong Jew. Requires situating Paul's letters within the varieties of Judaism(s), reflected in Jewish sources of the time.

normalization: A disciplinary way of organizing people in terms of standards (or norms) that primarily classifies people, rather than actions, as acceptable or deviant (normal or abnormal). For Michel Foucault, this is a powerful form of social control that not only compares and differently values certain behaviors, but it also develops categories to which people should conform and, failing that, they should be excluded from the domain of the "normal."

performativity: Concept developed by Judith Butler that argues for how gender, sexuality, or other categories of identity come to *appear* "natural" and inevitable; rather, identity is demonstrated (or performed) by the constant repetition of a set of actions that are prescribed by a rigid regulatory framework (so one can be recognized, for example, as a "woman," or "straight"). While this constant repetition seems to give gender a sense of stability, the possibility of failing to repeat these actions properly or loyally reveals gender's inherent instability.

postmodernism (adj., postmodern): A way of thinking that calls into question the certainty behind the modernist understanding of many ideas but especially claims about knowledge as objective Truth or about language as inherently stable and transparent in meaning.

postcolonial: May refer to the time period since the formal end of colonialism (*post-* as "after") as a structure of domination (*see*, however, neocolonialism, above). More broadly, though, postcolonial refers to the historical and discursive effects of colonial exploitation on individual people and cultures and, often, the efforts to resist or undo these effects.

Septuagint: The Greek translation of the Jewish scriptures (known alternately as the Hebrew Bible or Old Testament) begun in the third century BCE.

standpoint epistemology: Recognizes that much of what an interpreter sees in a text or in the world directly reflects their individual experiences and social location. What appears to be true depends upon where one stands. *See also* humanization, above.

Torah: A Hebrew word meaning instruction, teaching, or law, it can refer simply to the first five books of the Jewish scriptures. However, according to the tradition of uses, Torah can also mean all of the Jewish scriptures, can exist in both written and oral forms, and can include the Mishnah, Talmud, and other sources that are studied in Jewish communities to further understand what it means to be Jewish (and how).

womanism: A term coined by Alice Walker, as a form of feminism (*see above*) that is reflective of the experiences of African American women, or "women of color," in general. Particularly highlights how sexism, racism, and classism intertwine in their effects on African American women.

wo/men: A way of writing the term "women" that takes into account the varied social, racial, and economic experiences of women and resists a monolithic understanding of the female experience. This demarcation, as an alternative to the androcentric bent of the English language system, also includes men who have been disenfranchised by kyriarchal rule. *See* kyriarchy, above.